MARCI MCDONALD is currently Washington Bureau Chief of *Maclean's* magazine. Before being posted to the United States in 1984, she spent eight years as *Maclean's* Paris correspondent covering Europe and the Middle East and winning three National Magazine Awards. A graduate of the University of Toronto, she joined the *Toronto Star* in 1967 where she spent six years as chief entertainment feature writer. During that time, she first met Maureen Forrester for a 1971 magazine profile.

This memoir of my life and career is dedicated to all those who helped me along the way, but especially my parents, my husband Eugene, and our children, who allowed me to have a career; and our nanny Teta, who helped care for and nurture the children while I was frequently away on tour. And to my dear friend Irene Bird who managed, organized, and kept things in order during my absences.

My admiration and thanks go to writer Marci McDonald, whose sensitive probing enabled me to recapture memories and events, and without whom this book would not exist.

MAUREEN FORRESTER

Out of Character

A MEMOIR

with Marci McDonald

M&S

An M&S Paperback from
McClelland and Stewart
The Canadian Publishers

An M&S Paperback from McClelland and Stewart

First Printing October 1988

Hardcover edition published in 1986, reprinted 1987
Trade paperback edition 1987

McClelland and Stewart
The Canadian Publishers
481 University Avenue
Toronto, Ontario
M5G 2E9

Canadian Cataloguing in Publication Data

Forrester, Maureen, 1930–
Out of character

(M & S Paperbacks)
ISBN 0-7710-3229-3

1. Forrester, Maureen, 1930– . 2. Singers –
Canada – Biography.   I. McDonald, Marci.
II. Title.

ML420.F67A3 1988   782.1′092′4   C88-094286-X

Cover photograph: Peter Paterson

Printed and bound in Canada by Gagne Printing Ltd.

Lyrics reproduced on page 110 are from the song "I Know an Old
Lady Who Swallowed a Fly," words by Rose Bonne and music by
Alan Mills © 1952 and 1960 by Peer International (Canada) Limited.
Used by permission.

Lines from "A Great Big Baby," reproduced on page 335, © 1974
James Herbert (Eubie) and Andy Razaf. Used by permission.

Lines from "And I Was Beautiful," reproduced on page 336, are from
Dear World, music and lyric by Jerry Herman. © 1968 Jerry Herman.
All rights controlled by Jerryco Music Co. Exclusive agent: Edwin H.
Morris & Company. A Division of MPL Communications,
Inc. International copyright secured. All rights reserved.
Used by permission.

The lyric reproduced on page 362 is from the song, "From the Cradle
to Today" by David Warrack. Used by permission.

Every effort has been made to secure copyright information and related
permission. Further information would be welcomed.

Contents

O Sublime Art,
In how many grey hours
When the wild tumult of life ensnared me
Have you kindled my heart to warm love?
Have you carried me away to a better world?

– *An Die Musik | Ode to Music*
by Franz Schubert: Opus 88,
no. 44, 1817

Prologue

THE PLANE was late as usual. I landed at Montreal's Dorval airport only three hours before a Bach concert with the McGill Chamber Orchestra. By the time I got to my hotel, I was already frazzled; then in the middle of unpacking I realized that I had forgotten the evening slippers that went with my gown. It was summer and all I had were the heavy navy blue clogs that I was wearing, hardly the thing to go with a gossamer white dress. I rushed out to St. Catherine Street but all the shoe stores had just closed and none of them would take pity on a maniac blonde woman banging on the glass outside. Finally I thought, Well, I can't have a heart attack over this. On with the show. When it came time for the performance, I slipped on my gown and stockings and sort of swept out on stage. For the next ninety minutes I sang Bach cantatas and do you know that not one soul in the audience noticed that I was barefoot?

But then I've always suspected that nobody knows the real character that lies beneath the public image. People think because of the music I sing that I'm worldly and deep – some sort of intellectual. But as my husband Eugene always said, I'm a happy peasant. The Voice is one thing and I'm another.

I never take The Voice too seriously. It was a gift the gods gave to me. Some singers are always pampering themselves, having palpitations over every breeze. But I've been blessed with the constitution of a Clydesdale and the energy of a racehorse. I only need five hours of sleep a night and I scarcely ever practise. As far as I'm concerned, if singing isn't a joy, you shouldn't be doing it.

In nearly thirty-five years of performing and five pregnancies, I've only cancelled twice because of sickness. Once when I was singing with Tatania Troyanos and the Handel Society in Washington, I woke up with half my face swollen from an abscessed tooth. The dentist said he needed to do a root canal immediately and he would have to work on it over two days. But I was singing that night and I couldn't afford to risk my diction with my face muscles and tongue numb from Novocaine. "Go ahead and do it," I said, "but you can't use any anaesthetic." He thought I was out of my mind and the pain was horrendous. But then it was over and I carried on. That's my theory in life: Get on with it. I never look back.

I've had an extraordinary life. I've worked with some of the greatest names in music of this century and been honoured in my own country with its highest accolades. But there have also been some tough times that nobody knew about, not even members of my own family. That's why I agreed to write this book. Who knows, maybe my story might help someone else. After all, if a girl from a simple background like mine who left school at thirteen can make it, anybody with talent can.

Sometimes I stand back looking at my life and think: Why me? What made me so different from the rest of my family? I never feel that more than in Montreal where it all began. These days when I visit there my life can seem rather glamorous – headlining at Place des Arts with some of the great orchestras of the world, trading quips with Mstislav Rostropovich who happens to be passing through town, dining at the tables of some of Canada's most distinguished citizens whom I now call my friends.

But some afternoons I slip out after rehearsal and climb into a rented car, heading toward a corner of the city where those people would never dream of venturing – a humble, nondescript pocket of northeast Montreal. This isn't the newly trendy stretch of rue St. Denis, spruced up with cafés and chic boutiques. It is further east along boulevard St. Joseph past the giant green spires of the Église St. Stanislas which towered over my childhood. I negotiate the maze of one-way streets until I come to a little red brick church on a corner. It looks so shrunken from how it is etched in my memory. A black and gold sign with Latin letters announces it as the Romanian Orthodox congregation of St. Jean Baptisste. My mother woud spin in her grave to see what has happened to Fairmont Taylor Presbyterian where she spent so many of her days and pushed me into the choir almost as soon as I could open my mouth.

I turn the corner onto a narrow tree-lined street called rue Fabre. It is still much as it was: banks of three-storey row houses of different colours and shapes all attached to each other and strung with wrought-iron staircases that spiral up from the sidewalk to second- and third-floor flats. How I hated those outside metal staircases. To me, as a young girl, they were the emblems of working-class life. Now a new wave of immigrants has moved in and painted icons on some of the house fronts, but in each narrow building there are still five families piled on top of one another with postage-stamp gardens front and back.

The railway tracks barricade the end of the street and halfway down the block an enormous delivery van turns into the anynymous brick garage with a neon sign marked "Usine en Opération" – the only clue that Durivage Bakery has grown into a giant which now turns out bread for half the city. Its enormous smokestack still wraps the street in the sweet aroma from its ovens.

The smells! I always say that children today miss out on half the joys of life because their nostrils are anaesthetized by a world full of synthetics and chemicals. But if I close my eyes I can still scent the crazy pot pourri I grew up with – the soot from the incinerator by the railroad tracks mingled with the linseed fumes from a paint factory three blocks away and the heady sweetness drifting over from Cadbury's chocolate vats. Hovering over it all was the everyday fragrance of manure dropped by the horses that delivered Durivage's bread and ice and pulled the rag-picker's cart down the back lane.

There weren't so many cars then jamming the curb, making rue Fabre look narrow and diminished. Coming back after all these years, I have the feeling that I'm Gulliver landing in Lilliput. But to the child I was, this street was an entire universe and the centre of it was the small white house, number 5334, where lace curtains are now tacked up at a cockeyed angle in the front window.

Pulling up in front of it, I can sit unrecognized and remind myself of just how far I've come. But there is no nostalgia in the remembering. In fact, returning to rue Fabre, a feeling wells up in me once more that is almost as strong as it was then – the overwhelming desire to escape.

ONE

The Entertainer

Fᴏᴍ ᴛʜᴇ first I was a wanderer, off to see the world without anybody's help. Before I had even started kindergarten or could read, I was hitting the road. I couldn't have been more than four years old, but I knew where the streetcar stop was, four blocks from our house. I had figured out that the secret to hitching a ride was that I had to pretend to be with an adult. I would wait for a woman to come along who looked as if she could be my mother and clamber on behind her without paying.

What a thrill as I settled in to see the sights, delighted with my private rebellion. I strained high in the seat to look out the window at the houses of Outremont as the streetcar churned up the hill along Côte St. Catherine. I was hungry for a glimpse of the life behind those stout stone façades with their gingerbread and turrets, but all I could see were steep terraced lawns and heavy brocade drapes glimmering through the windows. I loved to imagine that I lived in one of those houses with a fabulously set table and a kitchen with a real refrigerator, not an icebox that leaked all over the linoleum in the middle of the night like ours. Sometimes back at home, sitting on the toilet seat, I would pretend that I was interviewing servants for those houses. At four, I had delusions of grandeur.

When the streetcar came to the end of the line, I would climb off and then try to repeat the same ruse I had used to get on. But occasionally my expeditions misfired. I would end up in suburban Cartierville, scooped up by the police. But I was never afraid. The stationhouse would call my parents and when they came to pick me up, I would be sitting on a policeman's knee, eating an ice cream cone. To me, there was no mischief in my outings. I just wanted to know how other people lived. I always yearned for a better life than ours.

I guess I came by it honestly enough since both my parents had left their roots behind. My mother sailed from Belfast when she was only seventeen. Her father, Matthew Arnold, was a yarndresser in a linen mill there and even then times were tense in Northern Ireland. She grew up in a Protestant neighbourhood but she and her sister, my Aunt Bertha, remembered there were streets they couldn't walk down for fear a Catholic would knife them. Some nights they would have to hide in the basement from the Sinn Fein. In that family of three girls and two boys, my mother, Marion May Dumican Arnold, was the second oldest. Her mother had realized early that she wasn't scholarly so she pulled her out of school and sent her to work in an aunt's tearoom in another neighbourhood. After a time, she noticed that my mother wasn't bringing home any salary. When my grandmother asked the aunt why she wasn't paying her, the aunt said, "Because May sits on the table in the kitchen all day long and entertains the cooks. She does nothing but sing."

My mother should have been a singer herself. She had a lovely untrained alto voice a lot like mine, and all her life she sang at church teas and socials; she was in the choir until five years before she died at seventy-six. But in those days in Belfast there was no money or opportunity to cultivate something as luxurious as a career in singing.

She had an Aunt Nellie who had come to Canada years before and married, and wrote wonderful tales home about life in Montreal. So at seventeen, lured by those letters, my mother was off to see the world herself, boarding the tender down the loch to the ship that would take her away from Ireland forever. It was the middle of the

First World War and she sailed on the *Lusitania*, which the Germans sank months later. She loved to recount what a harrowing crossing it had been.

She was never to see her own mother again. Within a few years of my mother's arrival in Canada, Ann Arnold died. All that my mother had from her were four dessert plates from a set of Royal Crown Derby her parents had sent her as a wedding gift. What that china must have cost a poor Irish family to ship, and when it arrived, every piece was smashed except those four plates. My mother always kept them on the wooden rack that ran high up around the dining room walls – the place of honour. I used to love those plates edged in black, orange and gold and I dreamed of inheriting them. But years later, when there was a fire in my mother's apartment, the firemen came in and blasted them off that perch with the force of their hoses, shattering the last souvenir that tied us to her roots in Ireland.

When my mother first came to live with her Aunt Nellie in Maisonneuve, outside Montreal, she found a job as a maid with a family in Westmount, the McBrides. But she had a disastrous career as a maid: she hated cooking and she loathed housework. When I was growing up, our house never seemed clean to me. That's why I became such a cleanliness fanatic. Today, whenever I work in an opera, the first thing I do as soon as they allot dressing rooms is turn up with a bucket and a great big shopping bag full of my Spic 'n' Span, Ajax and mops. I can't bear to start rehearsing until I've scrubbed the floor, the counter-tops and the bathroom. It's a joke among my friends that I show up at the stage door looking like a cleaning lady.

Once in San Francisco, I had arrived to play the wicked stepmother in Brian Macdonald's production of *Cendrillon*. I had been given a luxurious star's dressing room in the newly refurbished War Memorial Opera House and it came complete with an enormous make-up mirror framed in hundreds of bulbs, all covered in dust. I took them out one by one and cleaned them. When the two girls who played my ugly step-daughters caught me, they couldn't believe it. They just roared. But I explained that it all went back to having a mother who wasn't tidy.

My mother's career as a maid was short-lived. She went on to work as a waitress in a tearoom called the Irish League, which was more her style since she was gregarious and liked to make people laugh. Even as a young girl with auburn hair and sparkling brown eyes, she was large and jolly with a build not unlike mine; but the main difference between us was that she had a weakness for hats. She was once stopped on the streetcar by a hat-maker who asked her if she would model his creations. Watching my mother, I learned that no matter how big you were, you could carry yourself down the street like a queen.

I've always maintained that my mother ought to have been a minister's wife. She was in her element in church choirs or at bazaars and visiting shut-ins. She may once even have had her chance: for a time, she kept company with the Reverend John McIlroy who had come out from Belfast too. But then she met Thomas Forrester and that was that.

He was tall with receding reddish-blond curls, a shy, quiet man with a serious air and a big crooked Scottish nose. He had a slow, dimpled smile and one look from those soft, grey-blue oysterish eyes could pierce you to the heart. He had emigrated from Glasgow with his parents when he was a teenager and his father found work with the CPR in Montreal's Angus Shops. His mother died soon after they arrived so all seven children left school early and took up a trade. My father, who was the eldest son, became a cabinetmaker.

One night when he was at a Caledonia Society party, he saw a big lively brunette standing on the fringes of the crowd. He asked her to dance, but she said she didn't know how. "Well, I'll teach you then," he said in his Scottish burr. He was a beautiful ballroom dancer and they fell in love that night. They courted until my mother came of age and didn't need two witnesses to sign the permission to wed. Her twenty-first birthday was March 27, 1917, and on March 28, they were married.

My father didn't have much money and they never had an easy life. Their first two children were stillborn and so was their last. But finally Beryl came along and two years later Arnold and two years after that Jean. I was the afterthought child, ten years younger than Beryl and six years younger than Jean. By the time I was born, July 25, 1930, Montreal was still caught in the depths of the Depression, and my father was out of a job, struggling to make ends meet by building houses out in Longueuil on the south shore of the St. Lawrence. We had so little money that he would trudge across the frozen river to work, fighting that cruel winter wind just to save carfare.

Our family was still living then in a third-floor rue Fabre flat. My first memory is of being carried in a wooden crib down the street with my father at one end and my Uncle Dick at the other while I peered out at the world between the slats. My mother always said it was impossible I could remember back that far since I was only nine months old at the time. But I have a clear recollection of that day when we moved down rue Fabre to the first-floor apartment where I was to spend the next twenty-one years of my life.

Cave-dwellings, I've always called those Montreal row houses, because they were so long and dark. There was a regulation central hall with two rooms on each side, but windows only at the front and back which made the ground-floor flats depressing and damp. There was no central heating. Exposed pipes ran through the house and when you wanted hot water, the electric jacket heater would only warm enough for a four-inch bath once a week on Saturday nights. In the winter we would hang the frozen washing from the pipes to thaw and I remember suits of my father's long underwear ballooning up in the heat until they looked like Bonhomme, the snowman king of the Quebec winter carnival, bobbing above the dining room.

The living room had two ersatz Greek columns holding up an arched doorway and there was a fake electric fireplace with metal logs that would glow with a little red light when you switched it on. On the walls were brass plates with pseudo-English hunting scenes and framed copies of Gainsborough's *Blue Boy* that Woolworth's turned out by the thousands. Everything was an imitation of something else, tokens of a grander style my mother aspired to.

Still, we didn't have much in that house. My mother never had a washer, we didn't get a real refrigerator for years and the day we bought a wooden stand-up radio with a green magic-eye tuner on top, which looked like an ominous cyclops, was a day for a full-scale celebration. But everything we did have we owed to Mr. Levitt. He would come round on Saturday mornings selling his wares – sheets, dishes, the latest gadgets, even my first good black velvet dress – and my mother would pay for them on time, $2 a week for life. When she didn't have the $2, she wouldn't answer the door. "Hush," she would say, "don't let him see your shadow." Mr. Levitt was like the original credit card.

But despite his persuasive powers, in our house nothing ever matched. The plates were a mishmash, and my mother never used the napkins that went with the tablecloth because they might wear out. In the end, when the tablecloth wore out, we were always left with piles of orphaned napkins. The first thing I bought when I began to make money was tableware. Most people go out and splurge on a mink coat but I wanted matching sets of china, crystal and linens.

All through my childhood, I never had a room of my own. Beryl, the eldest, had hers behind a curtain at the end of the living room, but as the youngest I always had to sleep with somebody else. Once even after Beryl got married, when she came home because her husband was away on a hunting trip, she bunked in with me. In the middle of the night I woke up in the dark sticky all over, with a strange, pungent smell filling the room. It turned out that she had been pregnant and had miscarried in the night. I was lying in a pool of blood. From my earliest years, I longed for privacy.

At times we were eight in those five rooms on rue Fabre. After the 1921 uprising in Belfast, my mother brought her youngest sister Bertha out, and she lived with us until she quit her job as a Bell Telephone operator to marry my uncle, Dick Wallace. My father's father had lived with my parents since he retired from the CPR and he stayed almost until the day he died of a cold at the age of ninety-five. But he didn't like my mother and the feeling was mutual. It wasn't just the fact that he was Scottish and she was Irish. My grandfather was a dapper little man, no taller than five feet. He looked like Charlie Chaplin with his neat little moustache and his bowler hat, his waistcoat, spats and cane. But to get that way he spent an hour and a half in the bathroom every morning, which drove my mother wild

He also used to like his two or three glasses of wine a day – *whiskey blanc*, we children called it – and a glass of brandy before bed. Drinking was anathema to my mother, who was a teetotaller, and she made him take them in his room. The two of them were constantly at loggerheads. She would throw him out of the house and my father would have to go out to the pub and bring him back. My grandfather smoked industrial-strength Canadian tobacco, which he chopped up himself, and he liked a good cigar, so he always seemed to be lost in a cloud of thick blue smoke. Every so often he would rearrange it with little staccato expulsions of breath that grated on my mother's nerves. I sometimes wondered if he didn't enjoy smoking so much just because it annoyed my mother, who used to complain that you could scrape the nicotine off the drapes in our house with a knife.

But I adored my grandfather and spent a lot of time with him. My mother was always out at Fairmont Taylor Presbyterian Church or one of her part-time jobs and

Beryl and Jean and Arnold were off with their friends. They didn't want to babysit the runt of the family. I decided then that if no one wanted to look after me, I would look after myself, and that's when I began my wanderings. I knew there was a better life on the far side of the fence if only I could find it.

When I came back my grandfather would always be there, often frying up his favourite blood pudding and onions that my mother would never make for him. We would have to throw open all the windows to get the smell out of the house before she came home. We were co-conspirators. He was always saying to me, "Ach, Maureen, the others, they've got legs like your father. Ya have got good, straight legs like me."

But for me, the most magical thing was his lifetime railroad pass from the CPR. Part of my wanderlust came from my travels with my grandfather. Because I never fussed or cried, he would take me along on his trips to visit relatives in far-off Ontario. In those days, when people in our circle couldn't afford to travel, the next province seemed worlds away from Montreal, but the distance only intrigued me more.

Once when I was three, my grandfather took me with him to Toronto to visit his son, my uncle Jim, who had been shot in the stomach in the First World War and spent most of the rest of his life in the veterans' hospital. There, in that bleak place, amid the row upon row of grey-blanketed beds, my grandfather stood me on a table in my pink coat and matching muff and I performed for the whole world.

I sang a song I knew, "How'm I Doing? Hey, Hey, Chee, Chee, Diddle Dee Daw." He said I really hammed it up and at the end, I even took a little bow to the applause. My grandfather swore he knew from that day that I would be an entertainer.

TWO

The Price of Being English

PAPINEAU. Laurier. Masson. Marquette and Garnier and De Lanaudière. Those street names conjure up a world so familiar to me I could draw a map of it today. The Montreal I grew up in was the Montreal of Mayor Camillien Houde, an enormous, jovial man who was suspended from office for fighting conscription during the war and was totally without social graces. When King George VI and the Queen came to visit, he greeted them with, "Hello, Mr. King. Hello, Mrs. Queen." Everybody loved the joke when they nicknamed the public toilets in Place d'Armes "les Camilliens." This was the Quebec of Maurice Duplessis with road-paving contracts doled out like confetti at election time and the Church in stern control of morals and reading lists. But my universe was innocent of the politics that were simmering below the surface of the province around us. In our working-class enclave, we were poor but proud, nobody had anything but everybody mixed – French and English, Catholic and Protestant.

A number of artists were bred in those blocks – the singer Jeanne Desjardins lived behind us and the poet Sylvain Garneau across the street. Years after I left, Michel Tremblay, the playwright, grew up on rue Fabre and gave it a starring role in his plays. The life shown in those dramas like *Albertine in Five Times* is not so different from ours then.

In our neighbourhood the Fête de St. Jean Baptiste was such a celebration every June 24 that we assumed the whole world hailed it with a parade like the one we had through Lafontaine Park. On the Fête de Corpus Christi the priests would come swinging incense through the streets under a tiny canopy and all the Catholics would kneel right there on the sidewalk. We few Protestants who didn't stood out like interlopers. On the Sunday of First Communion, though, we would be green with envy when our Catholic friends filed through the neighbourhood on their way to St. Stanislas, the boys in their new suits with their hair slicked back in a helmet of Brylcreem, the girls dressed up in long white dresses with veils like little brides. At those moments, it seemed so boring to be Presbyterian.

There was no doubt that we were a minority. In all, there were only half a dozen English families on our block. Four French couples lived in the flats above us and there were French households on either side. Lajeunesse the druggist lived on the second floor and over him La-Belle the taxi driver. Monsieur Bussière's general store/*épicerie* was three houses away.

My father would get on the phone to order the weekly groceries from him. "Ah, Monsieur Bussière," he would say, "you geeve me two pound butter, one loaf bread. . . ." He would recite it all in a thick Québécois accent and he thought he was speaking French. My mother could utter two words of French at the most: *"bonjour"* and *"merci."* But I would come home from school and she would tell me about the latest neighbourhood catastrophe – say, how a delivery truck had run over the little Rivard boy at the corner – and she could relate it all right down to the goriest details.

"But Mother, how do you know all this?" I would ask.

"Why, Madame Lajeunesse told me over the fence when we were hanging out our wash." Madame Lajeunesse, who didn't speak a word of English! There they were, not knowing a sentence of each other's language, communicating over the clothesline all those years. I never understood how they managed it, but it was bilingualism in action over the back fence.

Madame Lajeunesse later reappeared in my repertoire. When I recorded some ethnic songs by John Beckwith, one was a child's counting ditty, "L'habitant de Saint Roch s'en va au marché," and I decided to sing it in a high, flat nasal voice which is typical of so many women in Quebec. The people in the recording studio roared. "*Where* did you pick up that voice?" they marvelled.

"That's Madame Lajeunesse," I said, "my former next-door neighbour."

We English kids spoke street French, and now when the Canada Council gives me a speech to read in both official languages, I always tell them that the vocabulary they put in my mouth is a long way from the vocabulary I picked up on rue Fabre.

The French children in our neighbourhood went to school at St. Stanislas Church and we Protestants went to William Dawson Elementary School, which was eight blocks down boulevard St. Joseph. It meant that we mostly played with our own kind, but, unlike my sisters, I had French friends as well. Although we all coexisted fairly easily in that time before language became such a sore point in Quebec, there were tensions between the lines of the banter. You would hear playmates griping about what some French kids had done – an attitude they no doubt picked up from their parents – but even in those days I hated prejudice of any sort.

One Saturday morning not long after I had started school, I was on my way to Verdun to see a Walt Disney movie. In Quebec at that time, a fire in a downtown movie house and the pressure of the Church had conspired to make it illegal for anyone under sixteen to enter a cinema, even with an adult, but everyone knew that Verdun winked at the law. Children from miles around would spend hours on public transit every week to converge on the two theatres there for the Saturday matinee. I was walking down rue Fabre to the car stop on an icy winter's day when, halfway down the block, a French boy from a few doors away came up behind me with an iron shovel and smashed me over the head. He knocked me out. When I came to in a snowbank, I was in terrible pain. I crawled across the street to the house of an English family I knew from our church and hauled myself up the spiral iron staircase to their second-floor apartment. A goose egg had started to swell on my skull but I told them that I'd fallen and hit my head on the ice. I didn't want my parents to find out what had actually happened because I knew my father would have come down and killed that boy. Afterward, because I hadn't pointed a finger at him or made a scene, I found that it was as if I had passed some test. From then on, the French gang accepted me without reservation into the neighbourhood: it seemed that I had taken my punishment for being English.

It wasn't a rough district but it had the raw edges of working-class life. Nine times we were robbed via the back lane as we sat out on the tiny front stoop taking the air. Once in the winter Beryl came running in to my mother with something she had found in a snowbank in the back alley. "Look at the funny doll," she said. My mother almost passed out. It was a frozen foetus, aborted or mis-carried, that somebody had thrown over the balcony into a snowdrift.

But although our streets were never dull, I yearned for a glimpse of the city beyond them. Friday nights and Satur-days at last I could venture farther afield when my father took me with him to do the grocery shopping. We would walk down to Mount Royal Street and St. Lawrence – "The Main" – where he taught me how to pick chickens by the colour and the feel of the breast. To me, those shopping trips were high adventure. Off we would go past all the stores spilling their vegetables and spices into bins on the street, past the kosher butcher shops on The Main with their red Hebrew letters swirling on the glass in front of the live hens sulking in their cages. We would wander sometimes as far as St. Denis and St. Urbain into another world entirely, which was mysterious and delicious to me. I would peer down the narrow streets into tiny synagogues which looked like storefronts, where men were gathering in the dusk in their *yarmulkas* and *talises*, rocking at their prayers.

I was always curious about other people, but my father was wary of customs that he didn't understand. He kept his distance. But at least he wasn't like some in our neighbourhood who whispered that the Orthodox Jews with their little velvet bags embroidered with the Star of David were carrying, not their *talises* and *tefillin* inside, but the knives they used for bloodletting. To me Judaism seemed an exotic world, and I never dreamed then I would some day be part of it.

On Friday nights when the shopping was done, my father would take me to a drugstore soda fountain and sit me up high on a stool at the counter. I could have anything I wanted – a soda or, in winter, a hot chocolate with a marshmallow melting in a puddle on top. I was in heaven, watching the Friday night bustle and flirtations around me at the counter. My father would ask the manager to keep an eye on me, then he would slip next door into the beer parlour to down a couple of glasses of ale. My mother wouldn't allow liquor into the house, except in the case of my grandfather whom she couldn't control, and somehow, though my father never said a word, I always knew enough never to tell her about his disappearances. It was an unspoken promise between us. My mother would have died if she had known that he had left me alone like that when I was barely knee-high. But it didn't frighten me. I felt like a grown-up, keeping a secret pact with my dad as he sat next door in that dark, foul-smelling tavern with sawdust on the floor.

I was accustomed to being left on my own. In winter, I would stay out all day long, skating or tobogganing in

Wilfrid Laurier Park, often without a playmate. I would only come home to change my snowsuit, which filled the house with the smell of burning wool when I threw it over the coal stove to dry. I never got tired or lonesome if I didn't have a pal. I was a happy-go-lucky kid and my mother never worried about my whereabouts.

Sometimes my father would take me to a baseball game with him or to watch the Junior A hockey matches at the Montreal Forum. The speed and the excitement of the game and gorging on popcorn and Coke in that enormous bright rink – that was my idea of entertainment. In those days hockey was still sheer sport, with no high-sticking or blood on the ice.

In a way, I was the son my father wished he'd had in Arnold. My brother wasn't interested in sports, which was a terrible disappointment to my dad. Arnold was a poet and a dreamer who wrote the most beautiful verses to my mother. Whenever he got in trouble, she would lie for him and I couldn't forgive her for that. He was not a strong boy and because of my mother, he never learned to stand on his own. It seemed that my father was always taking his belt to Arnold for something or other. He grew up moody and, although I was too young to understand it at the time, I'm sure that he tried to commit suicide once in his teens. My father had to go out and bring him in from the back shed where he was closeted with a shotgun.

The only time we escaped the neighbourhood for long was in summer when my father would take us up north to the foothills of the Laurentians. No matter how poor we were, there was always money for that seasonal ritual. Except for weekends when he would join us after work, he would leave us for weeks in some country village or other – St. Rose or St. Gabriel-de-Brandon and later Rawden where my two sisters came to live after they left Montreal during the rise of separatism. I wondered sometimes if he wanted to be rid of us all – to take his tea and read his papers in peace, to putter with his vegetables alone in his tiny back garden with its stubborn soil.

Since my father never owned a car we always had to ride up to the country by bus, and in the war years, the buses were ancient wrecks. Sometimes one of those rickety old coaches would rumble up Highway 18 with so much luggage stuffed inside and piled high on the roof that the driver couldn't make the hills. He would ask all the passengers to get out at the bottom of the grade and we would have to hoof it up to the top to meet him.

One summer we rented a minister's log house in the middle of the wilderness outside St. Gabriel-de-Brandon. The cabin was by a ruined mill left from the logging days, and miles from any neighbours. When my mother hung the laundry on the line, bears would often come and claw it off. Quite a shock for a girl from the streets of Belfast! My father would go out in the morning and catch fresh trout for breakfast and I can still smell them sizzling in the pan over the woodstove that my mother hated to stoke. There was a built-in bureau in the cabin and when we arrived, my father took a crowbar to the top and lifted it off. He made me a bed right there in the highest drawer. One of my earliest memories is of sleeping on that lofty mattress of pine needles.

I can remember, too, the summer storms that used to break over St. Rose. I would huddle in my father's lap in a wooden swing rocker on the verandah and watch as the black clouds blotted out the sun and the skies opened in a deluge. "Ah," my father would say with each crack of thunder, "it's the angels. They must be bowling." From that time on I've never been afraid of thunderstorms.

Later, we moved our summer escapes to Rawden where we had a flat – a second-floor quadruplex just off the main street of town. It was hardly rustic but that was what working-class people thought of as a country house in those days. The building had one of those sloping patterned tin roofs typical of Quebec and when it rained it sounded as if you were trapped inside an oil drum. Beside the kitchen, where a back shed would normally have been, an outhouse was attached and on a warm day, my, was that part of the house pungent!

Every night we went to Haddad's dance hall and soda fountain where we could feed nickels into a big coloured neon nickelodeon in the back room. I loved to hang out there and pretend that I was already a teenager, sipping on a Coke and watching the older boys and girls dance. Nearby there was a summer camp for the deaf, who would often come into town. One night at Haddad's one of the deaf boys beckoned me out onto the floor and he turned out to be one of the best jitterbuggers I've ever known. He could whirl and jump without missing a beat. I couldn't believe it later when I discovered he didn't hear a thing: he picked up the beat from the nickelodeon's vibrations pounding on the dance-hall floorboards.

To me, those days in the Laurentians meant freedom. They gave me a taste for the rocks and pines I flee to north of Toronto now every spare moment I can find. They were days of paddling in icy lakes or exploring the forests which would be starting to turn scarlet by the last weeks of August as we were packing up for the city. At night there would be campfires on the beach – hot-dog roasts and sing-songs in both English and French. The French kids would sing out their history – songs their parents and grandparents had sung before them. It's one of the reasons French Canadians have a strong culture: they pass on their traditions and myths in the songs they teach their children.

I often wonder if the reason I have such a lust for life is that I grew up in the boisterous jollity of Quebec. Back home on rue Fabre I would find any excuse to drop in on the French-Canadian families around us. They welcomed me like one of their own. The kitchen was always the biggest room in the house and family life seemed to re-volve around mealtimes, which made me dizzy with their intoxicating smells: ragoûts and Tourtières and thick pea soups studded with ham, not to mention my favourite, sugar pie – maple syrup or, if there was no money, just plain brown sugar drizzled over a buttered crust and baked till it perfumed the whole house. Everybody would gather around the kitchen table and tell the stories of the day and guffaw. They seemed so lusty and good-natured – my idea of what a family should be. Their meals weren't like ours where somebody was always looking at somebody else the wrong way and stalking off from the table in a huff, slamming doors.

In our house, by the time I came along, there was no sense of family. Except for Sunday lunch, our meals were helter-skelter – just eat and run. I believe, as I told Emmett Cardinal Carter one day, "It isn't the family that prays together that stays together, it's the family that eats together." Later, even when I was away on tour, I always insisted that my children sit down to a proper hot meal at night where they could talk to each other about what had happened to them that day. From my French neighbours, I learned early that mealtimes were the glue of family life.

But what I loved best about dropping in on the French Canadians around us was that long after dinner they would stay at the table and sing. Each person would take a turn with a solo, even the smallest child. The mother would sing about the loss of a baby – how the Virgin Mary came and took the infant away – and then an uncle would belt out a song about the bounty of the harvest. They sang out their happiness and their grief. In song they expressed all their emotions.

THREE

Prima Donna

"NO DIVA," a friend suggested I call this book. I am as famous for *not* having temper tantrums as Maria Callas was for indulging in them. The only time I admit losing my cool was a few years ago when I arrived ten minutes before a performance of the *St. Matthew Passion* at Montreal's Place des Arts. As I pulled up, a parking attendant yelled, "Move on, lady, it's full up." I can't count how many free concerts I gave to help build the Salle Wilfrid Pelletier, and when it opened in 1966 the one thing they forgot to include was parking space for the artists. "You can find yourself another singer then," I stormed at the attendant, but it didn't make any impression on him. I was left traipsing through the slush, hiking my couturier pale blue chiffon above my sodden evening shoes. I made such a fuss that night that I've had a parking space there ever since.

But that's the only incident I can recall. I have no time for theatrics. One of the reasons conductors re-engage me is that I turn up on time, I know my part and I'm cheerful. I feel that temperament is just an excuse for not knowing your work. But no wonder I can't stand a scene. In our house, my mother had the monopoly on melodrama.

One day will always stay in my mind. I was playing in the kitchen on Saturday morning after Arnold had just washed the floor and he was standing at the stove frying some bacon. Jean came in from the back lane with mud on her saddle shoes and he was furious. She started taunting him and he picked up the raw bacon and smacked her across the face so hard with it that he left a welt. They started screaming at each other, and my mother came running in and she started screaming too.

"Children, stop it," she shrieked. But nobody was paying attention to her, so she threw herself down on the floor and started writhing and moaning and gnashing her teeth. That was typical of my mother; whenever she didn't get her way, she would collapse and froth at the mouth.

Years later, after she'd had several heart attacks, I finally asked a doctor to run tests to see if she was even a borderline epileptic. For the sake of my children and grandchildren, I thought it was important to know. But the tests came back negative and the doctor explained that some people are able to pull off those symptoms just to get attention.

My mother was constantly having the vapours. She could turn tripping down the stairs of the choir loft into major histrionics with a Sarah Bernhardt swoon and an ambulance ride to the emergency room. Years later, it used to make my husband Eugene furious. I would limp home from a tour utterly exhausted after weeks on the road, and always twelve months pregnant, as Eugene used to say. My mother would have come to visit the children for a week and stayed six months so she would be sitting there when I came in. "How are you, Mom?" I'd ask.

"Oh, darlin', I'm so tired," she'd say. "Make me a cup of tea. I'm feelin' a bit poorly."

She didn't think people loved her unless she had their sympathy. It wasn't until after she died that my children told me stories about what she would do when I was away. If they misbehaved or were rude to her, she would flounce upstairs. Half an hour later the doorbell would ring and it would be a taxi. She would come down the stairs with her coat on, carrying her suitcases.

"Granny, where are you going?" they would cry.

"Well, I never thought I would live to see the day my

own grandchildren would talk to me that way. I'm going home."

"Oh, Granny, don't go away," they would wail. "Mommy will kill us." They would be crying and begging and feeling just awful, but off she would go in the cab, only to return three hours later, usually after seeing a movie. She would walk back in and say that there hadn't been any seats free on a plane. "But I'm going another day," she would warn, "unless you learn to behave."

As even those incidents showed, my mother was a terrific actress. She was a woman of enormous talent who loved to be the centre of attention and the way she told a story could convulse any crowd. She was always entertaining at church socials where she would dress up like Oliver Hardy of Laurel and Hardy with my father's jacket and bow tie and my grandfather's bowler hat. She would stuff a pillow in her pants and paint on a toothbrush moustache and have the whole church basement in stitches at her pratfalls.

The church was the centre of her social life. It pulled her out of the doldrums of lower-middle-class existence into a dream world of music and parties and fun. I suppose my mother was a disappointed woman. She had wanted to be somebody and have money, but it didn't work out that way. She had married a man who loved her and earned a living, but that wasn't enough for her. She longed to be a respected person in the community and the ticket to that was her church work.

With all the volunteering she did, plus her part-time jobs, my mother was never home. Stella Roy, her best friend who lived up the block, fed me more lunches than she ever did. Mrs. Roy was the kind of mother I dreamed of having. One day while I was playing hide-and-seek, I slipped and fell on a broken milk bottle under the stairs and blood started gushing from my leg. I had to run up the street to Mrs. Roy for a tourniquet, because when I went home my mother had promptly fainted.

She didn't have a domestic bone in her body. One night

at dinner I sat down to a fillet of sole she had made and when my father saw me screw up my face after the first bite, he was furious. "But it tastes of soap!" I cried.

"That's no way to talk of your mother's cooking," he said and sent me to my room.

Then the rest of them dug in and their eyes grew wide. "My God, but it does taste of soap," my mother said. It turned out that my sister had put her shampoo in the icebox and my mother had thought it was lard.

My father was the cook in our family, but he only displayed his skills once a week for the big Sunday lunch after church. He never went to the service himself. "If I wanted to pray to a god," he would say, "I can pray at my lathe." He would stay home and roast chickens and beef, and for dessert stud a blanc-mange with dates. He made the most wonderful winter soup from a brisket bone with parsnips and carrots and potatoes that he used to leave out on the back porch overnight, but I've never succeeded in duplicating that broth which I associate with some of the happiest moments of my childhood. We would all come in from church and there he would be, bent over the stove in his apron, whistling the theme song from the Sunday morning radio gospel singer.

Otherwise my father was a very formal man – a dour Scot, proper, almost prudish. When I was outside playing in my shorts, my mother would shout into the street for me to come in and put on a dress, in case my father got home early. He wanted to see me in a dress with a petti-coat, those little patent-leather Mary Janes and a bow in my hair, which I detested.

I can still see him coming up the street from work, a tired man walking so slowly up those three long blocks. After the Depression he had found a job at Northern Electric, installing switchboards for Bell Telephone wher-ever they were putting in a new plant, and he stayed there until he died. He kept his coveralls at work, setting off every morning in a jacket and tie with a gold pocket-watch on a chain at his belt, but by the time he came home at night, his tie would be shoved into his pocket and he would be carrying his toolbox. That picture is etched in my memory: my father trudging up the block, listing to one side from the weight of that heavy toolbox.

He worked so hard all his life. He would come home late from Northern Electric and when my mother would ask why, he would say, "Oh, they sent me a young carpenter today who can't even hammer a nail straight. I had to stay and re-do all his work. But he's a nice lad. I didn't want to get him fired."

He was a good man, a logical man. The emotional side of me comes from my mother and I've always fought it because I never wanted to be like her – out of control. The reasonable side of me comes from my father and, thank heavens, it usually wins out. Whenever I have a problem, I ask myself what my father would have done and I talk it over with him mentally. I've always believed that what I inherited from him is the best of me.

My father tried to be patient with my mother, even when he had given her money to pay the telephone bill and she had gone out and spent it on a new hat. My mother was a darling woman but she couldn't take responsibility. They would fight and she would stomp out of the house. Off she would go to a movie or to visit a friend and when she came back, he would say, "Well, I'm glad to see you've calmed down. Now, I've fixed you a little something in the kitchen." And there in the icebox would be her favourite lobster salad.

They loved each other but they bickered all the time. One day when they were fighting, I screamed, "Why don't you two get a divorce?"

They stopped dead and looked at me in shock; they were absolutely crushed. It was as if I had suggested stepping into the furnace – unthinkable. Bickering was just a natural part of their romance.

But how I hated it; I hate it to this day – screaming, scenes, confrontation of any kind. It makes me almost sick to my stomach. Whenever they fought, I'd run out of the room and sit down at the old upright Knabe piano in the parlour and start banging away.

From the moment I was big enough to crawl up on the piano bench, that keyboard was where I learned to lose myself when the world got too much for me. Even then, music was my refuge.

FOUR

The Sounds of Music

MY MOTHER took me by the hand and off we went, along St. Gregoire, up Papineau and across the railroad tracks to my first piano lesson. The house where we arrived was small and dark. Inside, the furniture was mock English, heavy with an air of dust and age. Faded maroon velvet sofas and worn red-silk lampshades crammed the room. A thick musty carpet hung over the top of the upright piano to keep the noise of the pupils from irritating the neighbours through the paper-thin walls.

I was barely five years old and when I slid onto the piano bench in my little smocked dress, my feet wouldn't touch the floor. The piano teacher, a woman in her sixties, sat down beside me. She went over the scales with me in her quavering voice and I followed patiently, but I had been doodling on the piano at home ever since I could remember and I could already play by ear. In that first lesson, all I could think about was the fact that the teacher smelled *old*. I gagged on the odour of decay and clothes that were never cleaned. After a few months, I would pretend to go to my piano lessons and disappear until my mother finally caught on. Parents should pay more attention to things like that. If a child doesn't like music lessons, I recommend that the first thing to try changing is the teacher. I would play better today if I had liked my first piano instructor.

From my earliest memory, there was always music in our house. I could hear it spilling out of the living room and up the long dark hall to the room where I slept. We gathered around the piano whenever there was a party or a christening or a wake. It was the hub of our entertainment, our only luxury. My father would sit down and play by ear the songs that he knew from the old country or from the radio. He would sing "Ye Banks and Braes, O Bonnie Doon," and, if they had company, he and my mother would perform their courting duet, he in his tenor, she in her alto, "Madam Will You Walk, Madam Will You Talk, Madam Will You Walk and Talk With Me?"

I don't remember a time when I didn't sing. My mother told me that even in the cradle I hummed to myself. It was something I just did, a natural part of my life. I never thought there was anything unusual about it.

On Sunday mornings, getting ready for church, my sisters and I would listen to a radio program called *The Bunny Bus*, emceed by Milton Cross, the announcer from the Metropolitan Opera, which was a sort of children's talent hour. Later, cleaning up after my father's Sunday lunch, Jean and I would harmonize over the dishes, repeating the songs on that show: "Sierra Sue" and "The Isle of Capri," and we knew every word of a crazy, corny tune by the Moylin Sisters called "Lazy, Lack-a-Daisy Melody." I was the youngest, so I always got stuck with the washing. I would lean over the sink with my forehead resting on the single low-slung dish cupboard overhead, scrubbing the pots, and we would try to imitate the Moylin Sisters' flat whiny sopranos.

Later, when I was in school, my best friend Ruthie Maclean and I would sit out front on the bumpers of cars during hot summer nights and harmonize to the sheet music of popular songs they used to publish in comic book form. I spent hours sprawled by the radio in the living room listening to the band singers whose voices would drift over the the airwaves between *The Green Hornet* and *Inner Sanctum*: Frank Sinatra, Rosemary

Clooney, Dick Haymes and Dinah Shore. Until I began taking singing lessons, I had barely listened to a classical piece in my life. I came from a family that didn't know the music I became famous for.

Choirs provided my mother's main social outlet and she took her singing extremely seriously. When she didn't win a solo she would be in a pique and when she did, she would be so nervous that the entire family knew enough to stay out of her way the Sunday morning beforehand. She was determined that all of her daughters would sing. Beryl and Jean were both in the Fairmont Taylor choir with her, but Beryl had a high thin voice and, although Jean had a lovely mezzo-soprano, my mother never managed to turn either of them into singers. By the time I came along, she focussed all her frustrated ambitions on me.

Even before I started school, she taught me the songs she knew as a girl from the ancient wooden trunk of Irish sheet music that she kept in the back shed: "Homing," "Think on Me" and "Bless This House." One of her favourites was "Macushla," an old Irish ballad. In 1985 when Prime Minister Brian Mulroney asked me to sing it at the Shamrock Summit for President Reagan on St. Patrick's Day, I realized that I couldn't remember the words. I had quite a time finding the text of that song, but when I finally located a copy at the CBC, I phoned Brian Macdonald, the director of the show, in a panic. "Are you sure you want me to sing this?" I said. "It's not a love song, it's a song about a dead girl!" After all, it was supposed to be a light-hearted variety show for President Reagan and so many people think he's embalmed anyway. But Brian just waved my worries away.

"The Prime Minister loves it," he said. "Sing it anyway. Nobody will ever notice."

He turned out to be right. But I had forgotten what a beautiful song "Macushla" was. Every time I would practise it in Quebec City before the show, the oddest thing would happen. The whole Place des Arts rehearsal hall would go quiet and suddenly all the RCMP and Secret

Service agents who were casing the joint would emerge from their hideouts to listen to it. I even caught one with a tear in his eye. It must have brought back their childhoods as well. That's the wonderful thing about a song; it can press the buttons of memory.

From my mother's flair for dramatics, I learned early how to throw emotion into the words of whatever I sang. By the time I was six, she had me booked up performing for Ladies Aid teas, where I was famous for my rendition of "Christopher Robin." I acted the whole thing out: the high little child's voice at prayer, the dramatic pause. I would have the ladies dabbing at their eyes with handkerchiefs in no time. For a natural ham like me, interpretation came effortlessly, as long as I liked the words to a song.

But those neighbourhood successes meant my life became a round of performing at church socials and suppers. The only one I never wanted to miss was the annual concert which always included a solo by a Scottish baritone from our congregation. For that, my friends and I always tried to grab a front-row seat. Every year, you could set your watch by it, as soon as he would hit a high note, his false teeth would come flying out and we would scramble trying to field them.

But most of the rest of my performances just seemed like a chore. Because singing came so easily to me, I never regarded it as important at all. I was a child soprano like so many others and I only performed to please my mother. What I wanted to do was skate and ski and play basketball. I would run in after school, excited about the prospect of going to a game, and my mother would say, "Oh, but the Women's Christian Temperance Union will be so disappointed. I've promised them you'd drop around after class and do your 'Lord's Prayer' and your 'Christopher Robin.'" For years, singing was a duty like homework: it just kept me from doing the things I liked.

From the time I was very young, I was a tomboy. I liked to play with miniature cars in the dirt and I loved to build fortresses with the boys in the back lane. I was never interested in dolls, but later I graduated to playing "dress-up" with my friend Ruthie Maclean. Since her father was overseas, people were forever giving her family old clothes and we would swan around in tattered crepe dresses and ratty felt cloche hats, pretending we were glamorous ladies from Westmount. But those cast-offs sometimes turned out to be full of lice. Once when I got home, my mother had to pour coal oil over my head to stamp them out and she chopped off all my hair into a bob. I dreamed of someday having flowing blonde curls and being pretty.

"Puddin'" or "Pie Face," my sisters called me because I was so short and pudgy. Adults thought I was cute, but I never liked my looks and an incident that happened to me when I was about to turn seven didn't help. My father had sent me to a lumberyard six blocks away with my girl-friend Phyllis Warrens to pick up some wood moulding that he needed to repair the house. It was May 12, 1937, I remember, coronation day for George VI after Edward VIII had abdicated his throne for Mrs. Simpson, "the woman he loved," and my mother was at home glued to the radio, as she had been all through the scandal. In honour of the occasion, I was dressed up in my Sunday best – an apple-green smocked dress and patent leather shoes. I was coming back with the strips of wood in my hand, waiting at the corner of Laurier and Papineau, when a streetcar came along and the conductor motioned for Phyllis and me to cross. She made it to the sidewalk but just as I got past the front bumper, a car came screaming around the corner and hit me. With the impact, the driver slammed on his brakes and went into a skid, but my dress had caught on his fender and he dragged me face down on the pavement for half a block. I was semi-conscious with shock. My right cheek had been torn away, the flesh and muscle sanded clear through on the asphalt so you could see into my jaw.

Some passersby carried me to a second-storey doctor's office which overlooked the corner while somebody else called an ambulance. When I came to, the pain was hor- rific and I screamed and screamed. But part of my terror came from waking up and recognizing the doctor. I realized that it was the same man from whom I'd fetched a prescription for Paragoric as a favour to one of our neigh- bours and the errand had made my mother furious. She said that this doctor was a shady character who supplied women with dope, as they called it in those days, and there were hints of other things going on in his office that I couldn't even fathom at that age. "Take me home to my mother," I started yelling as soon as I saw him. I imagined that he was going to perpetrate some evil butchery or drug me. But of course when someone drove me home to my mother, she promptly collapsed.

At last, the ambulance found me and sped me off to the Montreal General. There, they used a treatment they had just developed. Instead of a scalpel, they applied acid to my face to lift out all the embedded gravel and dirt. I can still relive that searing pain. I brought down the hospital with my shrieks, but that acid is why I have no visible scars today.

The doctors kept me in the hospital for three days, then sent me home with a huge dressing around my head. When I got back to the neighbourhood I was a star and I basked in all the attention showered on me. But the no- velty soon wore off and I hated having to wear a patch on my face for the better part of a year, which made me feel ugly and freakish. By the end of it, though, the skin had totally regenerated itself, leaving me with only a tiny dark cast on one cheek that you can see in certain lights. Now, make-up artists can always tell at a glance that the two sides of my face are not symmetrical and a dentist doing work on my upper molars on that side told me a few years ago that it was a nightmare trying to find bone, but it's a small price to pay for an accident like that.

Still, like so many people in those days, my father didn't have a cent of insurance coverage, and that mishap was just another financial burden to bear. He had one stroke of bad luck after another in the family. My sister Jean developed rheumatic fever and had to spend a year in a convalescent home across the river in Châteauguay. Then Beryl was caught in a freak accident. She had been skipping rope on the sidewalk near our house when a soft-drink truck came careening around the corner. A wooden soda pop crate slipped off the back and fell on her, breaking an arm, a leg and her collarbone. Years later, she had terrible back problems and the doctors discovered that she had three kidneys. They speculated that one of them might have been split into two by the force of that blow so long before in her childhood.

At the time of the accident, my father tried to sue, but the company claimed the truck was nowhere near our street at that hour on that day, and the case was thrown out of court. My father couldn't believe it and he knew the only explanation was that someone had paid off the witnesses. He never said a word about the case again, but it was clear that his faith in justice had been shaken. For me, it was a rude awakening: I learned early that poverty leaves people powerless.

FIVE

One Hundred Men and a Girl

GROWING up poor and English in the wake of the Depression in Montreal was like life anywhere else. There was one sure place to let your fantasies roam free: at the movies. Even in Duplessis's Quebec, Hollywood shaped our dreams up on the silver screen. One Saturday afternoon when I was barely eight, I sat mesmerized by the matinee in Verdun. In the film, Deanna Durbin, Winnipeg's own Hollywood pet, was a poor but spunky teenager who was trying to talk a conductor, played by Leopold Stokowski himself, into forming an orchestra of down-and-out musicians, including her father. In the end, when she finally succeeded, she won her own solo and of course she brought down the house with Mozart's "Alleluja" aria. The movie was *One Hundred Men and a Girl*. For months afterward, I went everywhere warbling "Alleluja," pretending that I was Deanna Durbin singing with Leopold Stokowski and the Philadelphia Orchestra.

What I loved about it wasn't so much that she sang, it was the fact that she had taken her fate into her own hands. I was impatient even at that age to get on with my own. Some people dream of a knight coming along and changing their lives, but I always knew I would do it myself. Like Deanna Durbin, I would make my own magic.

The problem was that for the longest time, I just didn't see how. It never occurred to me then that music was a boarding pass out of rue Fabre. All I knew was that I didn't want to be working class. I was tired of hand-me-downs and frayed edges and I longed for my own things, brand new from the store. I hated never having spending money. I'd want to go to the United Church film Friday night where they would be showing a Tom Mix serial but by the time my parents had chewed over whether to give me the dime admission fee, I would always end up missing the first scene of the movie.

My father didn't believe in allowances for his children and that may be one reason we all quit school so young to work. I couldn't even buy a chocolate bar without my own pocket money. I had to ask for everything. Needless to say, that kind of dependence didn't suit a personality like mine. Eventually, I got so frustrated at always having to beg that I began to pinch money from the change that my father would take out of his pocket and leave on his bedroom bureau at night. At first, I only took a dime now and then but once I pinched fifty cents. I'll never forget that night when he walked out of the bedroom and demanded with a hurt look on his face, "Who borrowed fifty cents?" His diplomacy hung in the air like the most terrible accusation and the whole house fell silent. I never had the courage to admit that I was the guilty one, although I was sure that he guessed. But the anguish I felt over disappointing my dad promptly made me look for other ways to get the money I craved for my freedom.

From a very young age, I found myself after-school jobs. One of the first was baby-sitting for my cousin Bruce, a task I was always volunteering for because it also meant spending the night at my Aunt Bertha and Uncle Dick's house in Maisonneuve, which I far preferred to ours. There, everything was spanking new and clean and a model of domesticity. One step inside the door and you could smell my aunt's fresh-baked apple pies and sense the order; her rows of pickles and relishes were lined up neatly in the cold cupboard under the stairs. They didn't have any more money than we did – my Uncle Dick worked in the furnaces of Canadian Car and Foundry all of his life, which eventually cost him his hearing – but I secretly wished that they had been my parents. As soon as they went out at night, I would go straight to their dining room sideboard where they kept sherry in a cut-glass decanter on one side and my Uncle Dick's pipe rack on the other. Then, after I had made sure Bruce was asleep, I would turn on the radio, pour myself a little glass of sherry, fill a pipe and light it. I would sit back in a chair, puffing away, imagining that I was Uncle Dick. It never occurred to me to pretend that I was Aunt Bertha. It wasn't until years later that I told them about my evenings' entertainment. "Well, no wonder when we got home, we'd have such a time waking you up!" they said.

Later I graduated to baby-sitting for a Syrian family who had a beautiful roomy apartment overlooking boulevard St. Joseph. I loved going there as well, admiring their exotic furnishings, and I adored the woman who hired me so much that I would do chores for her, like washing floors, that I would never have dreamed of volunteering for at our house. One day I was walking home from school, just across the street from their building, when her brother called to me. He was standing in the doorway of his apartment, which was downstairs from his sister's. "My sister just phoned," he said, "and she wants me to ask you if you can mind the baby later in the week." I was delighted at the prospect and followed when he beckoned me inside. I realized then that all he was wearing was an elegant paisley silk dressing gown with an ascot. It was a shock for me to see a man dressed in anything but a shirt and trousers, but he told me that he was ill and that he had to go into the hospital soon.

"Would you do me a favour," he asked, "and run over to the store at the corner for a Coke and some cigarettes?"

He gave me the money and off I went. But as soon as I got back in the door, he pushed me down on the couch and tried to rape me. I didn't really understand what was happening at the time, but whatever it was, I knew I didn't want it. I wasn't so much scared as I was wild with rage. I somehow managed to get my knees up under him and, with the force of my fury, I heaved him off me. I pushed him so hard that he staggered backward clear into the dining room. I leaped up and raced out of there, running the entire eight blocks home. When I finally got to the safety of our door, I was out of breath and my hands were shaking. I looked down and realized I was still clinging to his change from the Coke and cigarettes. I never told my parents about the incident, but I refused to baby-sit for that woman again. She didn't understand why and I could never tell her. That's the Anglo-Saxon mentality for you: neither excite nor disturb. I didn't want to cause a ruckus.

It was my first real brush with sexuality and it hardly left me feeling kindly toward boys. As a wholesome tomboy, I had never been the type to be popular with them. I would always end up as their best buddy, advising them on how to get dates with my girlfriends. In my heart, I longed to be one of the clique of girls who ruled the corridors after class, but from the first years of school I found out that there was another way to win friends: I had the ability to make people laugh. Even at that age, I knew I had a kind of charisma that made me comfortable centre-stage. With my musical ear, I could mimic anybody and whenever the teacher left the room, my imitations of her would have the other students rolling in the aisles. I was the class cut-up and I would do anything to be popular, take on any dare.

The other kids knew it and they dared me to go to Woolworth's to steal an eraser. I did it and then it got to be an ongoing challenge. *Bet you can't do that, Maureen!* So I would show them: I would nip something bigger or more showy – never anything very expensive, just enough to keep up my shoplifting laurels. I got quite good at it. Then one day, I suddenly asked myself why I was doing it. I realized that in a way I was the patsy, taking all the risks, and if I had ever been caught, my father would have been mortified. The thought of him made me put a stop to my brief life of crime.

By the time I was eleven, the chubby little strawberry blonde who had always been short for her age had shot up into a giant overnight. Suddenly I was tall and slim and looked more like twenty. But I still wasn't interested in boys my own age and their obsession with playing spin-the-bottle at house parties, which were all the rage. I had energy to burn and I was frustrated with how little there was to do in our neighbourhood, so on the sly I joined the youth club at St. Dominique's Church. My parents would have died if they had found out I was defecting to the Catholics, so I used to tell them that I was out visiting friends. But I've always been grateful to Father Connolly, the ebullient priest who later ran off with one of his parishioners and caused a terrible neighbourhood scandal. It was from him that I learned to figure-skate and play cards.

Finally, I landed my first real job – selling cigarettes and ice cream cones in a corner smoke shop on Laurier Street owned by a Greek we called Mr. Gene. The store must have been grander once – at the rear there was an abandoned marble counter with three wire-backed ice cream chairs – but by the time I came to work in it after school, it was dingy and faded. Everything was covered with grime. Old Mr. Gene just sat in his big armchair in the back room, wheezing and letting the dust take over. I always felt sorry for him until I learned later that he was one of the biggest gamblers in Montreal.

It was while I was clerking for Mr. Gene that I started to smoke. From the shelves, Ruthie Maclean and I would buy a package of Sweet Caporals, and after the store closed, we would run to the loft in her back shed and light up. I was only eleven and we thought we were pretty hot stuff. But I couldn't inhale – in fact, I still can't – so after a while smoking seemed pointless, although it's surprising how many singers are smokers.

Working for Mr. Gene, I made what seemed like a small fortune for a girl my age. With my own money at last, I could indulge myself in the things that I had craved: lipsticks and twin sweater sets – the symbols of sophistication. I began to acquire a taste for financial independence.

By then my sisters and brother had all quit school and gone to work. Beryl, who was a striking blonde with such perfect posture that my father always called her The Duchess, had found a job at Eaton's, where she later became a buyer. She was very fussy about her own clothes and none of us were allowed to touch them as they hung in her room off the living room behind a flowered drape. Before she got married, she saved to buy beautiful lingerie for her trousseau; she was so fastidious that she insisted on meticulously washing out every piece, unworn, and hanging it all on the line behind the house to dry. When she came back out, she found everything gone, stolen by some boys from the back lane.

Jean had been an excellent student and she could have had any career she set her mind to. But at the end of the eighth grade when she won a scholarship to go on to high school, the teachers decided to award it to another girl whose father was out of work and needed the money more. At the time it seemed so unfair and it was as if something went out of Jean then. She stopped dreaming of becoming a nurse and seemed to lose interest in school. It wasn't long before she quit to work at Eaton's too.

At one point, everyone in our family seemed to be in the employ of Eaton's. Even my mother had a part-time job in the cash office for a while. Eaton's was like family to us and, rain or sleet, my mother and sisters would get up and go to the store because they felt Eaton's depended on them. It was only later when that whole generation was nearing retirement and a lot of them found themselves laid off before their pensions were due that they realized the feeling hadn't been mutual.

My brother had dropped out of school to work too, but

by then the war news was crackling over the radio every night. For me, it was a blur of faraway battlefield names and longwinded political exhortations on the *News of the World* clips at the Saturday matinee, where Gracie Fields showed up in person on a war bond tour to sing "The Biggest Aspidistra in the World." But for Arnold and a lot of boys his age, the war meant adventure and escape from the humdrum confines of home. He had volunteered for the Air Force as soon as the call for Canadian troops went out, but they turned him down because he'd had pleurisy as a child and he still had a shadow on one lung. By 1941, though, when they started to run short of recruits, they finally accepted him. He looked so dashing in his uniform and cap of Air Force blue as he went off to Britain, where he was assigned to an Australian bomber squadron, but he seemed so young and innocent too.

Almost every family we knew had some member away at the war, even the French Canadians in our neighbourhood, despite the bitter fight in Quebec against conscription. Then one by one the ominous signs began to appear: the wreaths of black crepe leaves suddenly tacked up on a front door to signal that the family inside had lost a son or a husband.

In 1942, as soon as Jean turned eighteen, she joined the Canadian Women's Army Corps and went to live in a barracks. She had grown so pretty that they asked her to pose for the army recruiting poster and the boy they chose to photograph with her was a handsome, clean-cut young man named Fred Norman. Right there, in the photographer's studio, these two good-looking young corporals in their helmets and khaki uniforms fell in love, and they were married two years later.

Throughout the city there were thousands of jobs vacant because all the men were away at the front. The papers were full of ads and most of the mothers on our block were rolling bandages or working on the assembly lines in munitions plants or at Canadair, doing their patriotic duty and making enormous salaries. The temptation to get a job was tremendous. School just didn't seem relevant.

By the time I was six months into high school, I had come to hate it. I had never been a brilliant student, but I always made passing grades. Still, when the war came along, a tough crowd had taken over William Dawson Elementary and – with only old teachers who ought to have been retired left in charge – they would tyrannize the class. When the teachers would try to give a lesson in math, those roughneck boys would just cross their arms and glower sullenly back, demanding another session of art. I knew I wasn't learning anything and I was bored. I longed to quit and get a job like my friend Ruthie Maclean.

She had gone to work at Royal Insurance and she told me there was an opening there. At first my father wouldn't hear of it. Like most of that generation of Scottish immigrants, he believed in the importance of education. But finally when I promised him that I would go to night school, he gave his consent. I left William Dawson Elementary without a backward glance.

I was only thirteen, under age, but the insurance company looked the other way. They were happy to find anybody to fill the low-paying clerical jobs that no one wanted when there were such big salaries luring people into war work. For my part, I was thrilled finally to be out in what I considered the real world. At last, I was on the way to making a better life for myself.

SIX

A Woman of Independent Means

I'VE NEVER had any patience with people who resent their lot in life and go around with a chip on their shoulder. Whenever I'm in a store and a clerk is rude to me or I practically have to beg to be served, I always wait until we're finally in conversation and I suggest that they ought to think about getting another job. At first, they're taken aback. They tend to think I'm trying to put them down, which isn't what I'm after at all. But then I share a bit of my own story with them. "You know, I want to tell you something," I say. "You obviously don't like what you're doing, but you shouldn't take it out on the customers. You should try to better yourself. There must be something you're really good at. I quit school at thirteen and now I speak four languages and I sing twenty-six. I'm a singer and I travel the world, I've given concerts for presidents and princes. If there's one thing I've learned, it's that you can be anything you want to be in life. You just have to put a little effort into it." Often by the time I leave, they actually end up thanking me for making them think about their lives. Even though I never had a negative attitude like that, I always see a lot of myself in those sales-girls. If it weren't for singing, I might still be a file clerk.

I was perfectly content as a working girl. I loved the feeling of being grown-up, dressing up every morning in my nylons and high heels and taking the streetcar downtown to Royal Insurance. Overnight, I made the leap from childhood to having responsibilities, skipping over a teenager's carefree years. My duties called for me to file and make photostats. Filing was a breeze, but making photostats in those days was just like printing photographs – an incredibly complicated process which involved plunging elbow-deep into great vats of nasty-smelling chemicals. I hated that so I taught myself typing. I picked it up by watching the other girls in the office at their keyboards and then staying late to practise until I actually became quite a good typist. I was always reading the want ads with an eye to getting ahead and finally I saw what I had been looking for: an opening for a typist at Dominion Insurance for a little more money a week than I was making.

I landed the job in the typing pool at Dominion Insurance, but I didn't stay there long either. I was always moving on for a few dollars more a month. I turned over my paycheques to my parents and they would give me spending money back – only $2 a week – but in those days $2 a week was a windfall.

My next job was as an auditor in Eaton's accounts department. In that era before credit cards, comptometer operators sat all day going through Eaton's bills, typing the charges on the proper customers' accounts at their little machines. The auditors had to verify the statements. I had a good eye for signatures and suddenly I recognized a slight discrepancy in the handwriting. I brought it to the attention of the department head and a scandal broke loose. They discovered that six or seven comptometer operators, who were used to certain customers' vacation schedules, were charging things to their accounts when they were away. It was all small potatoes – stockings, make-up, nothing of much extravagance – but it added up. Because of that, half a dozen people were fired from the accounts department, which, needless to say, didn't make me very popular at Eaton's.

I moved on to the contracts department at McKim Advertising. I had never gone to night school as I promised my father, but finally while I was at the advertising agency I enrolled in a commercial art course after work and I did rather well. One day as I was going off to my class, the head of the company's art department noticed my big sketch pad by my typewriter and asked to look at my work.

"Why, you're very talented!" he said. "Why don't you come to work as an apprentice in the art department?"

"What do you pay?" I asked.

"Seven dollars a week," he said. I was earning eight dollars a week by then, so I declined his offer. I might have turned out to be a commercial artist, but I wouldn't work for one dollar less.

I loved that art course, and one night I came home from class full of enthusiasm. I showed my father my sketches of the nude female model who had been posing for us. "I'm so excited," I said. "Next week we're going to have a man."

That was the end of my art lessons. My father's Scottish prudery barred me from ever going back. It broke my heart.

Even as a working girl, I spent a lot of time on my own. After a falling-out with Ruthie Maclean, I had learned to be wary of girlfriends. I was thirteen, the age when teenagers get crushes on one another, and I had thought the world of her. She was older than I, sixteen, and to me she represented sophistication. One day we had a date to go skating together at a big rink downtown which was *the* place to be seen. All week I had been planning what I would wear. I spent hours getting ready but she didn't come and didn't come. Finally I saw her walking by the house with her older sister.

"I've decided to go to the movies," she said. "I don't feel like going skating."

The snub was all the worse because she knew I wasn't old enough yet to get into the cinema downtown. I locked myself away in my bedroom and wept my heart out. In retrospect, it wasn't such a terrible rejection, but from that day on I learned never to depend on anybody completely. In every relationship, no matter how close, I always hold a part of myself back.

I still saw Ruthie from time to time, but our lives were taking us separate ways. She ended up getting married very young and we had less and less in common. Not long after her wedding, she and her husband were out driving in the country when they had a terrible car accident. He wasn't badly hurt, but the police took Ruthie to a little local hospital run by nuns who didn't realize that she had suffered a concussion. By the next morning, she was dead.

Without a chum to share adventures, I often spent my evenings alone. On Friday or Saturday nights, my treat was to take myself to Danceland, a huge hall upstairs over Dinty Moore's Tavern on St. Catherine Street which featured big bands. I would dress up in my best imitation wool plaid skirt and the oversized sweaters that were all the fashion, then I would borrow a little detachable white Peter Pan collar and pearls from my sister. Bobby socks and saddle shoes completed that uniform which was to stay around for more than a decade. I would dare a little lipstick, stuff my bra with socks and stick my comb in the peroxide bottle to see if bleached blondes had more fun. I couldn't have been more than fourteen at the time, but already, as a working girl, I was trying to look ten years older than I was.

I would tell my parents that I was going to St. Marc's youth club downtown, where I sometimes hung out, then I would hop the streetcar to Danceland. The ceiling was strung in coloured lights, but that was the extent of the decor. There were no tables and people just clustered around the walls when they weren't dancing. Occasionally some young man would ask me to foxtrot but I wasn't interested in being caught in a clinch during the slow numbers with somebody I didn't know. What I came for was to listen to the music.

Every band leader I had ever heard of played at Danceland: the Dorseys, Woody Herman, Glenn Miller and Louis Prima with his stone-faced girl singer Keely Smith. But my passion was Stan Kenton and his progressive jazz. His arranger, Pete Rugolo, used to do fabulous orchestrations which brought very classical colours out of that band.

I would stand right up front below the bandstand so that I could watch the inner workings of the orchestra – how the theme would pass from the saxophones to the clarinets to the trumpets. When they would lower the lights for the slow dances and the big mirrored silver ball in the centre of the ceiling would throw its rainbow reflections wildly over the crowd, I would press myself up against the stage and close my eyes, swaying to the music. I would dream I was a singer with the band. That was the height of my musical ambitions then: I wanted desperately to be a band singer at Danceland.

At one point, I went so far as to call Johnny Holmes, whose orchestra used to play for the Saturday night dances at Victoria Hall in Westmount. I had heard his soloist had moved to the West Coast and asked if I could audition for him. But he said he had decided not to use a girl singer that year. I was crushed. Years later when I met him again, I reminded him of it. "You know, if you hadn't turned me down," I teased, "I'd have been a band singer."

Sometimes the price of admission at Danceland would take all my money and I wouldn't have anything left for the streetcar home. I would have to walk back alone following a route by the railway tracks, but it never dawned on me to be afraid. Once I got in late and my parents were already in bed. I had to creep on tiptoes into the bathroom which was just off their bedroom at the back. Suddenly a mouse ran out and I was so startled that I heaved myself up on the sink. That sink was so old that it came right off the wall. The pipes broke and there was water gushing out everywhere. I started to scream, waking up my parents, and before long everybody was running all over the house with mops and pails. We were all up half the night sloshing around in water to our ankles.

My working life continued to undergo its constant transformations. After McKim Advertising I found a job I adored – manning the switchboard as a Bell Telephone operator. I got to talk on the phone all day long and, even then, I loved to gab. I learned a lot on that switchboard about dealing with the public. Of course, Bell Telephone wasn't computerized at the time so 400 girls would sit in front of identical boards of flashing lights with their headsets on. When a call came in, the top light would go on and as many as six girls might plug into it, even though only one of them would end up channelling the call. When it was over, the bottom light would flash to signal that you had to disconnect, but sometimes an operator would pull the plug accidentally on a person in mid-call and he would start screaming. The supervisors at Bell taught us that if somebody was yelling, the trick was to lower your voice. The other person can't hear you so it forces him to lower his voice too. It was a strategy that I found came in handy later in all sorts of situations.

On the telephone, my zany personality came out. When I worked the night shift and it was quiet, I would play jokes on my father and my uncle in New Jersey. I would connect them, imitating the voice of an operator in both countries, pretending each one had called the other. "Meester Forrester, zees is long distance calling from Montreal. . . ." They never did catch on.

I loved to listen in on calls and guess what people looked like. A lady would come on the line and say, "I want you to dial this number in Chicago. If a woman answers, say you're sorry, it's the wrong number. If a man answers, I'll take the call." Or a man would place a call from a hotel room and you could hear partying in the background. Then when his wife picked up the phone back home, his voice would become terribly grave. "Honey, I'm stuck here in this darn meeting and I'm not going to make it back tonight after all." I learned all there is to know about men from working as a long-distance operator.

I was so happy at Bell Telephone that at one point I felt I could have stayed there forever. But after two years, the longest I spent at any job, I found a better salary as a receptionist at Canada Dry. Then from there I left for even more money at Gutta Percha Rubber, the tire company. *"Gutta Percha, la société des pneus. Un moment, s'il vous plaît,"* I would answer the phone. For a while I thought I had found my destiny as a receptionist. I not only got to talk on the telephone, I got to meet people as well. I was always good-natured and on time and people liked my voice. I was savouring the feeling of success. It wasn't until I received my first cheque for singing that my life would take a turn that I could never have imagined then and I would start to see my voice as a way out of poverty.

SEVEN

A Lower Key

V-E DAY! THE war was over! In that spring of 1945, people ran out into the streets of Montreal banging their pots and baking tins in jubilation. But for our family, the celebration we had waited for so long was delayed. My brother Arnold's bomber had been shot down and he was the only one of the crew to survive. He had to stay on in hospital in England for weeks after the other boys had started to come home. When he finally sailed home on the *Queen Mary*, we gave him a hero's welcome on rue Fabre. He had grown taller and more handsome, and to me he looked a lot like Leslie Howard. Even though I had been working for two years, in Arnold's eyes I was still the kid sister he left behind and he christened me "Mighty Mo," after the battleship *Missouri* – a nickname I've been saddled with ever since. He was full of war jokes but it didn't take long to see that his good humour was only on the surface. The war had changed him forever. It seemed to me that the Arnold we knew had really died in that bomber crash.

At times he would sit and stare into space, oblivious that you were talking to him, and for the rest of his life he would plunge into terrible depressions. It was guilt, I think – the same guilt that was felt by the survivors of Auschwitz. He could never work indoors again or stand confinement. Later, the only job he felt comfortable in was working as a telephone lineman in Sept-Îles where he went to live with Nan, the sweetheart he came home to marry.

It was Arnold who, newly back from the war, had heard me warbling around the house and remarked that my voice had changed. "You're going to be an alto like Mother," he predicted. I was just fifteen and my soprano had started to crack like a pubescent boy's. I had noticed that I couldn't cut the high notes anymore in the Fairmont Taylor choir. The choral director moved me back to join the mezzos in the second soprano section, but as time wore on my voice kept darkening. Finally, one day he said to me, "Okay, Forrester, why don't you go help out the altos?" In choir terms, it was a demotion. Altos sing the harmony, they never get to sing the melody, so nobody was clamouring to be an alto. But the move didn't particularly faze me, since I still had no ambitions to be a singer.

At the time, Arnold suggested that I take lessons to smooth out the new bumps in my voice and he said that he had heard of a teacher named Sally Martin who lived in Westmount. He even offered to foot the bill. Although I liked singing in the choir well enough, I considered studying voice a waste of time. But Westmount was the magic word – the golden enclave where the wealthiest Montrealers lived in incredible mansions. I longed to see inside those houses. I followed his advice and signed up with Sally Martin but, in the end, I had to pay for all the lessons myself. It turned out that the only reason Arnold had talked me into studying singing was that, even though he was supposed to be engaged to Nan, he hoped to meet a girl who he knew was one of Sally Martin's other pupils.

Once I'd begun with Sally Martin, I was hooked. I loved taking the bus to her apartment in a gracious old stone building on Sherbrooke Street across from Westmount City Hall. She was a voice teacher like so many others, with a little clientele of teenage girls who sang in choirs, but to me she was the grandmother I had never known – a vivacious figure, short and plump with curly grey hair over laughing blue eyes. She had never heard the dictum that singers shouldn't sing on a full stomach and she would spend half the lesson feeding me cookies and milk and scones and jam. Sally Martin seemed to think that all her pupils were suffering from undernourishment.

I suppose that's where I acquired the capacity to down a full meal right before a concert, unlike any other singer I know. John Newmark, my accompanist, dines out on stories of my appetite. He is always recounting how we arrived for a concert in Calgary late, not having had time for lunch, and I sat down to shrimp cocktail, a steak, French fries and a salad less than an hour before going on stage. I saw the horrified look on his face as I started into the pumpkin pie. "Don't worry, John," I tried to reassure him, "I won't eat the crust!"

I'm blessed by a good digestion. Still, there are certain things I've learned never to eat before a performance: creamy sauces give you a frog in your throat, fish dries you out and of course onions and spices are risky. One deep breath and they're doing an encore.

Sally Martin's husband would play the piano for the lessons. He was tall and gaunt with a tiny pencil moustache, which made him look like a haughty French waiter. I always expected him to appear with a white napkin draped over one arm and offer me a menu. But Sally was the opposite, bouncy and gregarious. She taught me the rudiments of breathing and she would show me how, musically, a phrase was linked from one bar to the next. But most important, she taught me my first German song. It was "Still Wie Die Nacht" by Karl Böhm. I didn't understand German at the time, but I could mimic anything, and I was thrilled by my new accomplishment. I ran home to my mother to enthuse, "You've got to hear this. I've just learned a song in German." I sat down at the piano and sang it for her.

"Ach, that's lovely, darlin'," she said unimpressed. "Now sing me 'The Old Rugged Cross.'"

While I was taking lessons from Sally Martin, someone recommended me for my first paying job as a singer. Doris Killam, the organist at Stanley Presbyterian Church, hired me as an alto soloist for $12 a month in her choir. For that $12 I had to sing two services on Sunday and attend choir practice after work on Thursday nights when Doris would also coach me. The church was so far away from our house that on Sundays I spent hours on the streetcar, making the long trip there and back twice. All through most of my teenage years when my friends would be off skiing in the Laurentians, it seemed that I was stuck the whole day singing at church.

After a while, St. James United, where my mother had joined the choir, offered me more money – $20 a month – so I went there as second alto soloist. For me, it was an important move. St. James's organist and choir director Warner Norman played one of the most significant roles in my life: he helped form my musical taste. The solos I had been used to singing at church were mostly the usual old chestnuts from the hymnal. But Warner Norman opened up a whole new world to me, a world of classical music I had never known. The solos he gave me were from Handel's *Israel in Egypt* or Bach's *B Minor Mass*, and he introduced me to the great French composers. He had his girlfriend Marie-Josée Forgues – a soprano who had won the CBC's *Singing Stars of Tomorrow* contest – coach me in French pronunciation that was more elegant than my street joual. I began to realize that there was so much Warner could teach me that I asked him to give me coaching lessons himself. Coaching is different from voice lessons. A singing teacher concentrates on the actual technique of producing the voice, but a coach teaches you how to interpret and shade a phrase. By choosing the pieces he did for me to learn, he launched me on a voyage of discovery, leading me on to technical challenges and vast sweeps of thought and emotion in music that I had never dreamed of. If I had stayed in my neighbourhood church, I would still be singing "Abide with Me."

Warner Norman was a former Navy officer, overweight with bushy black brows, but all the ladies in the choir had a crush on him, including my mother. One girl, a beautiful redhead, got entangled with him more seriously and, even when their affair had ended, she couldn't get over him, although by then he was taking out Marie-Josée. Whenever choir practice broke up, the redhead would be waiting at the door for him, no matter how he tried to escape. He had become her obsession.

After a coaching lesson, he would sometimes ask me if I wanted to drive with him up to Lachute, about fifty miles north of Montreal, where he conducted a men's choir. He liked company on the drive. I suppose I would have to admit that I had a crush on him like everyone else – certainly I idolized him – but he didn't have a crush on me and it was never a romantic entanglement. We would just talk about music and laugh a lot. But one day I came home from work and found my mother in tears.

"Well, I never thought I'd see the day a daughter of mine would be denounced by the elders of the church," she sobbed.

Someone had sent her an anonymous letter which read: "What would the elders of the church think of a divorced organist taking up with a young girl and spiriting her out of the city on long rides?"

"Mother, this is ridiculous," I said. "You know I sometimes drive up to Lachute with Warner Norman. The minister knows the situation too and we all suspect who sent that letter. Look, if I were guilty I'd leave the choir. But I will not be threatened by some anonymous misinformant." I told her that we were going to choir practice together that Thursday night with our heads held high and that we would act as though nothing had happened, because in fact nothing had. In the end, of course, it all blew over. But who ever said church choirs were dull?

Not long after, Warner staged Mendelssohn's oratorio *Elijah* and he gave me the part of Jezebel, the temptress. It was only a small role, two or three lines, and I thought nothing of it, but it won me my first review. Eric McLean, who was then the music critic of the *Montreal Star*, singled me out in passing when he covered the performance. He said the young alto showed great promise. Later Eric and I joked how that review could hardly have launched a career: he hadn't even mentioned my name because it wasn't printed in the program.

Someone else was in the audience that night: George Little, the musical director for Erskine and American United Church, a huge downtown congregation which a lot of wealthy Montrealers attended. He phoned me after the performance and offered me $30 a month to become his lead alto soloist. I knew that George Little also directed the Montreal Bach Choir on the side, which performed a lot on the radio – a prospect that made the invitation too tempting to resist. But I felt guilty leaving Warner Norman's choir and arranged to continue my coaching lessons with him. He never uttered a word of reproach, but he had been my mentor and I knew that he was hurt by the fact that I seemed to be outgrowing him so soon.

Some voice teachers warn young singers not to get involved in choirs, for fear that they might strain their vocal cords, but I've always advised just the opposite. Choirs were my musical training ground. And after all, if you don't learn to blend your voice with those of other people singing around you, how can you learn to blend it with an orchestra?

Choirs also transformed my social life. On Thursday nights after practice, a group of us would always end up in a makeshift party. Sometimes we would wind up in Warner's studio where one of the tenors, Harry Elsie, would produce a bottle of his home-made booze. I didn't drink then but often I would have a taste, just to go along with the crazy mood. Then one day he spilled a little on the floor and it burned a hole in the linoleum. That put an end to my drinking days for a while, I can tell you.

The gang from Erskine and American would hang out

at a restaurant on St. Catherine Street called the Old Mill. It was long and narrow and European, with an alcove at the back where a trio would play chamber music. The regular members of the group were an aspiring violinist and a woman pianist who looked gaunt and grey. Everybody knew that, although they were married to other people, they had been having an affair for years. But to look at them and hear them play, it was impossible to believe that those two were capable of passion.

Whenever they performed a selection we knew, we would leap up and stage an impromptu amateur hour. George Bragonetz, a wonderful bass from a Russian family, would sing the "Volga Boat Song," and Guy Pichet, a tenor, would sing one of the Puccini arias. I would often do an aria that Warner Norman taught me, which has stayed in my repertoire until recently, "Mon coeur s'ouvre à ta voix" from Saint-Saëns's *Samson and Delilah*. People from other tables would send over half a dozen beers for the boys to drink. It was good, innocent fun. I often think that if more people in cities – young and old – could join choirs and choral societies, it would cure a lot of loneliness.

Not long after I had joined the choir at Erskine and American, Sally Martin left Montreal. Her husband had suddenly inherited money in the old country, which they couldn't transfer out, so they moved back to Scotland. I was sad to see her go, but the timing worked out well for me in the end. I was so fond of her that I might have gone on taking lessons from her forever but I realized later that by then she had already taught me everything she knew.

I asked around for another teacher and finally found him in the back room of Belanger's Music Store on Amherst Street: his name was Frank Rowe. In his day he had been a famous British oratorio baritone and by the time I met him, when he was almost eighty, he could still make a wonderful sound. Even then, he could still sing the role of Elijah, and to me, he looked the part. He was an imposing figure, always impeccable in his waistcoat with a gold watch-fob, and an ascot at his throat.

In the front of the store a formidable maiden lady, who wore her hair pulled back severely into a bun, sold classical sheet music to piano and violin students and, in a cubbyhole at the back, barely bigger than a dining room table, Frank Rowe taught voice at an upright piano. He had the most amazing roster of students, many of the names that would go on to put Canada on the musical map, including André Turp and Louis Quilico – or Luigi, as he was still officially known on concert programs in those days. I remember sitting outside Frank Rowe's studio on a tiny wooden bench one afternoon, waiting for my lesson, and hearing this baritone pouring through the door like liquid velvet – the most magnificent warm voice I had ever heard in my life – and out shambled this enormous teddy bear, Louis Quilico.

Louis's father owned a bicycle repair shop and the family had no money for him to study at all. At the beginning of his career he didn't sight-read music, and his high-school sweetheart, Lina Pezzolongo, a pianist who later became his wife, would play the pieces for him until he had memorized them. She helped him build his repertoire. Louis is a sweet man, just as warm as his voice, and he always credits me with playing a role in his career. Once when the Ladies Club of Outremont approached me for help in planning a special musical afternoon, I proposed a program in which I would share the bill with Louis. "But he's very good," I warned. "You'll have to pay him." It wasn't until years later that Louis told me it had been his first fee. They had given him the grand sum of $5. In 1974, when I was a director of Comus Music Theatre and we were staging Gian Carlo Menotti's *The Medium* on television, we hired Louis's son, Gino, a baritone as talented as his father, in the role of Mr. Gobineau. Again, it wasn't until afterward that Louis told me it had turned out to be Gino's first paying job too. "You're the godmother to the whole family," he always jokes with me.

Under Frank Rowe, I flourished. He had the ability to bring out the voice and he would show me how to pronounce and breathe. My singing improved markedly and I began to get offers for small engagements around Montreal. One of the first was a regular job singing in Temple Emanu-El, a Reform synagogue on Sherbrooke Street, for the High Holidays. The Hebrew was all written out phonetically and the cantor would help me with the pronunciation. Some of my mother's friends thought it was strange, but to me it was just another church job.

I was eighteen and still working full-time, but I was staggering my hours at the Bell from 6 a.m. to 9 a.m. and from 6 p.m. to 9 p.m. so I could study and practise in the afternoons. By then I knew that I wanted to make singing a career. I remember exactly the day it happened. I was doing a CBC Radio broadcast of Vaughan Williams's *Music Makers* with George Little's Bach Choir and I had a solo – probably not more than forty-two bars – but because of union rules, soloists earned a special rate. When they handed me my fee afterward, it was not for the usual $18, but for $72. I realized I had been paid more for those forty-two bars than I had for the thousands I had sung with the whole choir. As my family likes to point out, the secret of what makes Maureen Forrester run has always been the next cheque!

It dawned on me then that singing could become a full-time job like any other. But deciding that was one thing, figuring out how to make the leap was another. Frank Rowe pushed me to start entering competitions. I had noticed in reading reviews that whenever the critics mentioned someone as up-and-coming, she had invariably won a Sarah Fischer Scholarship. Sarah Fischer, a one-time soprano who had enjoyed a brief fling on the world stage, was an incredibly theatrical woman. She looked like Helena Rubinstein with her flowing capes and her hair swept back severely into a bun. By the time I heard of her she was retired and liked to give young talent a break with competitions which she held in the

Ritz Carlton ballroom. The programs featured her profile printed on the cover.

I entered one of them, singing "Amarilli Mia Bella," a
solo every student learns out of the *Anthology of Italian
Songs*, and to my shock I won. But the prize turned out
not to be money; it was a chance to sing at another Sarah
Fischer concert. I would have preferred the cash at the
time, but those two concerts gave me an important opportunity to be heard. Still, preparing for them presented me
with a problem I had never anticipated. Sarah Fischer
started phoning me all the time, always late at night, on
some pretext about the performance. I began to get a little
nervous about her. I didn't know anything about females
liking females at the time, but my instincts told me she was
interested in more than my voice. Finally I had my father
answer the phone one night. "My daughter is a very
young girl and we have rules in this house," he told her.
"Nobody gets calls this late unless it's an emergency. I
don't care what kind of a career she is going to have, she
has to get up for work early in the morning. You can call
at a decent hour or not at all." After that, in the weeks left
leading up to my prizewinner's concert, Sarah Fischer was
good as gold.

But the contest that most intrigued me was the Marian
Anderson competition at the Academy of Vocal Arts in
Philadelphia. Another singer had told me about it and I
wrote for the brochure. I looked on a map and Philadelphia seemed a universe away, but I saved my money for a
plane ticket. It was the first time I had ever flown and I
was air-sick the whole way. But as soon as I walked into
the hall and heard the other singers, I felt another kind of
queaziness: I knew I was vocally out of my depth.

It was one of the few competitions open to blacks at the
time and ninety-nine per cent of the entrants were black. I
had never heard so much raw talent and, even before my
turn came, I realized I was totally unprepared; I knew my
performance was mediocre. But at the end there was a
section for students who had won scholarships the year

before to be judged for a renewal of their grants, and I stayed around to listen. A stunning girl strode out on the stage looking like some African queen. She had an absolutely regal bearing. Then when she opened her mouth and I heard that soprano voice, I thought, God, what do I know about singing? I wanted to crawl in a hole. I made a note of her name: Leontyne Price.

Years later, in New York, I went to her formal recital debut at Town Hall. She was premièring the *Hermit Songs* that Samuel Barber had written for her, and all the critics were there. Again, I was staggered by what I heard. She emerged as a real star a few years before I did, but I was flattered when RCA included me on a record of new voices with her in 1957 called *Meet the Artist*, and later we worked together quite often. We sang Beethoven's *Ninth Symphony* together so many times that at one time she joked, "Honey, we are the B-9 girls."

That contest in Philadelphia spurred me to work harder on my voice. A year later I decided I was finally ready to audition for the biggest test I knew of in Canada, *Singing Stars of Tomorrow*. It was broadcast every Sunday over CBC Radio, with Elwood Glover as the announcer. A panel of judges would choose the winners. There were try-outs all over Canada and Rex Battle, the conductor, who had been a violinist with a group at Toronto's Royal York Hotel, came to Montreal for the auditions. But the show itself was broadcast live out of Toronto and I had to take the train down.

I stepped out of Union Station and took one look at the city I hadn't seen since I was a child with my grandfather and I could have wept. It looked so lifeless and drab compared with Montreal. There was construction underway on Front Street at the time, which called for planks over the sidewalk. Hogtown, Montrealers called it with a sense of superiority, and at last I thought I understood why.

The sponsors had sent one of their officials to meet me. He told me he was my "escort." He took me to the Royal York and bought me lunch, then squired me to the CBC studio. Here I was, walking into the hallowed heart of the CBC, and all I could think was, What am I doing here? Am I ready for this? It was the first time I had ever sung with an orchestra and the closest I've ever come to the jitters. But I swallowed my self-doubts and went through with it, because once I make up my mind to do something I never back off. Besides, the first prize was $1,000, which would have allowed me to quit my job and buy all the music I dreamed of. I had to perform two numbers and I had chosen Grieg's "Ein Schwan" and the blind woman's aria "Voce di Donna" from *La Gioconda*. Years later, when I met Rex Battle again, he said he had thought at the time that I should have won, but I didn't even make the semifinals. I was still vocally unstable and I'd had almost no experience singing opera.

After I got back to Montreal, my "escort" kept calling me whenever he came to town. He began to get quite amorous. My mother thought he was terrific because he always brought her cleaned and filleted fish, and later I realized that he could have opened a lot of doors for me early in my career. But I had the feeling that he was married and I decided not to get involved. I didn't want to be somebody's mistress.

The next year, I entered *Singing Stars* again, without his help. That time I finished third behind Donald Garrard, the baritone from Vancouver who was runner-up, and a lyric soprano from Regina named June Kowalchuk who, despite her first prize, never went on to make a career. She had a beautiful voice but she became a doctor's wife and I never heard of her again until a few years ago when, at a reception in Hamilton after a concert, I felt someone touch my arm. I turned around and it was June Kowalchuk saying, "We're all so proud of you."

I was pleased enough with my third prize, but that contest gave me the first inkling of how unfair it is to make contraltos and bass-baritones compete with sopranos and tenors. When the higher voices sing an aria with a lot of flashy top notes, the audience goes wild. It's show-stopping. But the darker voices can't excite with only one number in the same way. We also develop later. A soprano is a soprano from the day she starts to sing, but a contralto doesn't form until she's in her mid-twenties.

I knew by then that I needed a great teacher. I felt Frank Rowe had given me everything that he had to give. He could bring out the voice but he didn't know what to do with it once he got it there. He could analyze what was wrong but he couldn't tell me how to make it right. I knew I wasn't making the sound I wanted to. I couldn't control it; it was hit or miss. My money was too hard-earned to waste any more time with him. It was sad because, coincidentally, all of us left Frank Rowe within the same year. Louis went to study in Rome, André in Milan, and I had my sights set on applying to the Juilliard School in New York. People told me later that it broke Frank Rowe's heart. But instinctively I knew it was time to move on. Now I always tell students that it's important to recognize that point in your career. You don't have to be ruthlessly ambitious but it's essential not to stand still. The ones who succeed are the ones who can pick up and move on to the next teacher they need to learn from.

I scrimped and saved and took the bus to New York. I couldn't afford a hotel so I stayed in the Rehearsal Club, a brownstone residence for girls studying acting. I dressed up in a red crepe dress with white polka dots and, feeling very chic, took the subway uptown to Juilliard. I was full of determination, but they wouldn't let me past the reception desk. The clerk refused even to give me an application form because I hadn't finished high school. I was shattered.

Someone had offered me the name of a teacher in New York, who had a studio in the Steinway Building. Although I was discouraged, I sought him out. I arrived early as usual and as I sat waiting in the hallway for him to see me, I could hear him giving a lesson inside. He would play, "La, la, la," and the girl would sing, "Fa, fa, fa," totally out of tune, and he would say, "Very good, my dear." I was horrified. I thought to myself, I could never study with that man. He's a total fraud. It wasn't until much later that I realized you have to teach an awful lot of rich debutantes to make a living in New York. But I didn't even wait to see him. I took the bus back to Montreal, utterly disillusioned.

What depressed me was that I didn't know of anyone in Canada who could help me learn what I realized I needed. Having struck out in New York, I began to wonder if I could ever save enough money to study in England, which was famous for producing contraltos, when I ran into Jean Scarth, a soprano whom I knew from the St. James United Church choir. She told me she had just found the most remarkable new teacher. He was a Dutch baritone who had spent the war trapped in Czechoslovakia, but after he had been liberated by the Russians, he decided to leave Europe completely. He had just arrived in Montreal. His name, she said, was Bernard Diamant.

As it turned out, he was giving his first concert in Canada the next week as part of Celia Bizony's Musica Antica e Nuova series in the Westmount High School auditorium. There was no way I would commit myself to spending money on lessons before I had heard the man, so off I went, slipping into a seat up in the balcony. John Newmark was accompanying him on a rare Clementi, one of the first pianos ever made, and Diamant was singing a program of Mozart *Lieder*. When he walked out on stage, he seemed extremely nervous. He was tall and angular and physically he reminded me of the French tenor Gérard Souzay, another nervous type, but I didn't like his voice at all. It was terribly reedy. Still, after the concert, I realized I had never heard anyone sing better with less equipment. He hadn't been born with a beautiful voice but he had made the songs come alive by the way he coloured the music and with the intonation he gave to the words. It was clear that Bernard Diamant had *learned* to sing.

I phoned and made an appointment to see him. He had an apartment in an elegant old red brick building between

Maisonneuve and St. Catherine. Inside, it was the picture of a Rembrandt interior, with a shawl over the grand piano and exquisite Dutch paintings in gilt frames on the walls. His collection of silver miniatures dotted the antique cabinet tops. In the hall, his dachshunds Peuchl and Peter were cavorting in booties. This, I thought, was class.

I sang some oratorios for him, just boomed them out in my plummiest voice. He was quiet for a few seconds afterward and he tried to hide his amusement by burying his face in the music. Diamant always had exquisite manners.

"Well," he said finally, "you certainly have a gift from God. That's a very big voice. But I must tell you something, my dear. You don't know how to sing."

Other students might have been crestfallen, but I wanted to hug him. At last, after all the years of flattery, somebody was telling me what, in my heart of hearts, I had suspected. I knew I would learn a lot from Bernard Diamant.

EIGHT

Opportunity Knocks . . . in Vain

MY FIRST instruction from Bernard Diamant was to stop singing. It might not have seemed like a promising start. "I'll take you as a pupil," he had said. "You have been blessed with a wonderful instrument. But I warn you, you'll have to stop singing for six months to a year and even out your voice. You'll have to cut out all your little choir and radio jobs."

I was shocked. I already had a blossoming reputation and a calendar filling up. "But if I stop singing, people will forget who I am," I wailed.

"Better they do," he said, "and as soon as possible. When I tell you you're ready to start performing in public again, they'll remember you forever."

I began to understand what he was trying to do, but when I told my mother, she went into a tailspin. There goes the bread and butter, she thought. My choir work was helping to support my family. But when Diamant phoned and told her he believed I had the potential of a world-class career, of course she was on his side. That was my mother's fondest dream.

I quit all my choir jobs on the spot. At first, Diamant made me sing in a whisper, almost no sound at all. He gave me scales to do in a tiny humming voice. I was so excited, I did them all the time. I would sing to myself in hallways or at the car stop on the way to work. It started to get around town. People who had known me began saying, "You know Maureen Forrester, that girl with the big, big voice? Well, she's studying with a Dutch guy who has ruined her. There's no voice left at all."

But I saw what he was getting at. He was building the inner core of my voice, expanding the range up and down. The middle range of an alto is around the G above middle C, but he pushed me an octave above that and half an octave below, while lightening the upper register.

I wrote everything he said down in a musical notation book and went home and practised for hours. Sometimes in those lessons I had a sense of *déjà vu*. I would know what he was going to say before he even got it out. He never ceased to marvel at that. We were on the same wave length immediately, as if we had known each other in a past life.

I was an uneducated girl from a simple background, so he chose easy analogies for me. He used to say: "Think of yourself as a car. The breath is the gasoline, but the accelerator is your diaphragm, that little muscle between the ribs. If you want to go faster – in singing that means higher, louder – you step on the accelerator. You push in the diaphragm or pull out the diaphragm like an umbrella opening or closing. To raise your voice, you lift your diaphragm so that last bit of breath floods up high into the lung." Or: "The voice is like a ball sitting on top of a water fountain. If you turn off the water – the breath – the ball falls. You need constant support of breath to make a sound."

Diamant made the complex mechanics of singing seem simple. But the most important gift he gave me was technique. Young singers like to think they sing naturally, but if you want to sing professionally, you have to plan the sound before it comes out. You have to see the sound and place it and be able to call it at will, so you aren't just good on a good day. You have to be good every day, even when you're tired or have a cold. I owe the fact that I've never not been able to sing when I'm sick to the technique I learned in those first two years studying with Bernard Diamant. He turned me into a performer.

Students often try to imitate the voices they hear on records, but that's not a method which can carry them very far. To make a career as a singer, you have to develop habits you can fall back on for a lifetime: to be able to lift your diaphragm and open the resonators in your head. You have to release the tension in your nose so you feel the air between the bone and the skin – that way the sound won't emerge narrow and pinched. The words may come out of your mouth, but the sound comes out of your whole head. People make the mistake of talking about chest notes, but you don't sing out of your chest; you resonate there. It's like turning on another speaker for a bass note on your stereo. You add to the two speakers you already have in the forehead and the two in the cheeks. I tell students, "Think of a rock group. The more speakers they have, the more impressive they sound."

Diamant had told me it would take at least six months to build my voice to the point that it was ready to be unveiled in public again, but I was so excited by my progress I couldn't wait. One day after only a few weeks he turned on the radio by chance to a CBC talent show called *Opportunity Knocks* and whom did he hear? His most devoted pupil! He was furious.

But with my newly acquired technique, I had decided to make another try at a competition. For me, *Opportunity Knocks* represented the big time. John Adaskin, the cellist from the famous musical Adaskin family, was the host. He went from region to region across the country auditioning young talent – drummers, clarinetists, jazz singers, musicians of every stripe. In Montreal, the show was held in the Imperial Theatre in front of a live audience and, to my delight, I won my audition.

On the night of the broadcast, my mother and sister were in the audience and friends were tuned in to listen at home. I dressed in the most sophisticated black gown I owned, with pearls, trying to look mature. My solo was "Ombra Mai Fù," the king's first aria from Handel's *Xerxes*, which years later I recorded in Vienna. I've sung it so many times since and I always tell the audience, "Now, I'm going to do a number that you usually hear at funerals and pompous occasions – what musicians call Handel's 'Largo' – and everybody thinks it's such a sad, soulful song. But in reality, it's when King Xerxes walks out into his garden and sings 'Ombra Mai Fù,' an ode to a tree which translates: 'In the shade of my beautiful vegetable'!"

In the end, I only finished second to the Montreal jazz trumpeter Maynard Ferguson, who was brilliant. But *Opportunity Knocks* marked a turning point for me. John Adaskin was very complimentary – cellists are sympathetic to contraltos because they play in the same register – and when he went back to Toronto, he began to spread the word about me. After the show, the orchestra players all came up to me too and said, "You have a wonderful voice. We'll be hearing about you again." For the first time I sensed that I might really be destined for a career in music.

Diamant had been so angry at me for breaking his ban on performing that at first he refused to give me any more lessons. "What good will it do if you're going to insist on performing in public before you're ready?" he said. Finally, my mother went to see him without telling me. She begged him to take me back. "Her only fault is that she's so keen," she coaxed. Diamant adored my mother, so at last he relented.

But I couldn't help being impatient. It seemed I had waited so long to turn singing from a sideline into a career, I didn't want to waste one minute more. I was still supporting myself, working by this time as a receptionist for a quarrying, road-building and cement plant called Highway Paving, up in Ville St. Michel, northeast of the city. The company was owned by James Franceschini, a remarkable character who had come to Canada from Italy with a pick and a shovel and ended up a millionaire, building many of the roads in Quebec. He had a beautiful country house at Mont Tremblant where he kept palomino horses. It seems there was a sort of fraternity of palomino horse lovers around the world at that time and one of them was Benito Mussolini. Franceschini had sent Il Duce a palomino and as a result the Canadian government had interned him during the war for fascist sympathies. But as soon as they released him, he went right back to amassing his fortune.

Franceschini had only half a voice. He had had cancer of the throat and one of his vocal cords had been removed. There was this great big stocky Italian body on short legs with a thin foghorn rasp of a voice. When I heard Marlon Brando in *The Godfather*, I thought that he must have heard about Franceschini.

Franceschini used to love me to sit on his knee at Christmas parties because there weren't many girls in the office. "Ya know what I would give for your health?" he would croak. "I tell ya, half my fortune." Not the whole thing, of course. Everybody was petrified of the man but me. When one of his truck drivers would see his car on the highway heading toward the plant, he would call in an alert, "J.F. is on his way." The whole place would be buzzing because J.F. was on his way.

He would get on the phone and say, "Gimme Leonard." I'd say, "Leonard is talking long distance to Toronto. I'll call you when he's free." He would just grunt. Whenever people heard me, they would say, "For heaven's sake, disconnect Leonard. Tell him his brother wants him." But I was only the receptionist. What reason did I have to be afraid of this old man?

One day I gave my notice. He called me into his office and said, "Why're ya leaving? Ya want more money?"

"No," I said, "I'm studying singing and I can't work all day. I need time for my lessons and practice."

"Can ya get up at 5 a.m.?" he asked.

"Of course I can," I said.

"Alright, ya got a job," he said. "Come in and open up

the office when the plant starts up every morning before the road crews come in to work."

I don't think Franceschini was particularly musically inclined but he liked me because I was gutsy. He arranged for one of the drivers to pick me up on his way to work at 6 a.m. and at 7 a.m. I would open the office, which I then had all to myself. I did all my practising in that enormous empty quarry headquarters.

On the switchboard, I used to like to imitate the Italian I heard around the plant. But my accent turned out to be so good that people would immediately start to answer me back in Italian. "Hey, wait a second," I would have to interrupt, "that's all I can say." Years later at La Scala when they asked me where I had learned my Italian, I told them it was at Highway Paving.

I dated two of the boys who worked there. Leonardo Giovanni Francescuti was more beautiful than any film star I had ever seen, with curly hair and teeth like diamonds. He was an immigrant from northern Italy, where he had trained as a veterinarian, but he wasn't qualified in Canada and had been forced to take a job as a labourer. His brother made him stop dating me after a while because he was supposed to save his money and bring another member of the family over from the old country.

The second was Sicilian, dark-skinned and sloe-eyed, very passionate. One day he said to me, "Hey, you talked to that other guy on the bus." I said, "Yes, he's a very nice guy." "If you look at him again," he said, "I bring a knife to work." That was the end of my Italian boyfriends.

My father wasn't too sure about these Italian boyfriends anyway. When they brought me home at night, he would pace up and down the hall to force them to leave. His protectiveness always touched me. Once I had waited and waited for a boy I had a crush on to ask me out for New Year's Eve, but he never called as he had promised. When my father saw me sitting at the piano – a sure sign that I was sad – he said, "Come now. Get on your best dress. We're all going down to the Mount Royal Hotel."

"Oh, Daddy, it's alright," I said. I knew he couldn't afford the money, but I was so moved that he didn't want to see me hurting.

On my seventeenth birthday, my father had given me a watch. At the time I was going out with a friend of my brother's from the Air Force and I knew he was really quite crazy about me, but after a while he started to come around less and less. Later I found out that my father had taken him aside and said, "Don't get serious about my daughter. She is going to be a singer with a very big career and live another kind of life that is not for you. You won't be able to afford her."

When I heard that, I was so livid I stormed into the living room and threw the watch at my father. But after a while I was sorry because, of course, he was right. A lot of the girls I had grown up with had already gotten married, and they were stuck forever in the neighbourhood, pregnant and poor. To me, their lives were over. I wanted another kind of existence but I never expected to marry it. I didn't want to turn into a woman like my mother who had to learn to lie so she could buy herself a new hat.

The one boy I was smitten with was Albert Nixon, who was so handsome he looked like an Ipana toothpaste ad. We went out together for quite a while but I knew his mother never thought I was good enough for him because he came from the right side of the tracks – Notre-Dame-de-Grâce, or NDG, as Montrealers call it. In the city then those distinctions were very important.

One day he phoned and said he had something to tell me. "You're getting married," I said. "How do you know?" he asked. I've always been psychic and often I can tell who will be on the phone when it rings. As it turned out, Albert Nixon had met a surgeon's daughter, who his mother had decided was a better match for him. I was not only hurt, but I made up my mind with even more determination that some day I would live on the other side of the tracks myself.

It was that rude reminder of social class which helped

persuade me to get my teeth capped. For years I had an embarrassing gap where a dentist had yanked out an inflamed eye tooth when I was twelve. The dentists that working-class people went to didn't know about root canals then; they would just reach for their pliers on any excuse. In our neighbourhood, if somebody had something wrong with several teeth, it wasn't uncommon to have the whole mouth pulled. Doctors often had the same sense of efficiency, and I can remember when one came to our house to take out my brother's tonsils on the kitchen table, he did mine at the same time even though there was nothing wrong with them. My whole family eventually ended up with false teeth. All through my teenage years I was so self-conscious about my missing tooth that I learned to smile by pulling down my lip to hide it. Finally, when I was twenty, I went to a dentist in the Medical Arts Building who I had heard capped teeth. He said it would cost $750 to do my whole mouth. I gasped since I was only earning $45 a week at Highway Paving. "Well," I said, "I'm going to be a singer and I have to have it done. If you have the patience to wait for me to pay you, go ahead." It took me quite a few years, but I finally paid off that dentist's bill.

With Diamant, I learned early that there would be sacrifices to make if I wanted a singing career. From the time I began my lessons with him, I didn't have a normal girl's life. When I wasn't working at my job, I was working at my vocal practice. Even friendships had to be shoe-horned into a packed schedule. I knew several girls who constantly had problems, which they were always pouring out on my shoulder. One day Diamant took me aside. "Maureen," he said, "you've got a talent which will take you a long way, but you have to dump all these girlfriends. They're leeches."

"How can you say that?" I was shocked. "That's terrible."

"The minute you stop solving their problems," he said, "they will find somebody else. You need time to study and concentrate on your music. You don't have time to mother the world."

Within six weeks after I had started lessons with Diamant, he lifted his six-month performance ban. One of the reasons I had learned so fast is that I was no ordinary student on scholarship or one whose parents were footing the bill. I made every lesson count as ten because those $10-an-hour fees twice a week were like blood money to me. Sometimes I couldn't pay him but he agreed to run me a line of credit until I could. "Don't worry now," he said. "When you start making money, you can pay for every lesson twice." Still, when people ask me about the struggle I had, I can only tell them that I never thought of it as hard work. To me, singing came naturally. I let music take over my life because it was a joy.

After a year of studying with Diamant, my voice sounded completely different. One day during a lesson he said, "Now take everything I've taught you and magnify it ten times." I looked puzzled. But he explained that he didn't want me to sing louder, he wanted me to create more depth of feeling. "I'm an introvert," he said, "but you're an extrovert. It will suit you to display your emotions large." In fact, that advice made all the difference in my performances. Engagements started to stream in.

Gifford Mitchell asked me to sing Brahms's *Alto Rhapsody* with his Montreal Elgar Choir. Gifford was a tall, handsome man who looked more like a football coach than a choir director – and sometimes sounded more like one too. "Okay, girls, suck in those tummies!" he would bellow. But I adored working with him. It was the first time I had performed the *Alto Rhapsody* which is in my repertoire to this day.

Brahms had composed the piece to be sung with full orchestra but the Elgar Choir could only afford an organist, Doris Killam, my one-time coach from Stanley Presbyterian Church. The *Alto Rhapsody* was written on a poem by Goethe about a winter's journey through the mountains at a time Brahms was in anguish over his loneliness and childlessness. It's really an alto reflection on the solitariness of life's voyage, punctuated by a beautiful transitional chord which then leads the solo to float above a male chorus, answering in a hymn of consolation and hope. Its message is that, after all the miseries of the world, what saves man in the end is love. Mahler's music has much the same kind of transcendental quality, especially the *Second* and *Third Symphonies* where, after long movements summing up man's trouble on earth, the chorus rises to a vision of a world without end. That's always been the musical message that attracted an optimist like myself.

The critics were very complimentary about my performance and my reputation around the city began to grow. One day I was coming out of the International Music Shop when I ran into Bill Stevens, a pianist I knew. He told me that Rudolf Bing was in town and wanted to audition me. Even then Rudolf Bing was the general manager of New York's Metropolitan Opera Company and his name was almost a household word because of the Met's weekly radio broadcasts. For the city's musical community, it was as if God himself had landed in Montreal. Right there on the sidewalk, Bill Stevens went down on his knees and started genuflecting at my feet. "Allah, Allah," he joked, bobbing up and down.

"I don't want to audition for Rudolf Bing," I told him. Bill was shocked. Most students my age would have killed for the chance. But, in fact, I didn't feel ready for it. I knew that if I sang badly for Rudolf Bing, I would never get the opportunity to sing for him a second time. On the other hand, if I sang well, he would want to put me in the Met's chorus and nobody would ever hear of me again. Even then, I realized that in order to make it at the Met, you had to arrive there as a star. And I knew that in opera there weren't many starring roles for contraltos.

At that time, the notion of singing opera still made me nervous. I hadn't been exposed to it very much and my one and only trip to the Met had been an eye-opener.

Through Jean Scarth, my friend from the St. James United choir, I had met Senator Charles Howard and his second wife. Whenever I was singing in Sherbrooke, they would invite me to their lavish country house outside the city and offer advice on my career. Once, in the hope of inspiring me, they asked me to New York for the weekend to attend the opera. It was to be a black-tie opening and I wore a daring black strapless gown with long black satin gloves. I felt so sophisticated dining in the Met's glittering restaurant, then taking my place in the Howards' box just down from Mrs. Astor's, and I fantasized that I belonged in that life.

The program was *Madame Butterfly*, starring the great Italian soprano Licia Albanese, but Albanese had fallen ill that night and Dorothy Kirsten was filling in. While Kirsten was singing "Un Bel Di," my eyes strayed to the next box. There sat Albanese. She had been too ill to sing, but not too ill to show up so that her presence loomed over the performance all the same. Right in the middle of Kirsten's incredible aria, Albanese let out the most ostentatious yawn. That was the first thing I learned about opera: the size of the egos.

Although in many ways that first trip to the Met had been magical, it also showed me that if you were going to sing there, you had to be strong. Diamant had already taught me that doing things before I was ready for them could end up in wasted chances like my impetuous bid to win *Opportunity Knocks*. I saw that he was preparing me step by step for another course which could take me on a different route to the Met. I thought to myself: It's not time yet for Rudolf Bing. For now I'm going to put my trust in Mr. D.

NINE

Solo Flight

"ARE YOU SURE you don't have any German ances- tors?" Bernard Diamant kept asking me. I was big and blonde, not to mention the fact that I had an obses- sion with cleanliness and order. But the thing that most astounded him was that I would only have to hear a Ger- man song once before I could repeat it perfectly. He couldn't believe that this uneducated young Anglo-Saxon girl could sing German *Lieder* so movingly. In fact, I can't explain it myself. He would give me a song to learn and when I came back to go through it with him for the first time, I would have the shading almost the way he said the composer meant it. I had never listened to recordings of *Lieder* and I couldn't speak a word of German, but, in- stinctively, I knew how a *Lied* – a song – ought to be sung.

Lieder were the popular songs of Germany in the late eighteenth and nineteenth centuries. They were based on lyric poems by writers such as Heinrich Heine and Goethe and set to music in a form that attracted all the great composers from Brahms and Schubert right up to Schu- mann and Mahler. In their day, *Lieder* weren't considered high-brow or esoteric. They were simple thoughts for ordi- nary people which were given extraordinary melodies. In a way, they were the height of Romanticism since they always expressed such great feeling.

Canada had no real tradition of *Lieder* singing when I was growing up, but after the war, the generation of Europeans who had fled Hitler brought it with them, just as they brought a whole range of Continental influences to music in this country. I don't know what it was that instantly attracted me to the form – maybe the rawness of the emotion – but it was that attraction which sealed my fate as a concert singer.

Lieder were Diamant's specialty and he knew how to pace my development in them. At each lesson he would give me something more challenging to sing to build up my voice or expand my interpretation. Unfortunately nobody seemed to realize the rate at which I was also maturing in the rest of my life. By the time my twenty-first birthday came along, I couldn't stand the restrictions of living at home any longer. I felt I was being cannibalized by my mother who, as I became more and more involved in music, was constantly demanding to know everything I did. She wanted to go everywhere with me.

When I told my father that I wanted to leave home, he hit the roof. He was so upset, he made himself quite ill. In our circle, nice girls didn't leave their parents' houses until they went to live in their husbands' and he thought at first that I wanted to lead a life of ill repute. But eventually I made him see that my mother was driving me crazy, leaving me with no private life. Besides, with my choir practice and radio broadcasts often finishing so late at night, it made sense for me to live downtown. Finally he calmed down and gave me his blessing.

I found my first apartment on Stanley Street, the right side of the tracks, at last. It was in an old stone house which had once been a graceful mansion, and was now sub-divided into flats. I rented what had been the front parlour with a lovely bay window. The only furniture I had was a fold-down lounge chair with chrome arms that I used as a bed, two horse-hair chairs I had scavenged from somebody's cast-offs in the street, and a baby grand piano which a friend had asked me to keep when he moved to New York to become Kaye Ballard's accompanist. At first I was thrilled at having my own baby grand, but it took up three-quarters of the room. I could barely budge in that studio apartment.

As soon as I moved in, it occurred to me that I had nothing to serve if someone visited. I decided that if I was going to be a sophisticate, I had to buy some cordial. I went into a liquor store, but I knew nothing about liquor then and I chose a bottle with a name that I had heard of which looked rather elegant. For a long time I had no callers, so every night when I came home from work, I would sit down and turn on the radio and treat myself to a cocktail hour – a little glass of Benedictine!

By that time, I was constantly busy with my choir work and the engagements that were increasingly coming my way. Chorales, oratorios, CBC broadcasts – I leaped at almost any invitation. I got to be quite seasoned in the limelight, but I had never sung a full program of *Lieder* all by myself. At last, Diamant decided I was ready. The YWCA on Dorchester Street held a series of free concerts on Sunday afternoons, mostly for Europeans who had just immigrated to Canada and couldn't afford to hear the music they loved. The Y invited me to give one of the recitals. There was no question of paying me, so Diamant arranged for his friend John Newmark to accompany me for free.

John came from a wealthy ship-building family in Bremen, Germany, and even though he was born Jewish, his mother had had him baptized as a Lutheran when the Nazis began to emerge as a force. But that hadn't helped when Hitler came to power and he couldn't get work as a musician. He fled to England just before the war broke out, but by then the British wouldn't let him work there either. In London, all the enemy aliens were rounded up and sent to internment camps. John was shipped off to Canada – first to a compound outside Fredericton, New Brunswick, then to one near Lennoxville, Quebec. That was his introduction to this country. But what incredible musical company he kept there. Interned with him were Walter Homburger, later the director of the Toronto Symphony; Helmut Blume, who became dean of music at McGill University; Eric Koch, one-time head of the CBC's arts and science programming; and Franz Kraemer, who went on to be the executive producer of so many CBC specials that he was dubbed "Mr. Music." It was forced networking. When John was finally released, it took him three years to find steady work in Canada, but when he did, he quickly became the leading accompanist in Montreal. By the time I met him, he had played for all the big names who came to town, and he had accompanied Kathleen Ferrier, the greatest contralto of the day, on her North American tour in 1950, and recorded with her.

When Diamant first introduced me to John, I didn't like him very much and later I found out that the feeling had been mutual. Because I was just starting out at the time, he intimidated me with his experience and knowing airs. For quite a while when we first practised together, he would look up at me from the piano with his bifocals slipping down his nose and give me a withering glance over an interpretation. He would just shake his head slowly, "No-o-o-o." I would think, Oh my God, I've done it in the most awful taste. Finally, after a few years, I got up the nerve one day to say, "That may not be right, but that's the way I want to sing it." From then on our relationship changed to mutual respect and John and I have been together now longer than most married couples. He's like a brother to me. We've shared so much over the years, laughter and tears and hilarious times on the road. He has been with me every step of the way, always elegant, always cheerful and supportive and one of the most sensitive pianists I could ever have found. Through his coaching, I learned a sense not only of the music, but of how to perform it.

John and Diamant were excited about my solo debut, but they never let on what opportunities they suspected it might open up for me. For a month we prepared my program: a group of Handel and Purcell songs, then three from Schumann, three from Fauré, three by Strauss and last a trio of Negro spirituals. A recital is usually made up of seventy minutes of music. The songs are grouped to create a mood, relate an unfolding drama or even to evoke an era. Normally, you do a twelve-minute group, then go off stage, mop the sweat from your brow, take a sip of water and come back out and do the next group, slipping into the new change of character. People think that singers only act when they do opera, but in a recital the acting is much more difficult because it's more subtle. With no help from lavish costumes or a set or even plotline, you have to convey all the meaning with only an eye or a shoulder or the flutter of a hand.

That program meant an enormous amount of music for me to memorize, especially when I was still working at Highway Paving every morning. The night before the concert I wasn't nervous, but I wanted to be sure that I didn't forget any of the lyrics. Just before I went to bed, I read through the texts of the songs in the order I would sing them, noting any musical markings I might need, then I turned off the light. Even before anyone had written about it as a memory technique, I'd found that reading a concert program just before I fell asleep meant that I would wake up in the morning totally confident that I had memorized the poetry, no matter what language it happened to be in. But once I had performed it, I could also forget it just as fast. Ask me to repeat what I sang last week and I couldn't do it for you.

The red brick barn of the YWCA was hardly the most chic place for a debut – a combination dance hall/auditorium with turquoise trim and a minuscule stage. Montreal's most elegant recitals were held in the ballroom of the Ritz Carlton, but I was happy with any hall at all. Diamant had sent me a nosegay beforehand with a card that read: *"Liebes Maureenschen, Toi, toi, toi,* Mr. D,*"* and just before I walked out on stage, John sort of half-spit three times behind my left ear, muttering, *"Toi, toi, toi,"* an old German theatrical custom supposed to bring luck. Since then, whenever we perform together, John always insists on going through that damp ritual. But in fact I've never been superstitious or nervous. Diamant couldn't get over my cool. "What good does it do if I get nervous?" I said. "I just sing badly. I can't afford to be nervous."

Ever since I began performing, I've felt perfectly comfortable the instant I step onto a stage. I can't explain it. I walk out and something happens – it's showbiz time. When I'm on stage I always feel as if I have the spotlight just on me, even if I'm not singing at the moment. Other singers have told me they have the same sensation. It's an electricity of some sort, an energy that makes people want to come and hear you perform.

People told me that they felt it that day at the Y. At the end of the concert, applause swept over the hall. It went on and on in what seemed to me an interminable ovation. I couldn't believe it: I was a smash. The next day, Thomas Archer of the Montreal *Gazette* wrote: "Few if any contraltos on this continent could challenge her." What's more, he put me in a league I never dreamed of: he said I was of the "calibre of a Ferrier."

He was the first of dozens of critics over the next few years to compare me to Kathleen Ferrier, who was to die tragically of breast cancer later that same year at only forty-one. I had seen her once in Montreal when I was just starting to sing seriously and I had been knocked out by her voice. She sang with one incredible, haunting colour and she was warmth personified. She had a way of drawing the audience into her fold as she sang, which served as a lesson to me. It was as if she was sharing a secret with whoever heard her. But I had purposely never listened to her records because I was always wary of copying someone else's interpretation.

John, who had played with her, said we didn't sound at all alike. Still, in many ways, the comparison was inevitable. She was an English girl who came from a simple Lancashire background not unlike mine and, like me, she had started out as a switchboard operator before she was discovered. We also shared the same lack of airs. When Thomas Archer first compared us, I was flattered. But if you're talented you don't want to sound like anybody else and after a while I grew to hate being called another Ferrier. The comparison dogged me for years. I remember the first critic who said it was time to stop calling me "another Ferrier – she is a magnificent Maureen Forrester in her own right." He was a Swede reviewing a 1957 Stockholm concert and I could have blessed him.

Still, that recital debut at the Y changed everything for me. Suddenly, I was noticed as a name, and from that moment I never had to go seeking solo engagements. I was on my way to a concert career.

My mother was overjoyed. Whenever I performed, she would sit front and centre, six or seven rows back, the best seat in the house. She acted as if she were the star. She would try to mouth every word along with me even though she didn't know the lyrics. It used to drive me mad. I finally had to tell her, "Mother, please, could you sit somewhere else? You're throwing me off my concentration."

My father never came to concerts. At first I couldn't understand it because he was so proud of me. If I performed on *Singing Stars of Tomorrow*, he would lie at home on the couch with his ear cocked to the radio speaker and rate all the performers very critically. But gradually I came to realize that he didn't like to attend because he was deaf in one ear. Apparently there is no focus for the sound when it only comes through one eardrum, and he couldn't enjoy music sitting in a concert hall.

It is my lasting regret that I never had the opportunity to make my father's life easier. Less than a year after my debut, he died. For fifteen years, he'd had a heart condition and kept it a secret. Only my brother knew that he had suffered a coronary on a trip out of town for Northern Electric and my father had sworn Arnold to secrecy. He felt he couldn't afford to retire because there wasn't enough money to keep the family. But finally he had a really massive heart attack in Sherbrooke, and then another back in Montreal. His bosses found him collapsed over his toolbox and rushed him to the hospital in an ambulance. The doctors just shook their heads; they said it was only a matter of weeks until he died.

When I went to visit him, I found him in a huge ward, lying on his side, his back to most of the other patients. The grey eyes looked broken and sad. As we were talking, he suddenly asked, "What time is it, dear?"

"But Daddy," I said, "there's a clock right behind you."

Then I remembered that all his life he had been so shy that he had trouble looking people in the eye. I realized it must be excruciating for him to be surrounded by strangers at such a moment of weakness. I went right home and said to my sisters, "He's not comfortable in the hospital. We're going to rent an oxygen tank and a hospital bed and bring him back here. He's going to die at home." It was crazy and I couldn't afford it, but I decided to do it anyway. Overnight I, the baby, became the head of the family.

My sisters had their own husbands and children to look after by then, but we organized ourselves into shifts to make sure that someone was with my father all the time, feeding and caring for him. My mother, true to form, was hysterical, crying and carrying on. She was impossible to handle, so we plied her with brandy and kept her drunk – my mother who had been such a teetotaller! It was the guilt that set her off, I guess, because all her life she had played at being sickly, complaining of her health, making my father's life difficult, and here he was, the one who had really been ill.

He developed pulmonary edema and the suffering as he tried to gasp for breath was almost more than we could bear. You could hear that death rattle reverberate through the house. No sound I have ever heard has haunted me like that sound of my father dying. It will stay in my ears for life.

Years later, I was to play the old Russian countess in *The Queen of Spades* with Jon Vickers at the National Arts Centre in Ottawa. There is a scene in which the countess returns from a ball and undresses off stage. The servants come out of the dressing room carrying her yards of glittering gown, then her underskirts and pantaloons and finally her huge powdered wig. When she walks on stage, she is a fraction of her former self. In just a skimpy cotton nightgown and her bald pate sprouting only a few tufts of hair, the countess suddenly isn't formidable at all, just a frail little old woman. She sits down in her boudoir by a table with a deck of cards on it and tells her servants to leave her alone. Then she starts to sing a touching French song about her long-ago life at court. One day at the rehearsal the director said to me, "You have to think of something to do to signal to the audience that not only are you old, but you are not very well, so they aren't surprised later when you die." At first, I didn't see what I could do, but then a sound came back to me. As I nodded off to sleep in my big chair, I began to wheeze, my chest heaving and rattling for breath. At the performance it rivetted the audience. Little did they know that what they were listening to was the sound of my father dying.

No one in our family had ever been faced with death. We didn't know what to do. But we had friends in the funeral business so I volunteered to go down and ask them how we ought to proceed when the time came. I was in the director's office at White's Funeral Parlour when Beryl called and said that Daddy had died.

The funeral was on a bitter, icy winter's day. By the time of the service, my mother, who was suffering from varicose ulcers on her legs, among other things, was so distraught that her nerves snapped. There, in the freezing wind and snow, she tried to throw herself into the grave with the casket. She'd had a kind of breakdown. Before we'd even left the cemetery, I said to her doctor, "She's sick. We can't cope with her. You've got to take her to the hospital."

While she was there, I decided that our house on rue Fabre had to go. I've never had any attachment to the places I've lived or my possessions. I sent the landlord notice and, without telling my mother, I pitched out everything. I rented an upper duplex on Oxford Street in Notre-Dame-de-Grâce and, when my mother got out of hospital, I moved her in with me. The apartment was spanking new with two bedrooms and a back parlour, and I bought all kinds of new furniture to add to what I already had accumulated or had salvaged from rue Fabre. At first, my mother was in seventh heaven. But after a while she would say things like, "Where did my sieve go? The sieve I had from the time I got married?" She never forgave me for dispensing with that old junk.

But then the problem began: my mother wanted to be with me all the time. Everywhere I went, she would tag along. She loved all my friends in the choir and she adored going out with us after practice. She was in her element then, witty and full of wonderful stories. But when I was doing a concert, I'd have to get dinner ready and do the dishes and then, when I was trying to dress, my mother would say, "Would you do my hair, dear?" It became *her* show. When I had a radio broadcast, we would be ready to go out the door and she would have to go back to the bathroom. Getting her to the theatre became more of a job for me than singing. I realized I had to draw the line. I didn't want to spend the rest of my life as a duet – Maureen Forrester and her mother.

Finally I spoke to her doctor and he explained that I had replaced my father in her life. "Now you've become the parent," he said. "You're going to have to be firm with her." So one night after choir practice I said, "I'll see you at home later, Mother. I'm going off with the gang." When I got home she was in a terrible sulk.

"Well, I may as well just turn on the gas and stick my

head in the oven," she sniffled. "I'm just a lonely old woman, no use to anybody. Nobody wants me around."

"Maybe you should, if you want to," I said. I was furious.

She went out to the kitchen and I could hear her banging around, whipping up an off-stage drama as only the Irish can. I was trying to pretend I was watching television when suddenly the noise stopped. Oh my God, I thought, maybe she *did* put her head in the oven. I was sitting there wrestling with what to do when she reappeared. She walked into the back parlour and said, "You're absolutely right. I'm behaving like a child. I'll never do it again."

From that moment, my mother and I got along just fine. I knew that, in a way, she had been responsible for whatever success I had. It was she who'd had more ambitions for me than I'd had for myself. But from then on she left me free to live out the dream she had dreamed for herself.

TEN

Angels

T HE TELEPHONE summons had been mysterious. J.W.
McConnell, the distinguished founder and publisher
of the *Montreal Star*, had phoned to say he wanted to
meet me. I had never heard of J.W. McConnell but I had
certainly heard of the *Montreal Star*, and I was stunned.

I dressed up in my very best business suit with a hat and
little white gloves – the *de rigueur* outfit of the day – and
went down to his office on St. James Street. It was very
grand, panelled in mahogany with overstuffed leather
chairs. McConnell must have been eighty, but he was still
quite a presence – handsome and erect, proud in his bearing and a little gruff.

"I have a proposition to make you," he said. "How
much money do you need to stop singing?"

It seemed like a bizarre proposition to me. But it turned
out that he had read in his own paper a review by Eric
McLean, which noted that I was singing all over the place.
What a shame, Eric had written, that a young singer had
to spread herself so thin at the very age she needed to be
studying and expanding her repertoire. He had warned
that such a taxing schedule could threaten a beginner's
voice and health. McConnell, who already had a secret
history as a philanthropist, had called Eric in to ask about
me and then he had launched an investigation of his own.
The review had been written when my father had just

fallen ill and McConnell had learned that I was supporting my family. Finally I understood what he was offering me – a scholarship of sorts.

"Oh, Mr. McConnell," I said, "it would be a terrible mistake for me to stop singing now, just as I'm beginning to get steady engagements and build a reputation." But I explained to him my real problem was that performances were often costing me more than I earned from them. Sometimes my fee was as little as $25. By the time I paid for my transportation and my accompanist and got my hair done or bought a pair of nylons, there was nothing left. My expenses for sheet music were as much as $400 a year while I was trying to build my repertoire and, of course, there was still the price of my lessons from Diamant twice a week. I was constantly in the red. There were times I hated to answer the door in case it was the bank manager again announcing another overdraft.

When he heard that, McConnell offered to make up whatever deficits I accumulated. But he said there was one condition: I could never tell anyone publicly that he had helped me as long as he was alive. Otherwise, every mother with a talented child would be on his doorstep. I was flabbergasted by his offer, but suddenly, as I was leaving his office, a thought occurred to me. "I'm curious, Mr. McConnell," I said. "Where did you hear me sing?" It turned out that he had offered to pay my way on the strength of what he had read in his paper: he had never once listened to me.

For the next three years, J.W. McConnell staked me to my career, even though I went on working at Highway Paving for quite some time. In all, he gave me at least $25,000. I know I could have asked for more, enough to sing full-time, but my pride wouldn't allow me to do that. I didn't want charity from anybody. Still, he made a major difference in my life when it counted most. There are crucial make-or-break-it years when young artists need that extra cushion to bolster them. The big breaks came to me on their own, but they would have taken five years longer without J.W. He made all sorts of opportunities possible for me.

Soon after, when my father died, J.W. called me into his office and asked me what I was going to do about my mother. "Oh, I can support her," I said. "I've moved her in with me."

"And what about the funeral?"

I told him I was paying it off slowly, week by week. "Well, I'll look after it," he said. And then and there, he dialled White's Funeral Parlour and picked up the tab. I had lost a father but I had gained a guardian angel.

From then on, whenever I sang I would send him the reviews and stop by his office to keep him up to date on how I was progressing. Sometimes he would lock his office door. Then he would disappear into his private washroom and when he came out, he would be wearing this ratty old brown tweed jacket with leather patches on the elbows and sleeves that were too short on him.

"You know, once I was poor," he would say. "This was my first jacket."

It was very touching. He wanted to show me that he had come from a humble background too and that no matter how successful he had become, he never forgot that he was a self-made man. I always thought that he must have been a lonely man as well. His wife was very social and mad for royalty, and his children were all off doing their own thing. Nobody had time for him anymore. He liked me because I was independent and I think he needed somebody to talk to. Sometimes he would hug me and give me a little peck on the cheek. At first I was afraid he might make a pass at me, but I came to see that it was the kind of physical contact a father would have with a daughter. I suppose he was a little sweet on me, but he was, after all, eighty years old and there was no question about who would have been able to run faster around that desk.

After my recital debut at the Y, another mentor sought me out: Gilles Lefebvre, who ran Les Jeunesses Musicales du Canada. Gilles had been a violinist, but when he was in the Air Force in Europe during the war, he had learned about an organization in Belgium that sent budding artists on tour throughout the Catholic school system. It was both a way of helping young careers and developing a taste for music in children early. He was so enthusiastic that he brought the concept back to Canada and established Les Jeunesses Musicales in the school system here. Later, it was Gilles who founded the music camp at Mount Orford and the Orford Festival, which in turn gave birth to the Orford Quartet. In 1984, when I took on the chairmanship of the Canada Council, who should be there as associate director but Gilles, still doing the same thing he has always done – helping young artists make their way.

When I first knew Gilles, he was a travelling salesman for music – a handsome, wiry dynamo with curly black hair and piercing eyes. He was always rushing off somewhere, persuading some nuns or priests to join the Jeunesses program. He was a holy terror in a car, constantly smashing himself up in a rush to get to another concert. But none of Gilles's dashing about was for his own glory. His great mission in life has always been to launch careers. Still, once he'd started talented young people on their way, he never tried to hold on to them or make them feel they owed him something. Like a mother bird, he gave them their wings to find whatever destiny lay waiting for them.

It was Gilles who turned me into a professional. He was a friend of John Newmark's and together with Diamant they decided I was ready to do a Jeunesses tour – forty-five concerts throughout northern Ontario and Quebec. They were spaced out over nearly six months in neat clumps. I was to travel with an accompanist and a *commentateur* – an emcee who would spend the last twenty minutes of each concert hour giving a lecture on the music to the students. But best of all, Jeunesses was offering me $25 a concert, plus a per diem allowance for my meals, while the parochial school board picked up the hotel bill. At last, I could quit Highway Paving. Singing had finally become a full-time job for me.

The *commentateur* chauffeured us from town to town in his car. We would drive for hours through the Quebec countryside and then, in the distance, we would spot a church spire towering over the landscape for miles, marking our next stop. The motels we stayed in along the way were travelling salesmen's haunts. They smelled of cigarettes and beer, and carpets that had been washed and never quite allowed to dry. Sometimes the organizers would put us up in tiny hotels on the main street above a store, where the rooms would feature a single light bulb on a cord from the ceiling and flocked wallpaper peeling in ribbons.

I cut my teeth on that tour. Who else but Jeunesses would have scheduled a singer at that stage in her development for forty-five concerts? It was better to master stage presence in Chicoutimi and Arvida than in Toronto or Montreal where the critics could crucify you and ruin your career even before it had started.

I learned how to pace a concert and what pieces worked or didn't to hold an audience. And I found out what it was like to sing on the road day after day, getting up at 6 a.m. to drive for hours, then arriving in a little town with only enough time to go and see the hall, do an interview with the local paper, put my hair up in curlers and change my clothes. Then after the concert, there would usually be a reception at somebody's house where I would be expected to rave over the home-baked pies and tell lots of amusing stories before getting up early the next morning to travel on to the next town. Sometimes we would have two concerts in a day. It really was a question of the survival of the fittest. On the Jeunesses tours you found out if you were cut out for this life, which can be a hard, hard life. Singing is not for the delicate.

My accompanist was Gaston Arel, an extremely

talented organist, who always had to get to the halls early to check out the old pipe organs, which, in that era before they all became electrified, invariably had a half-dozen stops which didn't work. Even more than a pianist, an organist on those pedal organs had to see you sing, so that he could anticipate where you were going to take a breath and pump accordingly. That meant I had to stand in the choir loft where the organ was – invariably at the back in a Catholic church. Nobody in the audience could see me. The first aria I did was always "Divinités du Styx" from Gluck's *Alceste*. It's set in a very, very low key. The minute I would begin singing "Divinités . . ." all these little heads would snap around and waves of snickers would roll up the aisles. Those youngsters couldn't believe that sound was coming from a woman.

Jeunesses catered to students from kindergarten to college, and some of those audiences included children barely four or five years old. They wouldn't make any noise – the nuns kept them in line – but they would wriggle for the entire hour, picking their noses, climbing out of their snowsuits, climbing back in again. It was certainly a test of a performer's concentration. The ones who were nine or ten would come backstage and say things such as "Loved the Vivaldi, hated the Schumann." Children never like Romantic music, but these students in the Catholic schools really knew their composers, and my, did they have strong opinions!

The students would line up backstage after the concert with their programs and even if they really didn't want an autograph, they would pretend they did because all their friends seemed to be asking for one. In a seminary, the boys knew they could stay up later at night if they waited for an autograph, so, after a gruelling day on the road and two concerts, I would sometimes be faced with the prospect of signing 700 programs.

Once, in Grand'Mère, I was singing up in the choir loft at the back when suddenly something came flying at me. I had dislodged a bat. They're sonic creatures and every time I would hit a certain note that bat would zoom closer and closer. I must have been on his frequency. But it wasn't the last time I proved to have such an attraction. Years later, I was singing Bach's *B Minor Mass* with the Tudor Singers in Montreal's Notre Dame Cathedral and whenever I hit one particular note in the "Agnus Dei," bats would come swooping out of the belfry, dive-bombing me. Suddenly, I could see 5,000 people in the audience staring, not at the choir, but up at the ceiling.

At another stop on the tour, I had a second minor disaster. I had started into a group of Fauré songs, one of which was called "Absence." It begins, "Je veux que le matin m'ignore . . ." "Je veux," I sang, "I wish . . ." and then I drew a complete blank. I stopped and put a hand over my mouth. *"Mon Dieu,"* I said to the audience, "I wish I knew what I wished." They burst out into laughter. Mind you, this is not a technique I recommend. Now I always advise students that they've got to learn to fake it when they forget the text. "Don't get a blank look on your face or stop," I tell them. "Just put any old sound in, but do it with an accent. Most people won't know the difference!"

My Jeunesses Musicales outings were quite a success. From Shawinigan to St. Hyacinthe, I was a minor celebrity. Some people still come up to me today after concerts and say they remember me from that trip. At the time, I felt as if the whole world knew I was doing a tour. Fortunately, I was too busy to discover otherwise.

In between the concerts, when I was back in Montreal, I was learning new *Lieder*. As I always point out to pupils, they can never learn enough repertoire when they're young. Sometimes a singer will audition for me and I'll say, "Alright, now what else do you know?" It often turns out that one program is the sum total of their knowledge. "For heaven's sake, what are you going to do when your career takes off or somebody asks you to fill in overnight?" I ask. "Tell them that you need a month to learn another program?" Early in my career, I became known for being able to substitute for an ailing star such as Elisabeth Schwarzkopf on only a day's notice. Not only could I step into her shoes, I had such a vast repertoire that I could even sing the same program, which never failed to impress impresarios and critics.

During one of the breaks in the Jeunesses tour, Diamant suggested I learn Robert Schumann's *Frauenliebe und Leben* (Women's Love and Life). From the instant I read the text, I adored that cycle. There it was in eight songs, all the joys and heartbreak of a woman's existence from the girlhood meeting of her sweetheart to the birth of their child to, in the end, the first pain he has ever inflicted on her – his death. It was such grown-up music. There was so much ecstasy in it. That piece presented a wonderful test of a singer's budding emotional range and from the first I loved to do it. But when you're young, you take every note so seriously. You give them all equal weight, which ends up in a kind of blandness. John Newmark used to say to me, "Oh, *Maureenschen*, I really want to hear you sing this when you're older, after you've had a baby." I was very hurt. I thought, What does he mean? Am I not doing it right? But now I understand what he meant. I was twenty-three, but there were things I had never known or felt. I was still poised on the brink of a woman's life.

ELEVEN

They're Playing Our Song

I BUILT THE early years of my career on some of the most unlikely stages. High school gymnasiums, church basements, mining town halls – I've sung in them all. From Joliette and Jonquière to Estevan, Saskatchewan, there's scarcely a hamlet in Canada that I haven't performed in over the years. Long after that first Jeunesses tour, I began accepting offers from the Canada Council Touring Office for whistlestop circuits in several provinces. People say to me now, "What are you doing singing in Port Perry and Red Lake, Ontario, at this stage of your career?" But audiences in small towns aren't jaded. They've been waiting months for you to come and when you do, it means something to them. You look at those faces and you know it's all worthwhile. What's more, they really listen to the music. In New York and the rest of the culture capitals around the world, often you look out and see glazed eyes. The audience has already seen too much and heard too much that week. You can feel the men in the tenth row wishing their wives hadn't dragged them away from the football game on television or the latest episode of *Dynasty*. Maybe it was because I started out in small towns that I developed a soft spot in my heart for them. Certainly they've provided me with some of my liveliest memories.

Once, years ago, when John and I were touring ladies' clubs in Western Canada, we ended up performing in a church in Lethbridge, Alberta, where they had removed the pulpit from the front to make a stage. We were doing *Frauenliebe und Leben* and the concert seemed to be going very well. But when John and I looked out at intermission, there wasn't a soul left. "Oh, John, we really bombed," I said. Just then the sexton came along. "Guess you're wondering where everybody is," he said. "Well, there's a game going on in the hockey arena across the street and they've all gone to check the score. But don't worry, they'll be back." And sure enough, after intermission they were. Another night in Melrose, a man came up to me at a reception after the concert and said, "Well, young lady, that was a full house tonight and that's a real credit to you. There were a lot of farmers out and this is seedin' time."

In small towns, people feel personally involved with you. Once, playing in Trois-Rivières without me, John was worrying about how he would get back to Montreal for a broadcast the next day. "Mama" Rousseau, who had been national president of Les Jeunesses Musicales, was head of the local committee. "Wait a minute," she said to him. When she came back, she had it all arranged. As her son pulled up in this big black Cadillac, John noticed that it wasn't your ordinary limousine. It had curtains in the back. He had forgotten that her husband was the local undertaker.

When you're a singer just starting out, the crazy places you end up performing in often teach you more than Carnegie Hall ever could. Mind you, Carnegie Hall isn't likely to knock you dead with the aroma of sweaty Adidas after a basketball game. One Sunday afternoon in 1953, I walked onto the stage of the Manor Park high school gym in Ottawa and whap, it hit me – the smell of over-ripe socks. This was no ambience for a concert whatsoever. I had been talked into doing it by a woman named Mary Gauthier, who had become a fan of mine while I was singing in Sherbrooke. She had just moved to Ottawa and begged me to do a recital there. Her husband's older sister was Eva Gauthier, perhaps the first Canadian *Lieder* singer who had made an international career, and Mary always talked of her as if I ought to know who she was, although at the time I had never heard of her. Still, I couldn't imagine the apparently fabled Eva Gauthier ever singing in a gym like that.

Like all auditoriums, it had a stage that was too high and lights that were too bright. You couldn't have missed a yawn at 300 paces. I looked out and thought to myself, What an audience! And then I noticed a face in the second row to the left. I took one look and knew in one of those psychic flashes of mine: That's the man I'm going to marry. Of course, it took a while before it finally came about, but that's how I met Eugene Kash.

Until that day I had never had the slightest desire to get married, but it was a case of proverbial love at first sight. The moment I saw that magnificent head, so dark and worldly and kind, I knew that if I were ever going to spend my life with somebody, it would be with him.

I once asked Eugene what his first impression had been of me. "Well," he said, "I thought: That girl is definitely wearing the wrong dress." It was blue moire taffeta with a short skirt and sequins that swirled around the hem. Sequins you *don't* wear on a Sunday afternoon, and although I have good legs, the skirt was too short, and blue has never been my colour. I don't know what I could have been thinking. I looked like a ballroom dancer.

But Eugene told me that when I had started to sing, he and his friend Karl Weiselberger, the critic for the *Ottawa Citizen* with whom he'd come, looked at each other, raised their eyebrows and agreed, "Hey, this is not bad." They hadn't expected this big healthy Anglo-Saxon girl named Forrester to be singing Schubert and Brahms *Lieder* in perfect German. In fact, they hadn't come to see me at all. I was sharing the program with a young violinist named Keith Milliken from the Ottawa Philharmonic, where Eugene was then the conductor.

After the concert, Eugene and Karl came backstage. It

was packed, mostly with people who had come to see the violinist because, after all, it was his home town. At some point I was standing on the stairway with a nosegay which Mary Gauthier had given me when Eugene came over. Mary introduced us. I twirled the nosegay in his face and said, "Well, I've got the flowers. Now all I need is the man."

He must have thought I was a cheeky brat. He was very European and sophisticated. As the Ottawa symphony conductor at the time, he was the toast of the capital. Eugene was also a violinist and, as I found out later, he had been a child prodigy. He was the eldest son of a Polish goldsmith who had immigrated to Toronto only three months before his wife gave birth. His parents discovered when he was very young that he had an enormous musical talent and sent him as a boy to study at the Curtis Institute in Philadelphia and then in Vienna. But in 1938, just before *Kristallnacht*, his mother had a premonition about the Nazis and ordered him to come home. During the war, he had been head of the National Film Board's music department under John Grierson, before being named to lead the Ottawa Philharmonic.

Eugene admitted later that when we first met, he had felt the chemistry too, but he was afraid of me. He had just come through a long, tangled relationship with a woman and besides, as he knew from the program, I was eighteen years younger, although you couldn't have guessed it immediately to look at me. When I took the train back to Montreal that night after the Manor Park concert, Eugene's face stayed in my mind, but I wasn't to see him again for months.

At the time, a young Hungarian-born composer at McGill named István Anhalt had asked if he could write some music for me. "Sure," I said. "I'm very flattered that you'd want to." What did I know about modern music then? He composed five horrendously difficult songs based on news items he had read in the paper. One was about the murder of a Balinese dancer and there was a line in it that went, "And Sampi's manager, Mr. John Coast, said . . ." Years later, when John Coast became my manager in England, I liked to tease him, "You know, John, I had you in a song before I met you!"

We were to perform Anhalt's song cycle at McGill's Moyse Hall, but at the last moment the violinist fell ill. Who should show up to fill in for him but Eugene. Because the pieces were so difficult, there were endless rehearsals so we saw quite a bit of each other. We got along marvellously but after each session, he would just walk me to the streetcar stop, say goodbye and rush off.

At the end of one rehearsal, his friend Alan Mills, the folksinger, came to pick him up. Alan was a fan of mine and we would all kibitz together. "Hey, Maureen," he suddenly asked, "do you ever get to Ottawa?"

"As a matter of fact," I said, "I'm going next month to sing in the *Messiah*."

"Okay, Kash, do me a favour," he said. "Take this kid to your famous Chinese restaurant."

"I sure love Chinese food," I hinted, but Eugene only smiled and made some vague remark. All through the Anhalt rehearsals and performance, he was charming to me and he seemed interested in my career. I had just done the first group of my Jeunesses Musicales tour engagements and he was very encouraging, but I couldn't get him to ask me out. I knew that he was staying in town for New Year's Eve and, praying he would ask me for a date, I bought myself a really spiffy new dress – navy *peau de soie* with a full skirt and a bodice that was cut into deep petals, then covered in net. It was very provocative, but I knew what I was doing – I had quite a figure in those days. I waited and waited for the phone to ring, but silence. I hoped right up until New Year's Eve itself, but I sat in that bloody expensive dress for nothing.

The next morning, the phone rang. Eugene said that Alan and Bernie, his wife, were having a New Year's Day dinner and they wondered if I could join them. He gave me the address, but he didn't offer to come and pick me up himself.

Bernie and Alan were a terrific couple and Alan was quite a celebrity in those days. In fact, he was really two people: a talented writer and CBC Radio actor who did very highbrow plays under his real name, Albert Miller; and Alan Mills, at that time the most famous folksinger in Canada. Later he had a children's radio show and wrote a song every youngster in the country came to know: "There was an old lady who swallowed a fly/ Now I don't know why she swallowed a fly/ I think she'll die." Alan had a feeling for the country's folklore and he was wonderful and warm.

He and Bernie lived in a lovely house off Atwater, and their dinner was very elegant – filet mignon with béarnaise sauce. But I didn't drink then and when Alan saw that, he blanched. I must have seemed so naïve to him. "Would you like catsup or anything on your steak?" he ventured.

"Heavens no!" I said.

"Thank God," Alan sighed. "You pass the audition."

We all became great friends during that dinner. That evening Eugene saw me home and kissed me goodnight.

Not long after, I went to Ottawa as scheduled for the *Messiah* with the Ottawa Choral Society. Although I don't remember much about the performance, I do remember the Chinese dinner afterward, and then the invitation back to Eugene's apartment. For me, that was it. This was no case of an older man seducing a young girl. I wasn't hard to get at all. For years, whenever we heard the *Messiah*, we'd say, "They're playing our song."

I was madly in love with Eugene. From then on, every time he came to Montreal, we saw each other. Eventually, because he came more and more often, he took a little apartment on Baile Street. It was minuscule – a tiny corner room with a kitchenette that I swear hadn't been painted in fifty years. It was dark and dingy, and, although he had a woman to clean it, he wouldn't let her move a thing. Music was piled everywhere. It was worse than his Ottawa apartment where I once found a tomato petrified on the windowsill like a piece of sculpture.

Of course, that drove me wild and I was always in there scrubbing the fuzz off things. I wanted to clean and cook for him. I think that's what made Eugene realize I was different than most girls he'd known. He was used to going out, taking dates to restaurants, but he had never been with anyone who worried about him. Sometimes when he was conducting in Ottawa, I would take the train down from Montreal and bring him a Swiss Chalet chicken to eat before the concert. You'd have thought there was no food in Ottawa.

"But I'm too nervous to eat," he would protest.

"You know what you call butterflies in the stomach?" I said. "That's gas from being hungry. You need strength to conduct." The overwhelming impulse I had with Eugene was to make his life beautiful.

We played house in that dingy little apartment of his in Montreal. It was just big enough for a desk and a bookshelf and an old split-level couch which, when you opened it out into a bed, had one side three inches higher than the other. We would laugh and laugh about it. When we finally married, Eugene's dowry was that sleeper sofa and it followed us from house to house for years. Finally when we moved to Connecticut, I said to him, "The one thing I'm going to get rid of is that couch. I've always hated it." But in retrospect, I realized I was fond of it. That was where we had started our romantic life together.

Through all this, my mother was never a big fan of Eugene's. She thought he was far too old for me and he didn't come courting with flowers and flatter her the way she thought suitors should. One night at 2 a.m. Eugene's phone rang. "Yes, just a minute," he said and handed the receiver to me. My mother was on the line sobbing. "If only your father were alive now . . ." she sniffled.

"Mother, I'm old enough to know what I'm doing," I said. "Go to sleep. I'll be there when you wake up in the morning."

I was twenty-four by then and I knew what I wanted. Sometimes my determination would scare Eugene. I was so psychic about him that, even if he didn't call me when he came to town, I could tell whenever he was in Montreal – right down to what building he was in. I would be walking along the street and it would come to me, "He's in here." I would walk in and, sure enough, there would be a violin-maker listed on the third floor. "Hi!" I'd pop my head in the door. It used to drive him crazy.

By this time I had resumed the last segment of my Jeunesses Musicales tour, but now, as I set off for another chunk of concerts in northern Quebec, all I worried about was how fast I could get back to Montreal and Eugene. I thought of nothing else night and day.

"Kutzerel," he called me, an endearment he made up, which he maintained summed up the little girl in me. I adopted Alan Mills's name for him: *"Kätsl"* – Little Pussycat. But despite the familiarity, I was still slightly in awe of Eugene. In my eyes, he was such a man of the world and it seemed to me there wasn't anything he didn't know about music. Every time I mentioned a piece I was going to sing, he had an anecdote to make it come alive for me. I would tell him I was studying a new work by Vivaldi and he would say, "Did you know Vivaldi was a red-haired priest who was made head of a school for wayward girls? He had to write something for mass every Sunday; that's why he was so prolific." He told me how, in Proko-fiev's *Alexander Nevsky*, the music was written for a mo-vie that Sergei Eisenstein made about a thirteenth-century battle where the Russians were fighting off an attack by the Germans. There is a part where Prokofiev recreates the sound of the horses' hooves crossing the frozen lakes. Ever since, I can't listen to that piece without hearing the timpani and visualizing the ice cracking under the horses as they sink from the terrible weight of those cannons.

Eugene couldn't believe that I could be so naturally musical and gifted on the one hand, yet so totally ignorant of music history and theory on the other. I knew nothing except what I sang in those days. I had no sense where a piece fit in the development of an era and often he would drop the name of some legendary composer in a conversation, only to be astounded when I asked, "Who's that?" Eugene helped provide my musical education.

But he formed me in other ways too. When I met him, I would blurt out whatever came into my head. In fact I found out later that John and Diamant kept catalogues of my faux pas. Diamant would be in the midst of telling me about a *Lied* based on a great love story and I would crack, "Hubba, hubba!" It was Eugene who taught me to edit myself before the sentences came tumbling out of my mouth. Discretion is still not my strong point, but in those days I was so naïve and brash that he thought I was some kind of screwball.

At that time I still talked in a very high, little girl's voice. Eugene made me see that it was probably a subconscious effort to save my vocal cords for singing but that it wasn't becoming at all. "Sweetheart," he said, "on a girl your size, that tiny little voice just doesn't go."

Ours was a great love affair, but from the first Eugene had warned me that I shouldn't get involved with him. "I'm not the marrying kind," he kept telling me. I insisted that I didn't care. I wanted only to be with him; I wasn't concerned about some piece of paper. But as soon as we would start to get too close, he would back off again.

"I'm older," he would worry. "You're young and you have a great career ahead of you. I'll only hold you back and it will cause us both a lot of pain." Once he even admitted, "I'm afraid you'll pass me by. I don't want to be the tail-light to a star."

But I waved off all his warnings. No matter what he said or did, Eugene couldn't discourage me. I knew that this was the love of my life.

TWELVE

Beyond La Belle Province

IN QUEBEC to this day, people introduce me as "Notre Maureen." French Canadians have a sense of proprietorship about their artists. They feel I belong to them and in a sense they're right; after all, they gave me my start.

After my recital debut, I had begun to win scholarships around the city. The Montreal Social Club, a businessmen's group, awarded me a prize of $500, and the Montreal Ladies' Morning Musical Club invited me to sing after giving me a $50 prize. The Ladies' Morning Musical Club met on Thursday afternoons and an invitation from them was very prestigious. Their concerts featured all the rising young musicians who came through town in the early stages of their careers, from Kathleen Ferrier to Leontyne Price. The organizers had an uncanny sense of taste. To be asked to sing for the Ladies' Morning Musical Club was a sign that I was on my way.

It's a shame that there isn't a circuit of clubs and concert societies like it today for young singers to gain experience. Now women work or play golf and go off to Hawaii; they don't go to daytime concerts. As a result, there aren't the outlets for a young generation of musicians to apprentice in quite the way that I did. In those days you could build a career step by step, but today you graduate from a conservatory, you give a recital and right away you're on the firing line. There's almost nothing between obscurity and going on television, where the producers are only interested in big names. In a sense my career came at the end of an era.

After the concert, Pierre Béique came backstage to congratulate me. The Ladies introduced us, but I already knew who he was. Everybody knew Pierre Béique, one of the most powerful figures in the city's music circles. For decades he guided the symphony on its course and he had such an eye for young talent that, long after I met him, he brought Zubin Mehta to Montreal and gave him his first big opportunity.

By then Igor Markevitch had become musical director of the symphony, but suddenly he wrote from Europe to announce that he wouldn't be coming back to Montreal. It was such short notice that even the worst conductors in the world were already booked up. Pierre was furious. But he had heard of Zubin winning prizes in Europe and being hailed as a promising young talent from India, so he hired him to fill in for one of the "Dollar" concerts sponsored by J.W. McConnell at the Forum. Zubin conducted Berlioz's *Symphonie Fantastique* and he was electric. Everyone was so knocked out by the fire and control of this young man that Pierre, with a gambler's instinct, persuaded the board to offer him a job. It was in Montreal that Zubin's career really took off. While he was conducting there, Fritz Reiner fell ill and the Los Angeles Philharmonic asked him to pinch-hit. Within a year Los Angeles had offered him the conductor's job too and at twenty-five, he was leading two of the continent's great orchestras at once. Overnight Zubin became a superstar, confirming Pierre's perspicacity.

When I met Pierre backstage after the Ladies' Morning Musical Club concert, he was young and debonair behind his perennial smoked glasses. He was very complimentary and courtly, as if I had somehow done him a personal favour by singing.

"Do you know Beethoven's *Ninth Symphony*?" he asked. Of course I didn't. I had never even heard it.

"Well, learn the alto part," he said. "I'm going to ask

Maestro Klemperer to give you an audition. I think it would be nice for you to debut with our orchestra."

Nice! What an understatement. It was the chance of a lifetime. An invitation to sing with the symphony made my Jeunesses tour pale in comparison. But even more important, it was an opportunity to work with the great Otto Klemperer who had held the city awestruck ever since he had become the symphony conductor through an incredible fluke. He had come to Montreal to guest conduct a concert in 1952, and, getting into his taxi at the airport, he slipped and broke a leg. He was already sixty-seven and infirm, and it was very traumatic for him to be immobilized for months, so he took an apartment in Montreal. Pierre, ever the gambler, decided to offer him the conductor's post. Klemperer not only accepted, he stayed on for two years. That's how the Montreal Symphony landed one of the twentieth century's great conductors.

Klemperer by then was paralyzed on one side of his body, including his face, after an operation years earlier for a brain tumour. He was known as a terrifying man if he didn't get what he wanted from an orchestra and the paralysis made him look all the more ferocious. He was enormous, towering above six feet, with wisps of hair and brows that swept out in wings over magnetic eyes. Once from backstage I watched him conduct and saw how he held the orchestra captive with the intensity burning in those eyes. Because of his height, he didn't need a podium but the management erected a railing for him to lean on and when he pressed against it and put out that crippled arm of his with its hand stiff as a claw, he made me think of a giant fierce bird. Years later, when I did Murray Schafer's *Beauty and the Beast* for CBC-TV, I sang both voices – the beast and the prince who was trapped inside him – and it brought the image of Otto Klemperer flooding back to me: the sick angry shell of the man and, imprisoned inside, just glimpsed through the light in his eyes, this soul who made beautiful music.

Backstage before that concert, he had asked me to crack open his score for him because it was brand new. "But Maestro," I asked, "did you lose your score?"

"No," he said. "Every time I conduct a work that I haven't done for a few years, I always buy a new score so I don't rely on my old markings. I want to think of the piece as if I'm seeing it again for the first time." That to me was a sign of greatness.

Pierre Béique arranged for me to fly to New York to audition for Klemperer. I met him in a small rehearsal studio where he had his daughter with him. She did a lot for him because his wife was frail and there were so many simple daily tasks that he couldn't manage. But there were rumours that despite his paralysis, there were some things he could manage very well: he reportedly had a voracious appetite for racy ladies. In fact, long after he left Montreal, he made the headlines for accidentally setting himself on fire in bed one night in London with a woman to whom he was definitely not married. Klemperer's inner core was certainly alive, although I can't attest to it personally.

At the beginning of the audition, he went to the piano and showed me how he wanted to do the *Ninth*'s alto part. I adjusted very quickly and he seemed pleased by that. As I was to discover later, if you tell a conductor that you can't do something his way, it's the kiss of death: you'll never be re-engaged. After I had sung something else for him, he turned to his daughter and said, *"Ja, ja."* He turned to me. "Fine," he said. "We'll see you in Montreal in six months for Beethoven's *Ninth*."

I flew home absolutely overjoyed. Imagine! I thought, I'm going to sing with this great conductor and the Montreal Symphony Orchestra. My mother was terribly excited. On December 8, 1953, she and my sisters came to listen to me. Little did they know they would only hear one note. In Beethoven's *Ninth*, there are four soloists – a soprano, an alto, a tenor and a bass-baritone. The soprano you hear a lot and the tenor as well. The baritone even starts out in a little solo, but, except for one note, the alto only sings along with the quartet or the chorus. The audience would miss something if she wasn't there, chirruping along, but it's impossible to pick out her voice from the rest. That performance was a total anti-climax for me. Since then, whenever I've sung that part, people have always said to me, "You looked so lovely up there. You were the only one smiling." I learned to smile through Beethoven's *Ninth* because, while the rest of the soloists are singing their hearts out, I figure that, since nobody can hear me, I might as well look pleasant.

That performance launched my career with the Montreal Symphony. Pierre Béique immediately re-engaged me for the next year and from then on, scarcely a season went by when I didn't sing with them. Each year, Pierre arranged for me to do a slightly more difficult work as I progressed and, within a few years, after I was established, he and Zubin asked me as a guest artist on the symphony's first European tour.

From the first time I met Zubin, I adored him and he became a friend. He asked me to do the Mahler *Second Symphony* and we were on the same wave length right away. He was so brash and dynamic then. Zubin is a singer's dream conductor. He breathes with you. He gets emotionally involved in the text and he looks at you as if to say, "God, if I could sing, that's the way I would like to do it."

When we made that first tour through France and Switzerland, we thought it would be a lark. I was to sing Mahler's *Kindertotenlieder* (Songs on the Death of Children) which by then I had done so often I could have sung them in my sleep. But Zubin is such an emotional conductor that every night in the middle of the piece, he would cry and the orchestra would cry and then the audience would start to cry. Sometimes even I would become emotional, although if you let yourself get too carried away while you're singing, you choke up and you can't get the voice out properly. But at the end, there would be handkerchiefs out all over the hall. The orchestra members would tap on their music stands and applaud and we'd all take our bows teary-eyed. It got to be a very depressing tour.

Zubin had already begun his affair with Teresa Stratas by then, on an earlier tour of Russia. They became a very hot item – it was no secret – although it was terribly painful at the time for Zubin's wife Carmen. But Stratas and Zubin stayed together for a long, long time. It was such a passionate relationship that there were rumours among the musicians that when they were separated they would phone each other and leave the receiver on the pillow all night so they could hear each other breathing. It was only hearsay but every woman dreams of an affair like that. In the end, that kind of intensity couldn't last – even though it broke up Zubin's marriage. But things worked out for Carmen in a wonderful way. When Zubin's brother Zarin came to Montreal to finish his accounting studies, he decided to stay on to work. While he was there, he fell in love with Carmen. They've been happily married for years and have beautiful children, and of course Zarin has now inherited Pierre Béique's job. Such are the behind-the-scenes adventures of the Montreal Symphony. No matter how many great orchestras around the world I may have sung with, it has always been a special orchestra in my heart – my hometown symphony.

All through my early career, my mother had set goals for me. First she would say, "Oh, wouldn't it be wonderful to be a soloist with a downtown church?" And I became a soloist with a downtown church. Then she would muse, "Oh, imagine if you could sing with the Montreal Symphony." At last I sang with the Montreal Symphony. But to her the crowning achievement was to sing for royalty. Like other women of that generation, my mother was mad for anything to do with the King and Queen. She was beside herself with delight in September 1954 when the Concerts Symphoniques de Montréal asked me to sing with three other soloists in honour of the visit of the Duchess of Kent and Princess Alexandra. The concert was held in the Chalet on top of Mount Royal, and Wilfrid Pelletier – the Montreal-born conductor who had become world famous and led the Metropolitan Opera orchestra in New York – came back to take up the baton for the night. My duet with a baritone named Denis Harbour in a group of arias from *Samson and Delilah* was not my finest hour, but to my mother it was a moment of glory. I didn't have the heart to tell her that in the receiving line later, that shaking Princess Alexandra's hand felt just like grasping a dead fish.

As long as I was working at what I liked, I had no great ambitions for myself. Because my horizons were so limited, I let my mother define what I should strive for. Her next dream for me was to sing Handel's *Messiah* with Sir Ernest MacMillan and the Toronto Symphony in the broadcast that the whole country tuned in to each Christmas over the CBC. One day, soon after I had auditioned for Otto Klemperer, I came home to find my mother in a tizzy. Sir Ernest had phoned! When I returned the call, his manager in fact invited me to sing the alto solo in the *Messiah* with the Mendelssohn Choir in Massey Hall on December 28, 1954. It was the first time I met Jimmy Milligan, the bass-baritone, and Lois Marshall, who had been singing the *Messiah* soprano solo with Sir Ernest for years.

When I had initially heard Lois sing in Montreal earlier, I had been stunned. The minute she opened her mouth, she had a quality which brought tears to my eyes. She can do that to me still. She can sing "A Fond Kiss," just a little Scottish farewell song, and make an audience dissolve, it's so beautiful. She puts her heart and soul into everything she sings and it becomes very personal. Maybe the suffering she had to go through as a child with polio contributed to her ability to bring so much emotion to her interpretation. On the surface Lois is always cheerful, always slapping people on the back with her big hearty laugh, but beneath that façade I'm not sure if anyone ever really gets to know her. She would never let on for the world that she's had to live with a lot of pain, but the one thing that took her out of it was her singing.

Jimmy Milligan was tall and ruddy-complexioned with piercing eyes and an incredible agility in his voice – a baritone that carried to the back of the hall. In those days I was still striving for projection. I wasn't used to singing with an orchestra and I didn't yet know that you couldn't sing softly with a full symphony in the same way you could with only a piano accompaniment. It's a colour rather than a volume that you have to achieve, and it can take five years to learn how to be heard *pianissimo* when you've got eighty-five musicians behind you playing their hearts out.

Those two performances of the *Messiah* also provided me with one of my first big tests of concentration. On opening night, while I was waiting for my part, I looked out over the audience in Massey Hall and what did I see directly in front of me but two frantic gum-chewers. One kept digging back into his teeth and extracting wads of pink goo. The other was pumping his jaws madly in 4/4 time. There must be a law among the gum-chewers of the world that requires they always chew hopelessly out of rhythm with whatever music they're listening to. For a musician, it can be incredibly distracting. Despite the packed house, I couldn't keep my eyes off them: I was mesmerized by those mouths chewing their cud. The next night, I thought: Well, at least I won't have to contend with them. But the moment we filed on stage, what do I see but two men in the same two seats masticating away as if there were no tomorrow. It was as if those seats had been monopolized by the gum-chewing lobby.

I was afraid that such an august figure as Sir Ernest would criticize my interpretation, but in fact he liked it immensely. And when Sir Ernest liked you, he would blow your horn. After I went back to Montreal, he kept saying to people, "Did you hear that broadcast? Now is that young lady not talented?" He opened up Toronto to me because, as former dean of the university music school, if Sir Ernest put his stamp of approval on you, everybody wanted to engage you. He was like a benevolent grandfather to talented young singers.

Sir Ernest had first heard me sing, not in the *Messiah*, but with Glenn Gould in a Toronto concert a few months earlier. He was one of only a handful of people who did. Glenn had invited me to join him in an all-Bach chamber program at the conservatory hall. It was a brilliant concert, but it was the day after Hurricane Hazel and, with all the devastation, only fifteen people showed up.

From my first meeting with Glenn I knew he was a genius. I was always in awe of his mind and I felt so inadequate in his presence. He was such an intellectual and I couldn't talk his lingo. I never analyze music, I just do it, and if a piece is too troublesome or doesn't sit well with me, I do something else. Once Glenn apologized to me because he was going to play from memory.

"I sing from memory," I said. "Why would I mind?"

"Well," he said, "it sort of looks as if I'm showing off. But it's not vanity, it's to save myself from embarrassing you." He explained that when he was playing a piano reduction in an orchestral piece from the score, he often looked at it on the page and mentally re-composed it in other keys while he went along. It worked for him when he was playing as a soloist but when he was accompanying someone, it could become very distracting, so once he had made up his mind how he would do something he memorized the part that way to keep himself from tinkering with it further. That was just one example of his brilliant intellectualization of music, which I couldn't begin to fathom.

Later, Franz Kraemer had us perform the "Urlicht," the four-minute vocal aria from Mahler's *Second Symphony*, on a CBC television special with Glenn conducting. But Glenn was left-handed and it drove the musicians insane. He led with the opposite hand to the one they were used to and for them it was like seeing a mirror image. They never knew what beat he was on. I think that was why he didn't conduct more even though he was clearly interested in it. Shortly before his death he was hiring orchestras so that he could conduct in secret at his studio in Toronto's Inn on the Park hotel.

Of course, when I first sang with him, Glenn was famous for his eccentricities. Once when we were both in San Francisco, he called me to join him for tea. I opened the door to his hotel room, and I could barely find a place to put my foot. Now, I'm a person who likes order – my shoes are all arranged according to colour and function and even the spices in my kitchen are stacked alphabetically – but Glenn was a real disaster in the tidiness area. He always looked as if he'd slept in his clothes, and his stage mannerisms were the subject of jokes all over the world. In 1956, when I had started to acquire a reputation myself, Vincent Massey, who was then Governor General, invited me to tea at Rideau Hall in Ottawa. He was a very dry, proper man and we were sitting in the formal Government House parlour when he asked me if I knew Glenn Gould.

"Of course," I said. "I adore Glenn."

"Well," he said, "I want you to do something for me. You have to tell him to stop those mannerisms and funny noises when he's playing."

"I would love to," I said. "But Glenn is a very, very gifted musician. That's just part of his personality."

"But it's very distracting to the audience," he insisted, as if he were issuing an order from Buckingham Palace itself. "You *must* tell him to stop it!"

I never told Glenn the story but I can't remember a time when he didn't hum. It never got on my nerves, but then Glenn Gould would have had to hum in a pretty loud voice in order to cover me.

Glenn Gould, Sir Ernest MacMillan, playing with Otto Klemperer and the Montreal Symphony, and falling in love with Eugene – so many things were happening to me so fast. Then suddenly that fall, Gilles Lefebvre came back from an international Jeunesses Musicales convention in Hanover, Germany, and announced that UNESCO had found some money left over in its cultural budget for a Canadian-European musical exchange. Gilles had played the board some of my CBC broadcast tapes and convinced them to choose me for a tour of eight countries on the Continent. In return, a German pianist was coming to Quebec.

Jeunesses had never before sent a Canadian abroad and the newspapers hailed me as the first singer to make an extended tour of Europe in more than twenty years. "Canada's Singing Ambassadress," the *Star Weekly* magazine dubbed me – a title that has stuck over the years. Jean Drapeau, who was already mayor of Montreal, called me down to City Hall for a farewell send-off to sign the city's guest book. The tour was the opportunity of a lifetime but I didn't want to go. I couldn't bear the thought of leaving Eugene.

But it was Eugene who finally persuaded me. "This is your big chance," he said. "You have to take it." Certainly, I had worked long and hard for it, but when he and Alan and Bernie Mills saw me off at the airport, my excitement was tinged with sadness. In those days you walked straight onto the plane across the tarmac and Eugene and I stood there at the chain-link fence with our gloves locked together in the freezing January air. I cried all the way to London. My God, what am I leaving behind? I thought. Do I really want this career?

THIRTEEN

Continental Rhythms

BRAHMS'S and Dvořák's *Gypsy Melodies* were tucked in my luggage and the Air Canada flight was beginning its descent to Heathrow Airport. I, who had never been west of Toronto or south of Philadelphia, was off to see the world at last. In the thirty years since that first trip to London, I've lived out of suitcases, crossing the Atlantic like a ping-pong ball, living the life of a gypsy myself. As much as I complain about the loneliness of life on the road, I like to keep on the move and wherever I've gone, I've never felt like a stranger. I was born to be a vagabond. Still, I have to admit that flight wasn't an auspicious start. In those days, planes weren't what they are now – we had to stop in Gander to refuel – and I seemed to be air-sick from the moment we struck cruising altitude.

During that two-and-a-half-month tour of Europe, there was no time to play tourist. John and I were scheduled for seventy-five concerts, one and sometimes two a day. After a while I began to wonder who had joked with me back home, "Be a singer and see the world." We were constantly racing from the hall to the airport or the train station.

In London, John was staying at the home of an old German actor friend, Anton Walbrook, who had played Diaghilev, Moira Shearer's ballet master in *The Red Shoes*. John asked me to come up to Hampstead, where Walbrook had a house, to have tea and sing for him. He was an exuberant man, full of wonderful anecdotes about his career. After I had finished singing, he said, "You have beautiful hands."

I blushed because in fact I never thought my hands were very nice at all and I was always pasting on false nails. "Why thank you," I said.

"Yes," he said, "you have beautiful hands but you use them too much. It distracts people from your singing. Keep them still." For the rest of my life, I remembered that lesson.

After London, where we recovered from our jet lag, it was on to Paris where I was to give my first performance – but not as part of the Jeunesses schedule. Diamant and John had arranged with the French impresario Maurice Dandelot that I would kick off the tour by making my European debut in the Salle Gaveau on Valentine's Day 1955 – the first by any Canadian singer in twenty-five years. J.W. McConnell footed the $800 bill to rent that elegant hall and he also picked up the tab for all the flyers plastered over Paris's kiosks. Before I left Montreal, Mrs. McConnell fluttered over me like a mother hen and she wanted to send me to Dior or Balenciaga for my dress but, dumb me, I declined. I didn't feel I was at the stage in my career when I was ready to wear lavish clothes. I thought that if I showed up in an elegant couturier gown people would expect me to be a world-class professional. I didn't want the audience to mistake me for a Metropolitan Opera star when I was still only a glorified student.

The program I sang was called *Le Lied*, a clever play on two languages. It was Gilles Lefebvre's idea to show Europeans that Canadians could sing *Lieder* after all. The songs spanned a musical history from Beethoven to Richard Strauss and, in order to catch the critics' eye, we had added something unique: a cycle of five Schumann songs composed from letters that Mary Stuart, Queen of Scots, had written back home to France from her prison cell before execution. Schumann had written the songs to

German translations, but on a trip through Washington, John had gone to the Library of Congress and unearthed the original French texts, which had never before been sung. When we had tried them out in Montreal before we left, that anecdote had been printed in the program but the English translation of it had people tittering in the aisles. It said that John had gone to the Library of Congress and brought back Mary Stuart's original "French letters"! In fact, the songs were even more poignant in French, climaxed at the end with a brief, touching Latin prayer. The Paris critics went wild and, even though I had competition for their attention from a Russian violinist's debut that same night, that concert set my tour off to a flying start on the Continent.

Right after the concert, the Paris Symphony asked me to come back and sing, and the organizers of the summer festival at Aix-en-Provence also extended an invitation. Everywhere I sang in Europe during that trip, I was re-engaged – and at fees that were ten times what I was making for the Jeunesses concerts. For me, that whole tour was like one big paid audition.

In each country we visited I tried to sing something in the native language, but in Lisbon, where we began the tour itself, Portuguese confounded me. I had taken Spanish lessons before I left, but when we arrived in Madrid, I realized that once I stopped singing I was in trouble. I couldn't wing it with what I remembered from my few lessons and some variations on French. In a restaurant when I was trying to get butter for my rolls, I asked for burro – a donkey! Then I innocently ordered what I thought was fish stew. The waiter brought me this lump of rubber swimming in a soup that was as black as coal. It turned out to be octopus in its own ink – horrifying exotica for a girl raised on roast chicken and mashed potatoes. But I got it down and that launched my gastronomic adventures. Now you can't restrain me from trying every delicacy I'm served, no matter how bizarre. But after months on the road, when I come home, the first luxury I treat myself to is a glass of milk and a fried egg sandwich with catsup.

On the trip, John collected stories about my gaucheries. I really had no conception of life in Europe. When he said he was going to Toledo to look at the El Grecos one afternoon, I didn't know what he was talking about. "No thanks," I declined his invitation. "I want to look at shoes." Since those days, I've learned to search out the museums and craft shops wherever I go from Helsinki to Humboldt, Saskatchewan. No matter how small the town there's always something to learn. Over the years I've educated myself on the road.

From Spain, we travelled back to France, but this time not to the bright lights of Paris. The Jeunesses tour was confined to small provincial towns – Angers, Le Mans, Tours and Nantes, to name just a few – most of which hadn't yet fully recovered from the war. It was a freezing February and their halls and old stone churches weren't heated. In Poitiers, the audience was swaddled in coats and mufflers up to its ears. Suddenly as I was singing I heard some people start to snicker. Oh, my God, I thought, has my slip fallen down around my ankles? Then out of the corner of my eye I saw this little man creeping forward with a heater on a long extension cord and he plunked it down in front of me. He had taken pity on me when he noticed that with every note I sang, the audience could see my breath.

In La Rochelle, a man on the welcoming committee provided my first lesson on the risks of naïveté on the road. He grandly told John and me to order whatever we wanted – it was all on him – so that night we went off and splurged on a dinner of oysters and lobster. The next morning when we went to check out of the hotel, he was nowhere to be found and the manager insisted that Jeunesses would foot only our hotel bill. That was the beginning of my education about managers.

Our program in France was so successful that an entrepreneur asked us to record it in Paris. It was to be my first real LP. We did it in a tiny studio on the Left Bank not far from the Eiffel Tower and it took only a day, which suited me perfectly. I don't like recording sessions which go on and on. When artists re-record things too much, I think it begins to sound boring. Years later, when I was under contract to RCA, the engineers would ask me to repeat one note but I would insist on re-doing the whole song. "If you splice it all together note by note, it's going to sound inhuman," I argued. In fact, I'd rather have a little flaw and end up with a warm, natural sound than have a perfect record that has all the spontaneity of background music. That Jeunesses Musicales LP, which was also called *Le Lied*, turned out to be so good that not long ago, Everest Records reissued it. The trouble was that they put it out as if it were a brand new record; I didn't get a cent of royalties and I hadn't been paid more than $300 for the original session. I was livid.

All along our route, I would phone Eugene and burble on to him about how well everything was going. It was a mad extravagance for somebody making $25 a concert to put through trans-Atlantic calls, but it was my way of getting over missing him. At the frantic pace we were scheduled, I had no time for letter writing. In France, we had twenty-five concerts in nineteen days. Then it was on to Brussels and Luxembourg, but getting there was no simple matter. The entire grand duchy was fogged in and our plane was forced back to Strasbourg. We put in frantic phone calls to the organizers who had a hall full of people waiting to hear us, and we assumed they would be so furious the whole thing would be called off. But they cheerfully said it would be no problem, everybody was willing to come back the next day, so we boarded an overnight train at 2 a.m. to get us there by noon for that faithful audience. Then later that afternoon we hurled ourselves onto another train for a concert 100 miles away. Thank God, I'm a good traveller. I almost never run out of energy.

But I was worried about arriving so frazzled in Bonn, our first stop in Germany. Even though I had taken diction lessons from a German historian at McGill before leaving, I was still jittery at the prospect of singing German in the cradle of *Lieder*. But the concert went very well. The critics declared I was a singer "to be classed in the world's top ranks," and complimented me on my diction. They went so far as to admire my five-foot-nine shape, which I was always desperately dieting and worrying over. "A proud, golden-blonde Juno," one reviewer described me. No wonder that, from the first, I felt as much at home in Germany as I had with its music.

After we played in Freiburg, a professor at the conservatory called ahead to his friend the director of the Northwest Radio Network in Cologne, to alert him to our arrival and recommend us for a broadcast. When we got to Cologne, John went to the station to make the arrangements and, at my prodding, he asked about the fee. "Fee?" the director said. "I'm not paying any fee. I've never even heard you. I'm buying a cat in a bag." But I refused to do it unless he paid us, and very reluctantly he gave in. The irony was that as soon as he listened to the broadcast, he asked us to come back for two more – and at four times the agreed-upon rate.

During the first show, we had noticed the hostile behaviour of the engineer in the studio toward us, so as a matter of self-preservation we made a point of chatting him up. It turned out that he had been a Luftwaffe pilot, shot down during the war and interned on Île Ste. Hélène in Montreal. When John explained that he had been interned too, but that all his recriminations had disappeared after the war and he now loved his life in Canada, the transformation in that engineer was amazing. In the end, he couldn't do enough for us.

After our German tour, John flew back to Canada, but as we had agreed, I stayed on in Europe to see if I could win any further auditions. I wanted to take full advantage of my trip. The train ride back to Paris was horrendous because I was sick all the way. When I finally got to my little hotel off the Champs Élysées, I hauled my bags up the stairs and fell into a deep sleep. I woke to the phone ringing.

"Mademoiselle," said the concierge, "the taxi driver just returned the purse you left in his cab." I had been so tired I hadn't even noticed that I had left behind my wallet containing $1,500 – all the money I had in the world. I could have kissed that honest cab driver.

In fact, for the first time in my life I seemed to be constantly tired – and constantly nauseated. I had noticed it as soon as we got to Portugal. Every morning when we had breakfast downstairs in the hotel café, the smell of the red sawdust that the busboys used to sprinkle on the floors before sweeping would make me sick. I put it down to an allergy. But the nausea didn't disappear with the red sawdust. Hmmm, I thought, but I never mentioned a word to John. I carried on with the tour. Finally, when it was finished and I had flown from Paris to London, I found a doctor. She told me what was wrong even before she tested me: Canada's singing ambassadress was pregnant.

I called Eugene right away. His first words were, "Oh, my God, you've got to do something! Jump! Drink whiskey! Take some medicine!" He made clear that under no condition was he marrying me. "It's your baby," he said, "not mine."

I was heartbroken, but I also wasn't surprised. He had warned me and he had never led me on, and by then I knew the man too well: I understood that it wasn't just commitment that he was afraid of. On her deathbed, his mother – who was a very strong personality – had made Eugene promise that he would never marry outside the Jewish religion. There was no question of my converting because, to Orthodox Jews like Eugene's family, conversion still doesn't make you Jewish. I knew Eugene was wrestling with powerful private demons.

Still, I didn't want an abortion. I was already at least three months pregnant and, at that late date, it wouldn't have been safe. Besides, I didn't believe that it was right. This was 1955, only six years after Ingrid Bergman had provoked an incredible scandal and denunciations on the floor of Congress when she walked out on her husband and daughter to give birth to a baby out of wedlock with Roberto Rossellini. I didn't know what to do. I wrote my older sister Beryl and told her I was pregnant, hoping that she would offer to take the baby. I was shocked at her reply: "This will ruin your career and bring shame on our family." Then unbeknownst to me, Beryl went to have lunch with Eugene and she told him that he had to do the right thing by me. I could have predicted what his reaction would be.

In fact, I didn't care about marriage or what other people thought of me. I wasn't promiscuous and I felt I didn't have anything to be ashamed of: I had gotten pregnant with a man I loved. But I did worry that my mother would be devastated by the news. In my heart of hearts, I had hoped that Eugene would have been so delighted at the idea of having a child that he would say, "Grand, don't worry about a thing. We won't get married but we'll live together and enjoy this baby." On Easter Sunday, when I phoned him again from London, he told me that if I insisted on going ahead with the birth, I ought to think about putting the baby up for adoption. How could I even consider making a career in Canada with an illegitimate child? I spent the whole $75 call in sobs. I felt utterly alone – trapped.

But I've never been one to feel trapped long. I dried my tears and decided to make the best of it. What the hell, I finally thought. I had toyed with the idea of going to Berlin to study. I would do it anyway. I had my $1,500 from the Jeunesses concerts and Berlin was still an occupied city so I could have a baby there who would be considered a Canadian citizen. I told my mother and everyone at home that I planned to find a great *Lieder* teacher in Berlin.

Ann Watson, a soprano I had known from George Little's Bach Choir, was also going to Berlin to study, so, with another girl, we set out from London in a new car she had just bought which she was going to ship home from Paris. But the route we took to Paris wasn't exactly direct; it was via the Riviera, Monaco, Florence, Rome and Milan, then back through the Alps and Switzerland. Everywhere we stopped, the other two wanted to shop, so after two trips through Europe I still hadn't seen a museum or a sight. The trip seemed to take forever and Ann was a novice driver, but absolutely fearless. One night we ripped through the Alps at breakneck speed, oblivious to the sheer drops we were blithely flirting with on those curves. The next morning when we saw the landscape in the daylight, it shocked us into slowing down. But no matter what our speed, I was sick the whole trip. Ann couldn't figure out what was wrong with me.

Along the way, a memory kept coming back to me. For the last concert I had sung before I left Montreal, Diamant had given me a new piece to learn – Benjamin Britten's *A Charm of Lullabies*. When I had arrived at McGill's Redpath Hall the night of the recital, he handed me what looked like a shoebox. I thought he must have brought me a corsage, but inside I found a rubber doll. "Now, I want you to think of rocking this baby doll whenever you sing those lullabies," he had said with a mischievous smile. Driving through Europe months later on that trip with Ann, I began to wonder if Mr. D., who had always been so psychic, had realized even before I did that I was pregnant.

FOURTEEN

Ich Bin Ein Berliner

BERLIN IN the spring of 1955: it was no longer the far-out, frenetic city of *Cabaret* and was still recovering from having been the site of another kind of folly – Hitler's. As the plane began its descent to Tempelhof Airport, I realized the full impact of its situation, stranded like a Western island outpost afloat in a hostile Communist sea. If I thought about the geography too much, it gave me claustrophobia. What a symbolic place to start my own confinement, cut off from everybody I knew and loved.

The city was sliced up into sectors like an unwieldy pie, wrapped in barbed wire and patrolled by soldiers dressed in the colours of different nations. The Wall hadn't yet been built but new office towers were going up madly everywhere on top of the ruins. Still, it was bleak. During the terrible winters of the war, the people of Berlin had cut down all the trees for firewood and the landscape looked shorn and impersonal.

Almost as soon as we landed, Ann got homesick for her boyfriend, who also sang in the Erskine and American choir, and she turned around and flew back to Montreal. I was left in Berlin alone.

I found a tiny flat in the Frohnau district at 38 Marienburger Allee. My landlord, Otto Sauber, was in public relations for the Berlin radio station RIAS and he and his wife rented out half their house to make ends meet. To celebrate the signing of the lease, we had a glass of *Berlinerweisse mit schuss* – a light beer spiked with raspberry cordial which was a local specialty – in their back garden. I loved the apartment, which had a little fold-down Murphy bed that dropped out of the wall and an upright piano.

Ever since I was a child, I had never been able to let my anger or sadness show. But when I felt emotions building up and I needed to let them out, I always knew I could go to the piano and play a child's piece by Schumann called *Träumerei* (Dreams) and make myself cry. I don't know why it had that effect, maybe because it was in a minor key, but it works to this day when I need to release what is pent up inside. It's full of so much longing. During those months in Berlin, I spent a lot of time at the piano playing *Träumerei*.

Physically, I felt fine. By the time I'd settled in Berlin, my morning sickness had stopped. I could wear ordinary clothes because up until the last month, I only showed a little thickening around the waist. On a girl my size, a five-pound baby was nothing.

I walked everywhere in those months and I got to know Berlin by heart. I would even take the U-Bahn over to East Berlin to see operas staged by Walter Felsenstein, the director of the East Berlin Komische Oper company, who was such a genius that the government allowed him to live in West Berlin. And of course I would shop for the baby.

When I first arrived, I could barely speak a word of everyday German. I could sing poetry by Goethe and Grillparzer but I had to struggle to make myself understood when I wanted to buy a loaf of bread. I had purposely sought out a German-speaking neighbourhood to live in and I made myself listen to German radio all the time. I went to movies where John Wayne looked ridiculous up on the screen, dubbed in guttural tones. With my gift for mimicry, German came quickly. But unbeknownst to me, it was a very particular brand of German. As Diamant was to exclaim later when he heard me back in Montreal, "What a thick Berlin dialect!"

For quite a while, I didn't know a soul. I wasn't anxious to acquire too many friends and have to produce explanations about my life. But that meant a lot of loneliness. What saved me, as always, was music.

I had arranged to take lessons with Emil Weissenborn, who had been the teacher of Dietrich Fischer-Dieskau, then probably the most famous *Lieder* singer in the world. The prospect was exciting, and when I met Weissenborn, I liked him very much. But after three lessons I realized he was past his prime. He was very old and had grown slightly deaf by then. I saw that I wasn't going to get my money's worth from him, so I began to look for another teacher. Later, I was glad that I hadn't stayed with Weissenborn because I noticed that everyone who had studied with him acquired a certain sound. It's a beautiful haunting colour but a highly controlled vibrato that I've always been able to recognize as soon as I hear it in a singer's voice. In 1982, when I was giving master classes in China, the minute I heard a young Chinese tenor sing, I said, "I'll bet your teacher studied in Berlin." Sure enough, Mrs. Liang Yi, one of the chief professors at the Peking Conservatory, had been one of Weissenborn's students at the Hochschule before the Cultural Revolution.

In my search for a new teacher I went to the Canadian Legation in Berlin, where I had already made myself known. The third in command, Richard O'Hagan, was a dapper Englishman who looked like the perfect British major and whose girlfriend was a Berlin opera singer. They invited me to a lot of concerts and were extremely kind to me, guiding me through the city's musical life. When I asked them who I ought to study with, they suggested Michael Raucheisen, who had been an accompanist to Fritz Kreisler, the violinist, and had known Richard Strauss personally.

Raucheisen and I hit it off right away. My German was still sketchy and he spoke almost no English, but he would give me twelve Schubert songs on a Tuesday and say, "Learn by Friday. Bring them for lesson." And off I would go and work like blazes and memorize them in three days. He couldn't believe that anybody could learn so fast. What he didn't realize was that I was used to having to learn vast amounts of music while also singing in choirs and doing full-time jobs. In Berlin suddenly I had a lot of time on my hands. I acquired an enormous repertoire in those months.

When I would come back to Raucheisen with what I had learned, he would say, "*Sehr gut*. In four days, we record for RIAS." We recorded hours and hours of Beethoven and Brahms and Schubert over the next six months and to this day I still get royalties from them. They didn't pay very much at the time, but it was enough to cover my expenses. Raucheisen kept me alive through those difficult days.

Oddly enough, it never occurred to me to take lessons from Raucheisen's wife, Maria Ivogün. She was a legendary Hungarian lyric soprano for whom Strauss had written the one-act opera *Ariadne auf Naxos*, and she had later been Elisabeth Schwarzkopf's teacher. But by the time I met her she must have been in her sixties and was going blind. Whenever I came to the house, she would be in the parlour listening to records of herself, just closeted there in the dark feeding on her past triumphs. It was the most tragic thing. I made up my mind then that I would never be like that, living on my faded reviews and my yesterdays.

I often wondered if Raucheisen suspected I was pregnant. I hadn't told a soul in Berlin about my condition except the obstetrician I found, Dr. Kos. When I first went to him, I had asked if he could help me arrange an adoption for the baby. I explained that I was a singer and that after I had paid my transportation to a concert, my hotel bills and my accompanist's fees, there was barely enough left just to support myself. The baby's father, I told him, didn't want to get involved.

Dr. Kos sent me to a Berlin social agency. I filled out all the forms. "Is the father white?" the social worker asked. She wanted a picture of Eugene and of my parents, just to be sure about the background. Later, she told me an American couple at the U.S. army base would be adopting my child. But about a month before I was due, I told her I couldn't go through with it. After you survive eight months of a pregnancy, you realize that having the baby is the least of the problem. I just made up my mind that, no matter what the financial and logistical burden, I would manage with a baby somehow. I knew I would never be able to live with myself if I put my child up for adoption.

Through all this time, I was writing my mother chatty letters from Berlin, brimming over with stories about what I was learning and seeing – weaving my fiction. Periodically, I would break down and call Eugene. He was the only friend I could share my secret with. I knew that he still loved me, even though he was trying to keep his distance. I sensed that he was afraid to show too much interest in the baby in case he found himself roped in. I was too proud to ask him for any financial support and he never offered any. All I ever asked Eugene to do for me was send a package of American-style diapers. For some reason I was convinced that Europeans knew nothing about diapering a baby.

One night in October I went to a concert with Richard O'Hagan and Donald Bell, the Canadian baritone who was studying with Weissenborn in the city at the time. It was the Berlin recital debut of the Finnish bass Kim Borg. We had a crazy evening and I walked home with them in my highest heels, laughing all the way. It must have been a distance of five miles. In the middle of the night, I woke up feeling strange. Well, I thought, this is it.

But when I called the Wartburg Clinic, where I had registered in advance, they couldn't take me. They said they were completely full and gave me a list of other clinics, including one run by nuns which finally produced a bed for me. Then Dr. Kos didn't show up and sent a midwife in his place. I was beside myself and the birth was a nightmare. My labour lasted thirty-six hours. Then, because the afterbirth hadn't been expelled and complications set in, they had to call in a surgeon to operate. The doctors told me later that I could have died.

The next morning, the first person I called was Eugene. "We have a beautiful baby girl," I said, "and she looks just like you. She's tiny, just five pounds, but she has black curls. What would you like me to call her?"

I was indefatigable in trying to get Eugene to take an interest in his child. Besides, he was the only person in the world with whom I wanted to share that moment. In fact, he did tackle the problem of what to call our daughter. In the Jewish religion, you never name a baby after someone living, he explained. "My grandmothers were named Poria and Pearl. Both their names started with a P."

"Paula," I said. "Let's call her Paula."

I loved the name but the nuns in the hospital hated it. *"Ach, das ist ein Name für eine alte Dame,"* they said. "That's an old lady's name." But she looked like a Paula to me, this tiny creature I could almost hold in the palm of my hand who already had Eugene's dark furrowed brows. Those nuns gave me a terrible time. It was as if they wanted to punish me for not being married. I was exhausted from the birth but they put Paula in a bassinet in my room where she screamed the whole time. Then they tried to force me to breast-feed her.

"But I can't," I cried. "I have to go and give a concert in Bochum in five days." I had engagements already lined up which I badly needed. I wanted her bottle-fed so I could travel and earn our living.

"You must," the nuns insisted. "We will give you pumps and you will send your milk back from Bochum." But how was I going to send milk back from engagements that I had waiting all over Germany? Finally the doctor had to come and explain the situation to them so they would let me alone.

When it came time to take Paula home from the clinic, I called Otto Sauber to come and pick me up in his car. I hadn't told him I was pregnant but he and his wife had guessed. When we got back to Marienburger Allee, a German *Feldmarschall* was standing on the doorstep. This horrible woman was demanding to know if I had enough money to support the baby or I wouldn't be allowed to keep her.

"She's alright," Otto sprang to my defence. "She always pays her rent on time." It was then that I realized I didn't have a moment to lose before I registered Paula as a Canadian citizen, safe from German bureaucracy. I called Richard O'Hagan and told him my predicament.

"Well, well, aren't you the tricky one," he marvelled. "How did you keep your secret from us all that time?"

Paula was born on October 14, 1955, and five days later I was singing in Bochum. In between, I had found a nanny, Frau Döbbelin. When the war broke out, she had been married to a dentist who was sent to the Russian front and never came back. In a way, even though she had remarried, her whole life had stopped with his disappearance. She seemed to wear a perpetual sadness. But she had been a nurse and she was wonderful with Paula. She never asked me for any explanations and I knew I didn't have to worry as I went off to my engagements.

But within two months, the bookings I had lined up were farther away: Paris, London and a cross-Canada tour that I had promised to do as my homecoming. There was no way I could get back to Berlin for a few months and yet I couldn't take Paula with me. When I told Frau Döbbelin my problem, she said it would be better if she took the baby to live at her house. She promised to keep me up to date on how Paula was progressing and said she would send snapshots every few weeks. It tore me apart to leave her like that but I knew that there was no choice:

more than ever I had to build my career and Paula would be in better hands this way.

In London, preparing for my British debut in Wigmore Hall over that Christmas holiday, I found the city depressing. It rained the whole time, and being so far away from home and the baby in that eternal London grey made me wonder more than once how I was ever going to manage. But no matter what happens, I try to take the philosophical approach. I always believe that things will eventually work out, so there's no point in having a nervous breakdown. Even about Eugene, I was the ultimate optimist. I was sure that he would finally come around and see things my way – that he would realize we could have a wonderful life together with so many things in common and a beautiful little girl to share. It was just a matter of time. Until then, all I had to do was carry on. Hidden in the bottom of my suitcase was a tiny grey plastic photo album filled with pictures of Paula which kept me going whenever I felt down. I carried it everywhere with me and at night when I was alone, I would take it out and stare in wonder at this secret child of mine.

In my mind, my London recital debut was not a great success. Because the artist has to pay for the rental of the hall, it had cost me money I could ill afford, and I didn't like my accompanist since I had been used to the best with John. Generally, I didn't feel in top form, although the critics were enthusiastic and Noel Goodwin wrote in the *Daily Express*: "A voice with a capital V. Let's hear this girl sing again." Still, I've never depended on reviews to tell me whether I was bad or good. I'm my own toughest critic and I know when the magic has been there and when it hasn't. Somehow I've never really felt that I made it in England, where they have so many good contraltos of their own.

I realize in retrospect that my life then was at a turning

point. If I had stayed on in Berlin and continued my studies with Raucheisen, I would have had a very different kind of career – a different kind of life entirely. In Europe, they treat their artists almost like royalty, bowing and scraping and bestowing on them a kind of cachet and glamour that you just don't find in North America where you're apt to run into a diva at the local supermarket. I suspect that I would have gone into opera sooner and become more of an international star. Maybe I would have ended up living in a chateau with servants at my beck and call. These days I would give anything for a butler to haul the groceries in from the car and have a drink waiting when I get in the door. But after living in the bell jar of Berlin, I longed to re-connect with a world I could feel part of. Besides, I've never regretted a decision in my life. After all, how could I, knowing now what lay waiting just around the corner?

FIFTEEN

"Mr. Mahler"

IWAS SITTING on the Air Canada flight to Montreal, going over Brahms's *Four Serious Songs* in my mind. In two months I had a date to sing them with Sir Ernest MacMillan in my solo debut with the Toronto Symphony and I was using a technique I had discovered to memorize *Lieder* texts while on the road: I would sing the whole thing silently to myself in my head. It was great for developing your concentration. But this trip was particularly rough and those old turbo-props were so noisy that I had to close my eyes to keep my attention from wandering. I was into the third song – a really doleful number about death – when suddenly I found this man hunched over me, patting my hand. "Now don't panic, honey," he said. "The pilot assures me we're going to land safely. Everything is going to be okay." Ever since, I've learned to keep my facial expressions in check when I'm memorizing on airplanes.

In fact, that man turned out to be right. Montreal welcomed me home like some conquering heroine. No one seemed to suspect that I had been up to anything other than studying, and the papers had reprinted my most glowing European reviews. "Montreal Contralto Returns!" ran a half-page feature in the *Star*, complete with photographs of me dishing up a huge homecoming, Canadian-style breakfast of bacon and eggs for my mother and sisters in the kitchen. There were also photos of me showing off my souvenirs and some concert gowns I had had made by a wholesaler in Zurich on the way back. The day after the story ran, a Customs inspector knocked on our door. "About these gowns," he said. "Did you declare them?"

"But I've worn them to sing in," I protested. "I've been living in Europe for a year. They're used gowns." But he didn't flinch. He made me pay duty anyway. A few days later I saw J.W. McConnell and cursed his paper for getting me into such a fix. But he had no sympathy. "You're going to have to learn to do interviews," he said. "Never say what you bought or how much money you make."

Of course, as soon as I got home, I started seeing Eugene again. I brought him pictures of Paula which he would stare at for the longest time. "Nice, nice," he would say and then change the subject. "How are your studies going?" But despite my hurt, the instant I saw him again, I felt the old electricity between us was still there. We resumed our relationship as if I had never left. I didn't bring up the subject of marriage or living together again, but I was sure that if I just bided my time, Eugene would finally come around. I'm not the type to give up.

Within weeks of coming back, I was on the road again, but this time instead of Paris and London, my bookings were Halifax and Lethbridge. For a month, John and I did a coast-to-coast recital tour. It was the first time I had ever really seen Canada and my year in Europe had made me appreciate what a great country it is. I realized that here people made me feel I belonged. It's different in the United States where audiences identify an artist as a New Yorker or a Texan. In Canada, from coast to coast, I'm regarded the same – as a home-country girl. People took pride in what I had accomplished and they gave me a sense that I was contributing to the national cultural life. In Europe, I would have been just another singer – a bit player in a tradition of music that was so old and venerable it could daunt a young musician. Nobody would have had any stake in me. But in Canada, I was one of a handful of artists bringing music to areas which were sometimes starved for it. Canadians know their music and they have very good taste. You can't sing down to them, even in small towns. In this country, when people recognize me in the street, it gives me a feeling of family.

Mind you, it hasn't always been clear just why they recognized me. At a big reception that Drapeau threw for me on Île Ste. Hélène that spring after I had won the Montreal Critics' Circle Award, a woman who had interviewed me on the CBC kept signalling to me across the room that I mustn't leave without talking to her. I avoided her all evening, because I couldn't remember her name. I was trying to think of some way to gloss over it when she came up exclaiming, "Oh, it's so good to see you again, Doreen."

Once a few years ago I arrived in Sydney, Nova Scotia, and the organizers were making quite a fuss about me in the hotel lobby. This small, greying man pulled me aside and said he was with the local newspaper. He asked if I would be kind enough to do an interview with one of his young reporters. "Sure," I said, "but I'm exhausted now after the rough flight from Newfoundland. Let's do it in a few hours."

"Oh, that's so wonderful of you," gushed the young reporter. "It's such a privilege to meet you. I can't wait." But just as I reached the elevator, she came running up behind me, breathless. "Excuse me," she said. "I hate to bother you. But who are you anyway?"

Later, when I was retiring from six years on the National Arts Centre board in Ottawa, where I had regaled the other members with the story, Don MacSween, the centre's director, had a T-shirt printed up as a goodbye gift with my reply to her emblazoned in black across the back. "Well, honey," I told her, "I am *not* Sophie Tucker."

That spring of 1956, I returned to sing with the Montreal Symphony whose conductor by then was Josef Krips. Krips had been one of the original Vienna Choir boys before becoming a legendary maestro. I was to sing often with him later and he was very helpful to me, but that first time, the piece he had chosen for me to do was Mozart's *Requiem* – the one the composer was writing for a mysterious patron when he died. I'll never forget working on it with Krips. I had just bought a brand new black-and-white tweed coat. For me, it had been a costly splurge and I put it on to go to rehearsal feeling like a queen. I walked down to the bus stop and, as I was waiting, a truck lumbered by and splashed me head to toe in oily black slush. The coat was ruined and I arrived at rehearsal in a terrible pique. I started to sing my part in the *Requiem* but suddenly I heard Krips going tap, tap, tap with his baton on the podium.

"Madame," he said, "this is not *Carmen*."

Later, he used me a great deal and I sang with him all over the States. He was almost bald and heavy-set in the face and when he conducted, his whole frame would shake, leaving his jowls quivering like Jello. He had a tendency to sweat profusely, so if you were sitting near him in a pale dress, you would end up looking as if you'd taken a shower. I always made a point of wearing a dark gown if I was singing with Josef Krips.

I felt so cut off from Paula and missed her terribly. But my trip home was becoming longer and longer as opportunities came flooding my way. Earlier that spring a Montreal agent named Monni Adams had taken me under her wing and arranged a homecoming concert in the Ritz Carlton ballroom. Eric McLean and the other critics all noted that my voice had acquired a new richness and maturity in the year since they'd last heard me. "A great deal has happened to Miss Forrester since then," Eric wrote. Little did he know.

Without telling me, Monni Adams had also taken it upon herself to send letters to every well-known conductor in the United States, trying to get me engagements and enclosing my reviews from Canada and Europe. Their agents all wrote back saying the same thing: that they'd love to hear me but unfortunately they were booked up for the next three years. The only personal reply she received was from Bruno Walter.

Bruno Walter had been a child prodigy in Berlin and conducted at the Cologne Opera House when he was only seventeen. He had gone on to Hamburg as an assistant to Mahler whom he later accompanied to Vienna at the turn of the century, helping him reorganize the Vienna Court Opera. He was considered not only Mahler's disciple but his walking testament. Every musician who wanted to play the composer's works would have killed for a chance to perform with the conductor known as "Mr. Mahler." But at the time I didn't know a thing about Gustav Mahler. All I knew was that Bruno Walter, one of the most famous conductors in the world, had written back to say that he wanted to hear me. He named a time and a place in New York. I looked in my date book and, to Monni's horror, I discovered I was booked to sing in Oshawa that night. I telephoned Bruno Walter in New York.

"Dr. Walter, I would love to come and audition for you," I said, "but unfortunately I have an engagement that night." I was so brash in those days, it never dawned on me to be awed by a great man. He suggested another date and then another, but I wasn't free on either of them.

Finally, in exasperation, he said, "Well, my dear, you're obviously much busier than I am. When *can* you come?" I picked a Sunday evening, March 25, and he said he would make time for me that night at 8:30 p.m. He asked me not to bring an accompanist and to prepare some Bach and Brahms.

When I told people in Montreal, they instantly went into a flap, but I wasn't nervous. To me, it was just another singing date. If it went well, fine, but if it didn't I still had a living to make in order to support my mother and my baby. I was incredibly nonchalant in those days.

I had been up until 2 a.m. the night before at a post-concert party in Toronto, and after only four hours' sleep, I took a plane to New York with Monni Adams. That Sunday afternoon, I had my first gall bladder attack. I had gorged on smoked meat at the Stage Delicatessen and I had to go back to the hotel and be sick before setting out for Bruno Walter's apartment hotel. Monni was having an anxiety fit that I wouldn't be able to sing, but I often make myself sick before a concert if something isn't sitting well with my digestion. I always feel better for it. By the time Monni and I arrived at Bruno Walter's door, I was fine. As soon as I set eyes on him, I felt as if I had known him all my life.

He was nearing eighty, and he had the kindest face and the most wonderful manners, which were European, almost courtly. All he knew about me was the clutch of reviews Monni had mailed him, so before I even had my coat off, he was asking me to sing for him. He seemed so excited to hear me, I couldn't believe it, but as I realized later, he had been searching for a new alto ever since Kathleen Ferrier's death. He looked for voices the way some people choose paintings – because they had the colour he wanted. I had prepared the aria from Bach's *St. John Passion* and he sat down at the grand piano in his suite and played for me from memory. "Bravo!" he beamed at the end. "You pick something difficult to start with." He said afterward that he had made up his mind after the first few phrases, but we went through some other pieces before he asked me to move to a far corner of the room to sing Brahms's *Alto Rhapsody*. It had been one of Kathleen Ferrier's signature pieces. She had been known as his contralto and together they had recorded all the great Mahler works before her death only three years earlier. After I finished singing it, he murmured, *"Wunderbar, mein Kind,"* in a voice I could scarcely hear. It was as if he were having a dialogue with himself.

"Now," he said, "what are you doing on February 14th, 15th and 17th next year?"

My eyes lit up. "Oh, I'm so excited," I enthused. "Jeunesses Musicales has booked me on a tour of Morocco then."

"Das tut mir leid," he said. "That makes me very sad. I've programmed the Mahler *Second* as my final performance of the season with the New York Philharmonic at that time and I wanted you to be my soloist, then record it with me."

I was stunned. Monni's jaw just fell. "Oh, Dr. Walter, for you I would not only drop Morocco," I blurted out, "I would even drop dead."

He laughed and, just like that, it was arranged. Then he sat down at the piano again. *"Ich habe noch Durst,"* he said. "I'm thirsty for more." And we went on making music together for nearly an hour – through Beethoven, and Schumann's *Frauenliebe und Leben*. He asked me who I had studied with, amazed that a Canadian girl could sing European works with such sensitivity. I noticed as he played for me that he did what a lot of older musicians do: he speeded up the tempo just a fraction too much, almost as if to show that he was still vigorous. I found it endearing in a man who was such a legend.

After we finished, he suggested some other works I ought to tackle that would be suited to my voice; then we set a date for our first rehearsal in Carnegie Hall in eleven months. When I walked out into the brisk New York night, I couldn't quite grasp what had just happened. It took me years to realize to what extent that hour had changed the course of my career.

But a hint of it began to hit me the next morning. As soon as Bruno Walter had called the New York Philharmonic to notify them that he wanted this unknown Canadian girl hired to sing the Mahler *Second* with him, the word went out like wildfire. When Bruno Walter chose a singer, it was like being anointed. Within twenty-four hours, every manager in New York was on the phone clamouring to represent me.

In Europe I had been taken in by a lot of managers who

put on a recital and then tried to get out of paying me. I got the glory, but they got the money. It had made me wary, even of Monni who began insisting on a percentage of the take although I had never signed anything with her. I decided to wait for the New York offers to come in while I fulfilled my other engagements and went back to Europe to see Paula. Then at the end of July, when I was home again, I flew to New York and met them all. One invited me for cocktails at home with his wife, but when I arrived there was no wife in sight and he started showing me nude pictures of artists. No matter how much I wanted a career, I certainly wasn't into that! I didn't like any of the rest, except one. He was the only person in the bunch I felt any empathy with: André Mertens, the vice-president of Columbia Artists.

His father before him had been a great manager in Europe and he himself handled some of the most famous musical names in America, including the pianist Gary Graffman and the diva Renata Tebaldi. But what convinced me that he wasn't just an opportunist out for the fast buck was that – unlike the others – he wanted to audition me.

"Listen, I've read all your reviews and they're very impressive," he said. "And to be chosen by Bruno Walter is like getting a stamp of approval. But I never manage anyone until I've heard them sing."

The next day was my birthday and I didn't want to hang around New York in the summer heat. I was anxious to get back to Montreal. "If I rent Carnegie Hall for the afternoon tomorrow," he said, "will you stay and sing for me?"

I demurred because I knew I didn't have time to fly John down to play for me, and I wanted to be at my best. "I can't sing with just any old pianist," I said. He promised me he would get me a good accompanist and as it turned out, he found one who wasn't bad. But the poor fellow was terribly nervous. He was so tense that he had stayed up the whole night practising the hour's program that we devised.

The next afternoon when I walked into Carnegie Hall to meet Mertens, I passed the soprano Nell Rankin hurrying out. She had been imported as the star in a Montreal Opera Guild production of *Boris Godunov* two years earlier, where I had sung a brief solo, the Innkeeper's part in the second act – and won some very good notices. But of course Nell Rankin didn't recognize me from a hole in the wall. She was all dolled up in black – black dress, black picture hat, black stockings and shoes, black parasol and long black lace gloves, on a sweltering New York's summer day. She reminded me of a perfect tarantula. In retrospect, I realized that Nell Rankin must have auditioned for André Mertens too that afternoon.

I sang for him and at the end of the second piece, he shouted, "Bravo!" from his seat halfway back in the hall. "Wonderful! Now come on back to the office and my assistant Nelly Walters will draw up your contract."

I walked forward to the lip of the stage. "Mr. Mertens," I said, "you asked for an hour and we prepared an hour's program. This poor man stayed up all night practising, and the least you can do is hear us out."

I don't think anyone had ever talked to André Mertens like that before. He was so taken aback that he just sat there through the rest of an hour's recital. André and I always laughed later that my real debut in Carnegie Hall was playing to a reluctant audience of one.

When we got back to his office, I scanned the contract and stuck it in my handbag. "I'll have to have my lawyer look it over," I said. "I want to be careful signing a contract for three years at a time when making money is so important in my career." André was aghast, but he was amused too. He let me take the contract back to Montreal. I don't know where I got the chutzpah. I didn't even *have* a lawyer. I had to ask Alan Gold – a friend who often dropped backstage after my performances and who is now Chief Justice of Quebec – if he would glance over it. I was determined then not to let anybody think he could take advantage of me.

That afternoon in Mertens's office, he had introduced me to his public relations assistant, Audrey Michaels, who became a lifelong friend. Audrey was amazed at the stack of flattering reviews from critics on both continents that Monni Adams had assembled. They made Audrey want to gamble on the way she would introduce me to the tastemakers in New York. Together, she and André devised a strategy. They realized that if I made my first New York appearance with Bruno Walter in the Mahler *Second*, he and the work would steal most of the thunder and the reviewers would devote only a paragraph to Walter's new contralto find. Instead, they decided I ought to make my debut beforehand in a solo recital where the critics could discover me for themselves. It was a clever plan. All it needed was someone to come up with the $1,800 rental on Town Hall.

"Don't you know anyone who would sponsor you?" Mertens asked. Of course I did, although I was at first reticent about asking him. But once more J.W. McConnell came to my rescue.

On November 12, 1956, I walked out onto Town Hall's stage to face the toughest crowd of my life. Eugene couldn't come but I had flown my mother down and given her a special box with my Aunt Eva, her sister who lived in New York. The reviewers from Montreal had all made the trip too and, as it happened, there was no other major musical event that night in New York, so all seven papers which existed at the time sent their first-string critics. In fact, the only person who almost didn't show up was the star of the concert herself.

After practising in the morning, John and I had window-shopped up Fifth Avenue all afternoon on the way back to the Wellington Hotel, a cheap little musicians' hang-out where the elevator boys and the switchboard operators always knew every guest's life history. We had agreed to meet in the lobby at 8 p.m. to walk over to Town Hall for the concert which was scheduled to start at 8:30 p.m. At 8:10, John phoned me in consternation from the lobby. "I'm coming, I'm coming," I said. But I didn't make it down until nearly 8:20 p.m. I had been sticking on false nails and the glue wouldn't dry.

We raced over to Town Hall and arrived at exactly 8:31 p.m., or so John tells it. Being German, he is always very precise. I had made him so nervous that he came down with an attack of Montezuma's revenge and couldn't go on right away. André Mertens was almost having a heart attack. He was dumbfounded when I just dropped my coat, took a breath and walked on stage cool as a cucumber.

Jacques de Montjoye, a Montreal couturier to whom Mrs. McConnell had introduced me, had designed a terrific gown for me – black jersey draped Grecian-style into an hourglass form that shimmered with a metallic thread as if it were beaded. I still have that dress in a trunk somewhere although now it would probably fit on one thigh.

I sang a program that I knew well: some Schubert, and Poulenc's cycle *La Fraîcheur et le Feu*, then Britten's *A Charm of Lullabies* and Wagner's *Wesendonk* songs. (It was a program that John and I were to do again on that stage in 1977 exactly twenty-five years to the day after that debut as part of an effort to resuscitate Town Hall. As one critic said to me at the time, "Boy, do you have courage!") But even that first time, I had sung a lot of the pieces before, some of them only the previous night in Winnipeg, so I felt comfortable in the music, which must have showed. "Canadian Contralto Displays Superb Voice," read the headline the next day in *The New York Times*. "The girl possesses a voice of remarkable power and freshness," wrote Louis Biancolli in the New York *World Telegram*, "and an artistry of phrase and style in German

Lieder phenomenal in one so young." Harold Schonberg called mine "a rich creamy contralto, voluptuous in sound." When Audrey Michaels came running into the reception that the Canadian ambassador to the United Nations was hosting in my honour at his Sutton Place apartment after the concert, she was waving the papers in her hand triumphantly. Without an exception, the reviews were raves.

For my mother, the reception was even more of a thrill than the concert. The ambassador had invited a guest list of diplomats and bright lights from Columbia Artists' roster to nibble on canapés of smoked salmon and caviar and sip Mumm's Extra Dry. It was the first time in her life she had sampled champagne. "My, my," she marvelled, her eyes sparkling, "it tastes just like soda water with a dollop of apple juice in it!"

No matter where else I performed after that, I think my Town Hall debut and the party afterward were the highlights of her life. She basked in all the compliments that came her way with the noblesse oblige of some grande dame. "You must be so proud of your daughter," people would say and my mother would positively beam. "Oh, yes, my late husband and I sacrificed everything so she could have this career," she would reply. I just smiled to myself, remembering how hard I had worked to pay for all those lessons, with not a cent of help from my family.

The reception passed in a dizzying blur of congratulations and gestures of kindness. Then Eric McLean sought me out and confided that at intermission he had overheard the editor of a leading American music magazine marvelling about what he had just heard. He had mentioned that Lois Marshall had made her New York debut two years earlier and Glenn Gould his only the season before mine. "And now this Maureen Forrester," the editor had declared. "God bless Canada!"

All evening, people kept marvelling at my youth. New Yorkers acted as if I were some primitive milkmaid who had stumbled suddenly onto the Town Hall stage with a veteran's miraculous emotional range. Little did anyone in that elegant Sutton Place apartment that night know the reason for the maturity of my interpretation was a tiny black-haired bundle an ocean away, who had just thrown another curve into my life.

SIXTEEN

Hasty Exits

THE WEEKLY letters from Berlin arriving early in that fall of 1956 had made me more and more uneasy, but most ominous of all was the last one. Herr Döbbelin wrote that Paula was transforming his marriage. "We've always wanted a baby," he said. "And now this child has come into our life as if she were our own. My wife is a changed woman, she loves the baby so. She is never depressed anymore. This child has been a gift from God."

I panicked. I had a terrible premonition that these people were going to try to keep Paula. I had just been discovered by Bruno Walter, been signed on by André Mertens and was in the middle of planning my New York debut. I was up to my ears in opportunities and engagements but, without any explanations to anyone, I caught the next plane for Berlin. I called the Döbbelins from the airport that morning. "I've come for Paula," I said. "I'm taking her to England with me today." It was cruel, but I realized I had to do it that way – like surgery. I was afraid that one day longer would be too late. There was no kind way of reclaiming my baby.

They took me to Tempelhof Airport and what a tearful goodbye it was. The plane taxied out and I thought, "At last, I'm safe." Then suddenly on the runway, the pilot turned around and we taxied back to the airport. An extremely unpleasant-looking official boarded the plane. "Fräulein Forrester!" he demanded in a very loud voice.

He made a point of calling me "Miss." "Whose child is this?"

"My child," I said. "I have the papers. They're all in order."

"Do you have a ticket for this child?" he said.

"Well, no," I said. "She isn't even a year old yet. In Canada you don't have to have a ticket for a baby."

"This is Germany," he said. "You need a ticket for the baby."

He was going to haul me off the plane until I persuaded him that I would pay when the flight stopped in Frankfurt. We taxied out again and this time we took off, but every passenger in the plane by then was staring at me with my illegitimate child. I'll never forget that the sister of Lilli Palmer, who was then Rex Harrison's wife, was sitting in front of me. "What a horrible man," she leaned back over her seat to say. "Good for you for standing up to him." I could have kissed her for that show of solidarity.

But what to do next? Here I was, trying to talk baby-talk to this child who only understood German and who knew me only as a strange face who had flitted in and out of her life once or twice. I hadn't had time to make arrangements in London but when we landed I phoned Murray and Libby Kash, Eugene's brother and his wife, who had taken over my flat when I'd left. I decided it was time to tell somebody my secret; I desperately needed help and a family. Besides, I knew they would be able to tell me if my former landlady, Mrs. Posnanski, had any spare flats to rent. Libby said that she had two rooms free in her third-floor attic.

I had rented a basement apartment from Mrs. Posnanski when I had first gone back to London after my Jeunesses tour of Europe and discovered I was pregnant. When I'd asked her then if she would mind my moving in a piano to practise my singing, she had said, "No, go ahead, but only on one condition: that you leave the door open when you practise." I knew that if anyone would understand my predicament, Mrs. Posnanski would. Needless to say, she was nonplussed to see me come back with a child, but she took it in her stride. And who did one of her neighbours turn out to be? Lilli Palmer's sister.

Paula and I settled into that attic apartment and I called my mother to tell her that I had some European engagements to arrange. I was already on the road so much that nobody knew where I lived anyway. But after a few weeks of hauling an eleven-month-old baby up and down three flights of stairs and wrestling with a pram, I knew there had to be a better solution. I remembered that I had met a woman with flats to rent through friends of John Newmark's on one of my trips through London. Her name was Branson Price. I went to see her and braced myself to tell her about my situation. "I have a baby," I announced solemnly. Well, a love child was nothing to Branson. It turned out that she had given birth to a baby out of wedlock ten years earlier.

I've met a lot of incredible people in my travels, but Branson Price was one of the most amazing. She was a Southern belle from Atlanta who had gone to work in Washington for the department of labour, fallen in love with an older man – married, I suppose – and found herself pregnant. In those days, it was still considered scandalous to have a child out of wedlock in America, especially for a girl from a wealthy, proper Southern family, so she just packed up and moved to England, where the British are very civilized about these things. She's been there ever since. One day Branson turned to me. "You know, darling, I've been here so long everybody thinks I'm British," she said in a Georgia drawl you could still cut with a knife.

After I had known her for some time, Branson told me a story about flying back to London from a holiday in France when an immigration officer at Heathrow stopped her and announced that she had overstayed any possible legal limits in Britain. He warned her that it was time to move back to America. Branson was horrified. She was telling her friends about it at a party one night when suddenly Breon O'Casey, the son of the playwright Sean O'Casey, spoke up and said, "I'll marry you, Branson." She hardly knew him and he was thirty years younger than she was, but she became Branson Price O'Casey. They later divorced, but they're still the best of friends.

Branson always attracted interesting people. She had been a close friend of Paul Robeson's in London, and she was so madcap that, in 1961, she took off for China with Edgar Snow's widow on only a moment's notice. After Edgar's sudden death, the Chinese government asked his widow to make the trip they had invited him on to northern China anyway. It was through Mongolia on horseback. When Branson arrived with Mrs. Snow, the Chinese organizers almost had apoplexy: they could see from her passport that she was no spring chicken. They insisted on posting a rider in front of her and one behind her, like nurse-maids. "Go away, darlings," she waved them off. "Don't worry, I was brought up on a horse." I laughed uproariously when she told me the story, but I didn't understand the full impact of it until by chance I asked her how old she was.

"Next November I'll be eighty-four," she said.

When she first arrived in London, Branson bought four houses on Balcombe Street, just north of Marylebone, which were almost flophouses. She modernized them with council grants and, at one time or another over the years, she played landlady to a generation of expatriate Canadian writers living in England. Branson and I felt a bond right away. She had raised her son Nicholas marvellously and we were the same kind of women – very positive. If there was a problem, we'd solve it; nothing was worth suicide. I've never had time for whining women.

Branson offered me a big ground-floor apartment with a back bedroom for the baby and a front room with a couch where I slept. Then she helped produce another miracle: a baby nurse named Elsie Farrell.

Farrell, she called herself, and she was the archetypal

British nanny – tiny and spry and no-nonsense. She reminded me of Mary Poppins. She had worked for the Grand Duke Popov in Russia and when the Revolution came, she had managed to escape the country by escorting two Canadian children who were ill back to England. You can imagine how old that made her – far too old for any agency to hire out – although she certainly didn't lack pep. Somewhere in our scrapbooks, Paula has a picture of Farrell a few years later when we moved back to Canada, whooshing down a playground slide with her legs in the air.

She always wore a white uniform and she talked incessantly in a perfect, clipped British accent, but Farrell was the most unusual Englishwoman I've ever met: she hated tea. As soon as her eyes opened in the morning, she would plug in an electric kettle beside her bed and make the first of countless pots of espresso that she would down all day. And no steak-and-kidney pie for her. She was a vegetarian who lived on Hovis bread and Branston pickle. When she came to Canada, she was horrified by the size of our steaks and would sniff that we were all cannibals.

From the first, I was frank with Farrell. "It doesn't look as if I'm ever going to marry the father of this child," I said. "But I want her brought up properly. I'm going to have to be away a lot earning our living – my career is on the road – but I don't want Paula to suffer for it. I don't have very much money, but I promise you that you will be paid."

She never batted an eyelash. She found herself in charge of a child who still understood only German, but that didn't discourage Farrell from talking to Paula non-stop in English. Every day, rain or shine, she would bundle her up until only her little eyes showed and wheel her in her pram down to Regent's Park, chattering away the whole time. The first word Paula ever said in English was "Down." She wanted out of that pram. There was a kind of nanny competition in the park and all the others would say, "Oh, ours have beautiful outfits. Your poor little girl has the same dress she had on yesterday."

"She's perfectly clean," Farrell would sniff. "Soap and water are cheap."

Farrell saved my life as I flew back and forth between London and Montreal or New York – shuttling between two worlds, one secret, one more and more public.

At one point when I was in England for a few weeks, Eugene was coming through town on a conducting course and he called me. At long last, I persuaded him to see Paula. I had talked about her so much whenever we dated back in Montreal and had inundated him with so many pictures that by then I thought he must be getting used to the idea of being a father.

Farrell had dressed Paula up in her very best and she came creeping out of the back room to meet him. She was an adorable baby with a solemn, square face and big blue eyes that took everything in. She stared at this man in front of her, another new face. "Why, she looks just like my mother," Eugene said. But he seemed reluctant to hold her. It was as if he was afraid that if he picked her up, he would get attached and never be free of us. I had hoped that once he saw Paula, he would realize what a wonderful life we could all share as a family. But he still insisted there wasn't any point in our living together to enjoy this child. "I'm not right for you," he would say. "You deserve another life. So many big things are starting to happen to you. Forget me."

Libby and Murray were furious at him. They began telling me how egocentric and selfish he had been as a child and accused him of terrorizing his brothers with his temper. "Eugene?" I said. "Don't be silly. He's the softest man alive."

I wouldn't tolerate a bad word about him. I knew I loved him and, despite the fact that he wouldn't marry me, I never doubted his love for me. Ours was a great romantic relationship. But I realized he was a complex man who was being eaten up by guilt because of his mother. Still, I never gave up. Once I had decided this man was for me, nothing could change my mind.

But in retrospect I think that the way Eugene behaved with me changed other people's minds about him. Unbeknownst to me, some gossip had started to filter back to a few of our musical friends in Montreal about my situation, and they told me many years later that people were very harsh in their judgment of Eugene for not doing right by a girl who was so much younger than he was. In thinking back, I realize that it was about that time they began to drop him socially and it may have hurt his career.

One day while I was still in London, I got a phone call from a reporter for the *BBC Times*, the little paper which told people about what was on the BBC. He wanted a quick interview with me for a blurb about a concert which was being broadcast. But Paula was in my arms and she had developed quite a voice of her own. "Mama, Mama," she started to holler and squirm.

"Oh, I didn't know you had a child," he remarked. Well, I could hardly deny the existence of someone calling me Mama and I couldn't think of anything else to say.

"Oh, yes, I have a child. Didn't you know?" I said airily.

"And who is the father?" he asked.

"A very fine Canadian musician," I tried to dismiss the question. "But I'm sure you wouldn't know him." He kept pressing me until I finally said Eugene's name.

I hung up grateful that it was only the *BBC Times*, sure that the paper would never use it. But in his blurb, the reporter did mention that Maureen Forrester was staying in London with her child. It was such a small item I prayed nobody would notice it, but Canadian Press picked it up on its wireservice and it ran in papers across the country. All I worried about was how I would explain it to my mother, but for some strange reason she never saw the story.

Someone else did, however: J.W. McConnell. I got a

letter from his secretary, very brief and terse. She wrote that Mr. McConnell felt, now that I had a husband, I would no longer need his financial assistance. I never heard from him again. I was crushed, not because I'd lost a patron, but because he had believed in me so much and regarded me as a daughter of sorts. I knew he must have felt terribly hurt that I hadn't shared what was happening in my life with him. In retrospect I wonder why I didn't write back and explain the situation – or why I hadn't worked up the courage to confide in him in the first place. I could have told him that I loved Eugene and that I wanted to have his baby. J.W., who had always been an understanding man, might even have helped me. But I was too proud and independent to involve him in my misadventures and somehow I felt that I deserved his punishment. Just like a disapproving father, he cut me off. I never saw J.W. again before he died.

Friends now ask how I could carry on with singing during that time and, looking back, I realize that all through the formative years of my career, I did have the most horrendous problems. But my career became my release. No matter what was happening to me, as soon as I stepped on stage, I forgot all my worries.

Marvellous things were happening to me professionally. My schedule was more and more hectic. But suddenly in the midst of all the elation, I felt some familiar symptoms. I started to be air-sick all the time. Dr. Adams, my gynecologist in London, announced that, sure enough, I was pregnant again. It was just a year since I'd had Paula, but I'd never thought much about the consequences when I took up with Eugene again. I was brought up by a mother who had never uttered the word sex, like so many women of her age, and contraception was a taboo subject. My idea of birth control was keeping my fingers crossed.

This time I didn't even bother to call Eugene. "I can't have this baby," I said to Dr. Adams. "It's taking every cent I earn to support the child I have now. It's almost defeating me."

I was heartsick but I knew what I had to do. Dr. Adams booked me into a private hospital to have an abortion. I would never have gone to a backstreet clinic or allowed it unless it could be done properly, but in London then it wasn't difficult to arrange such things. It was clean, it was safe and nobody asked you any questions. Still, for a girl from a background like mine, an abortion was a terrible thing. Years later, of course, when the women's movement brought so many other women of my generation out of the woodwork to admit that they had been forced by their circumstances to have abortions too, I realized that there were a lot of us at the time, each going through her own secret trauma.

I didn't allow myself to weep over it. I was pretty hardened to disappointment in my romantic life by that time, and, once the wonder of the great romance had worn off in so many tears, I had become very realistic. I had to do the best I could by the child I had already brought into the world. But later when I would look at my other children, all so healthy and talented and bright, I would think of that baby and wonder: Was it a boy or a girl? What would things have been like if it had been a brother for Daniel?

Finally when so many things were breaking for me in North America, flying back and forth to England became too much. I decided to take Paula home with me, at least for a visit. By then I had told my friends Walter Joachim, the cellist, and his wife Evelyn about her and they met us at the airport in Montreal, then brought the baby to stay with them. I, of course, had to stay with my mother in the apartment I was still renting.

Evelyn had thought it would be fun to have a baby in the house, but after three weeks we both realized that it wasn't quite what she had imagined having this creature around who cried during Walter's afternoon nap and piddled on the carpets. I knew it wasn't working. I realized there was nothing left to do but to confront the situation head on. One day I walked into our apartment and said, "Mom, get yourself dressed. I've got something to show you this afternoon. I want to introduce you to your new grandchild."

"Why, whose baby is it?" she asked, astounded. It took her the longest time to understand that it was mine. "So where *is* this baby?" she wanted to know when finally it sank in.

"With friends," I said.

"You mean you left her with strangers?!"

When we arrived at the Joachims, Paula was tottering just inside the living room, staring out with her enormous eyes as she held onto a chair. My mother, who I had thought would stick her head in the oven over an illegitimate grandchild, reacted to her as if it was the greatest thing to happen since the invention of strawberry jam. She just wrapped Paula in her arms and started cooing, "Now, do you love me? How much do you love your Granny?" From that moment, we took Paula home to live with us. After all my lies and fears, my mother could hardly be pried away from the baby.

Not that she was the type of grandmother who was into baby-sitting. In Montreal I finally found a young German nanny to look after Paula. I had vague misgivings about her after Farrell, but I was grateful to find anyone. Then one day my bank manager called and inquired if I had anyone by that name working for me. He asked how often I paid her. "Once a week on Saturdays," I told him.

"Well, she's paying herself on Wednesdays too," he said. What had tipped him off was that she not only misspelled my name, but she wrote it in German script. I called her in and offered not to report her in return for her paying me back, although I made clear she couldn't work for me any longer. She had just left after that interview, looking terribly remorseful, when we realized that while she had been there, she had stolen some more money – this time out of my mother's purse.

The next nanny was not a vast improvement. I came home early from work one day and found her naked on the sofa with her boyfriend. I was furious enough about that, but when I went into the bedroom, I couldn't wake Paula up. It turned out that she had drugged her with cough syrup to keep her quiet. That's when I decided to move Paula back to Europe. I called Farrell and told her we were returning.

After I had left England, Branson had rented our little apartment so I had to find another. At last I lucked into one on St. John's Wood Road – an enormous flat over a garage which looked onto a canal. It was so luxurious yet so cheap it seemed too good to be true. Then one morning I discovered why. I walked into the bathroom and found the tub filled with beetles big enough to make a meal out of you. I nearly died. English friends explained to me that I would have to plug the drains every night to keep them out.

That was how Paula began her life, being shunted from city to city across the Atlantic, hearing a parade of strangers talk to her in different languages and only knowing her mother as someone who came and went a little more often than the rest. It was a tough beginning and it must have been very confusing for her. Sometimes I think it's a miracle that she didn't turn out to be a disturbed child. But in fact just the opposite occurred. Paula grew up sweet and sensitive and giving, and it's she who now teaches disturbed children.

SEVENTEEN

Ja, Ja, Mein Kind

IT WAS SNOWING in New York and people were scurrying through the streets, heads down against the cold and screaming for taxis. But I love to walk in the winter air, especially before singing. It's a way of letting quiet into the mind and oxygen into the lungs. I get my rhythm going by moving. I arrived at the front door of Bruno Walter's hotel suite for my first rehearsal with him and he took one look at my apple-red cheeks. *"Ach, mein Kind, du bist so kanadisch!"* He shook his head. "My child, you're so Canadian!"

After my initial audition with him the previous spring, I had rushed back to Montreal and bought the Mahler *Second Symphony*, but when I first glanced at the alto solo, I wasn't very impressed. It was only a four-minute piece. I liked the music and the text, but frankly I wondered what all the fuss was about. I'd certainly sung longer and more difficult works before. Although Diamant had coached me in my part, I was so busy with other engagements and it seemed so short that I really didn't memorize it until I was on the plane to New York. Duck soup, I thought of the work which was to become my signature piece. What did I know of Gustav Mahler?

In the piano rehearsal, Bruno Walter showed me what he wanted and essentially he liked my interpretation. But it wasn't until I heard the full orchestration that I realized the depth of the *Resurrection Symphony*, as it's known –

how truly magnificent it is. I've always joked that Mahler suited me because I'm so melodramatic myself, but of course there's more to it than that. People either like Mahler or they don't; it's hard to explain the strong feelings he evokes. Who knows why you walk into a room and immediately gravitate toward someone? But it's like that for me with music: instinctively I was drawn to Mahler, as if I'd been singing his work all my life. It's strange because there couldn't be two sensibilities more different. I'm basically a happy person while he was a complex, tortured genius. I take life as it comes; he was morose and moody, constantly questioning the meaning of the universe.

Mahler was never recognized as a composer in his day and the critics at the time were devastating about the *Second*, even making fun of it as *Kapellmeistermusik* – a church conductor's handiwork. Some dismissed it as the result of his conversion from Judaism to Roman Catholicism. But there is something in his music – a lot of pain and nostalgia – which touches me. I don't know what it taps, but maybe it's the reminder that my life has not all been a bed of roses. I don't dwell on those sad times, but I can call on them when I interpret a piece and Mahler's music touches a chord in me that can make me weep.

In the *Second*, the alto sits interminably on stage through the first three movements before her solo comes in the fourth. Then at the end of the third movement, there's a bar which, without fail, makes my eyes fill with tears. It puts me in the mood for my part to come. In those few brief notes, I open up to all the memories I keep stifled in the rest of my life. Like an actor preparing for a role, I let myself think of all the things that make me sad: I think of my father dying or of aborting a child. I can call up a moment which creates a longing that you can hear in the voice.

Mahler was still held in low esteem until the late 1950s, when I was lucky to be part of the beginning of his revival, and the *Second* was not played often. I could see that even the musicians in the New York Philharmonic derided the piece as being too long-winded. In fact, it made me angry to see that many of these men playing in a great orchestra were bored with their work. When Bruno Walter wasn't looking, they would lounge in their chairs and all but chew gum. Some of them had been in the Philharmonic twenty-five years, they were nearing retirement and they had long ceased to be involved in the music they were playing. I thought to myself that the minute I became bored with music, I would give it up. But that hasn't happened to me yet. I still sing for the simple reason that I love to.

People often send me letters after I do a Mahler work saying that it's as if he had my voice in mind when he wrote, and in 1964 the Bruckner Society gave me an award for furthering his music. In fact, I would have liked to have known Mahler, although he had a terrible reputation for tyrannizing singers. I've often wondered if he'd once had a love affair with an alto because some of the most beautiful things he wrote are for that voice. Mahler gives a contralto a chance to do things that few other composers have allowed – to spin out high *pianissimo* phrases and to use different rhythms, all with an overlay of tragedy.

I've gone on to sing the *Resurrection Symphony* with so many great conductors. I love to do it with Zubin Mehta, who has such an affinity for the music and conducts it in such an emotional way that I'm knocked out every time. But there has never been a performance like that first one with Bruno Walter. Here he was, this man who had known Mahler, through whom Mahler spoke, leading the last orchestra that Mahler had led in his life. That performance was so moving that all through Carnegie Hall people were weeping. The ovation was staggering. André Mertens had been right in scheduling my New York debut beforehand, because most of the excitement that night was for Bruno Walter and the *Resurrection Symphony* – which is exactly as it should have been – and I shared in it. At the end, Bruno Walter came over and patted my hand. Other conductors have always kissed it, but he was very fatherly to me. Two days later we recorded the *Second* together.

After the third and final Carnegie Hall performance, he had called me into his dressing room. "Now, when are you coming to the West Coast?" he said. Ever since my Town Hall debut, I had been booked solid, but I discovered that I had a concert in San Francisco with a day free afterward. He asked me to come to his home in Los Angeles so that he could coach me on the rest of the Mahler solo works. If approval was re-engagement, this was the ultimate accolade.

Bruno Walter had lived in Beverly Hills ever since he fled Vienna at the outbreak of the war and had taken out American citizenship. That first time I arrived in Los Angeles to see him, I knew nothing about the city and I took a taxi from downtown all the way out Wilshire Boulevard – a $40 fare. I had very little money and I just about fainted when I saw the meter.

He lived with his daughter Lotta Lindt in an elegant mansion which was totally un-Hollywood; it looked almost like an old English country house, filled with solid European antiques and priceless paintings. But there was one feature which caught my eye. As we were discussing when I could return to Los Angeles to work with him again, he suddenly excused himself to get his date book. He went over to the staircase where he had one of those little built-in electronic chairs that slide upstairs on a rail, and in he climbed. He had already had a number of heart attacks, and he seemed embarrassed by that symbol of his frailty, but to me it was the most magical invention I'd ever seen.

After Lotta discreetly disappeared, Bruno Walter would sit down at the grand piano to work with me. Since then, every musician in the world has wanted to hear the pearls of wisdom that I picked up there from him. But in fact, he spoke very little, and I have come to the conclusion that great musicians are people of few words – you're either on their wave length or not. I picked up what Bruno Walter had to teach me almost by osmosis. I had an instinctive feeling of what he wanted or how I ought to correct a phrase and when I would hit what he was striving for, a smile would break over his face. I learned from that look. *"Ja, ja, mein Kind,"* he would say, nodding.

The one piece he shared an insight into which could only have come from knowing Mahler personally was *Lieder eines Fahrenden Gesellen* (Songs of a Wayfarer). In the very beginning of it, there is a bar of three, then a bar of four, and the music alternates like that, changing tempo, for quite a while in a way which had always puzzled me. But Bruno Walter explained that Mahler had forgotten to notate the score to show that he meant the different tempi to be painting two parts of a single scene – a wedding feast going on in a tavern and, standing outside, wistfully looking through the glass, the wayfarer watching the celebration of his beloved's marriage to someone else. From then on, whenever I've sung it, I've told the conductor that's what Bruno Walter said Mahler intended, but not all of them want to believe me.

I worked with Bruno Walter at his home several times more and the next year I sang for him twice: the Mozart *Requiem* with the Chicago Symphony in the spring and then Brahms's *Alto Rhapsody* for the opening of the first Vancouver Festival that summer. The *Alto Rhapsody* was one of the pieces I had originally auditioned for him and, as I prepared it, I remembered his advice at the time. "When you sing Brahms and Mahler," he had said, "think masculine. Even though the *Alto Rhapsody* is written for an alto, sing it dark like a man." That Vancouver Festival was quite a gala event, graced by the presence of Princess Margaret who danced with a handsome young lawyer named John Turner. When Bruno Walter arrived, it was obvious that he must have been under the impression that coming to Canada was like voyaging to the North Pole. On a day when the temperature had soared into the eighties – hotter even than that week's weather in Los Angeles – he turned up in a winter coat with a big fur collar.

After my first meeting with Bruno Walter, I began to work on *Das Lied von der Erde* (Song of the Earth) – the piece which will probably one day be my swan song. I had always hoped I might get the chance to sing it with him and, because he liked his musicians to memorize a work, I had started to learn it – no mean feat. The whole cycle takes an hour and five minutes and the last song, "Abschied" (Farewell), is twenty-nine minutes alone. In the spring of 1960, when he was invited to wind up the New York Philharmonic's Mahler Festival with *Das Lied von der Erde*, he asked me to be his soloist. The invitation was all the more meaningful because, since Mahler had never lived to conduct the piece, Bruno Walter had led the first performance of it in Munich in 1911, six months after his mentor's death.

He always said it was the most personal of Mahler's works. Mahler himself had called it his "symphony of songs" and it never fails to touch me. Written after his daughter's death and the discovery of his own incurable illness, it's the kind of music that can make me cry when I'm singing and I can't allow that to happen. If you get teary, you sap your breath and a veil comes over the voice which makes it husky. I have to call up the right colour for that piece without letting it get to me or else I've had it.

There are six songs based on ancient Chinese poems, three for the tenor – who was Richard Lewis for that performance – and three for the alto. My first song sets an autumnal mood, starting out with the lonely sound of oboe and strings. "My heart is tired," it says. "O Love's warm sunshine, have you gone forever? And will my burning tears be never dried?" My second song is light and charming – a tribute to youth and beauty. In it, maidens are picking flowers on a hillside while flirtatious young men are showing off on horseback for them down on the shore. But in the last one, the "Farewell," the narrator sees a rider standing off in the distance to carry him away

– death waiting like the proverbial horseman. Still, he isn't sad. He looks around at his beloved earth where the spring will come again and he sees it all as a world without end, everything eternally renewed, everything new once again to those who are born each time around – even the destination that he is setting off for with the waiting rider. Death itself becomes a glorious new journey. There is a point where the orchestra builds and builds and you can see the audience gasp. It really takes people off into another universe – even I get transported – and, at the end, every time I have done that piece, there is dead silence. That hush – just before the audience breaks into tumultuous applause – is the mark of Mahler's genius.

In 1960, one of the four Philharmonic performances was always a Friday matinee. On the Friday morning I woke up and decided I absolutely had to get my hair cut and bleached, so I went to a big salon called Larry Matthews, on 57th Street near Carnegie Hall, which all the artists frequented. Those were the days of lacquered beehives with hundreds of coils sculptured like works of art, held in place with enough hairpins to build a tank and armoured with a shield of hairspray. Suddenly I realized that concocting this engineering triumph was taking longer than I'd expected. The clock was edging closer and closer to concert time and I was getting more and more agitated, but I couldn't leap out of the chair looking like a drowned rat. The performance was to start at 2:30 p.m. and I got out of the salon at 2:10, raced back to the Wellington Hotel, threw on my blue brocade gown and tore out to Carnegie Hall half zipped up. On the street I ran into someone from Columbia Artists. "Hi, Maureen," he said. Then he did a double take. "Hey, Maureen, aren't you supposed to be singing right now?"

"Yes," I yelled, panting on up the street. I was out of breath when I rushed through the stage door, where they had just finished the Schubert *Unfinished*. Audrey Michaels, my publicist, was wringing her hands. I dropped my coat, threw on make-up and went straight on stage, blessing Mahler for giving the tenor the first song. Later, Audrey just rolled her eyes as people came backstage to congratulate me. "It's amazing," one of them said. "You always look so composed on stage."

The final performance of that series, on Sunday afternoon, was the most incredible of any I have ever known. Carnegie Hall was full of older Europeans and, as I was sitting on stage waiting for the final movement, suddenly it hit me: the audience felt it was watching Bruno Walter conduct *Lied von der Erde* for the last time. He was eighty-three by then and quite frail. It was a very emotional moment. There were handkerchiefs out all over the hall. But when I glanced up at him, he had an amused, almost mischievous, look on his face. I had never seen it before but I got the distinct feeling that he sensed exactly what was going through people's minds and he was saying to himself, "Ha, I've got a surprise for you. I'm going to be around for a while longer."

Certainly, he had plans. He wanted me to come to Europe with him to perform. But even more important for me, he had asked me to re-record in stereo, the new technique at that time, all of the Mahler works that he had originally done with Kathleen Ferrier. I was thrilled at such a chance to recreate classics. But when I told André Mertens about the offer, he was suddenly, uncharacteristically, silent. Only three days earlier André had signed me to an exclusive recording contract with RCA Victor and they wouldn't release me to sing with Bruno Walter who was under contract to Columbia Records. I had sung the concerts with him but when it came time to record *Lied von der Erde* and the rest of the Mahler songs, I had to watch Mildred Miller step in. It was a crushing blow. I've never signed an exclusive recording contract since and it's no exaggeration to say that was the biggest disappointment of my career.

RCA tried to make it up to me. They arranged for me to record *Lied von der Erde* with Fritz Reiner and the Chicago Symphony – and that is certainly nothing to complain about. Again I sang it with Richard Lewis, this time in a concert hall in Chicago, and let me tell you that session would have done in a person with vertigo. We were placed behind the orchestra on a platform teetering above scaffolding fifteen feet high, with no railings around the edges.

It was just one of a half-dozen performances of *Lied von der Erde* I sang that year. After that recording, I was going straight to Cleveland to sing the same piece with George Szell and the Cleveland Symphony to celebrate Mahler's centennial. From there, Szell had asked Ernst Haefliger, the tenor, and me to travel on to New York with him to repeat it there. When Reiner heard that I was going on directly to sing with Szell, he looked over the little half-glasses he was famous for and said, "Now let's work on your diction. I want to make sure you have every note perfect because Szell is tough." This from a man who himself was known as a little Napoleon!

Everybody had warned me that Szell was a tyrant. Musicians were petrified of him. There was a story about a young horn player from Toronto who went to play with the Cleveland Symphony; all through the rehearsal Szell glared at him. The horn player kept getting more and more uncomfortable. Finally, at the end, Szell snapped, "No crewcuts in my orchestra!"

He was a perfectionist. I once saw him nearly destroy a singer. He had asked me to do Cherubini's *Missa Solemnis* at La Scala. There were two soprano soloists and one of them couldn't read music; she kept getting her lead note wrong. Szell couldn't stand anybody around him who was so unmusical and it drove him to distraction. He humiliated her each time she made a mistake and she kept getting more and more nervous, making the situation worse. Finally, I couldn't bear to see her crucified like that. I leaned over to her and hummed the note so she could pick it up.

The stories about Szell had prepared me for the worst when I went to rehearse with him, but he wasn't hard on me at all. In fact, it was heaven to work with him. What he wanted was a perfect performance and in a way I'm similar; I can't stand people not to give their all. At our first piano rehearsal, he said he would accompany me himself, and he sat down and played absolutely magnificently. I didn't know it then but he had been a *Wunderkind* on the piano in his childhood and had even been sent on tour in his little velvet pants before he became a conductor at a very young age. After I had sung my part for him, he didn't say a word. Finally, I ventured, "Maestro, if there's anything you don't like, I'd be happy to adjust it."

"No, my dear," he said. "If I could sing, that's the way I would want it to sound."

I had had a similar vote of confidence when I recorded *Songs of a Wayfarer* and *Kindertotenlieder* with Charles Munch and the Boston Symphony – the other part of the compensation package RCA had arranged for me. I had always admired Munch, an elegant Alsatian, and was flattered to be singing with him, but unfortunately Mahler wasn't his specialty. At the very first rehearsal, with the whole orchestra present, he turned to me, a beginner who had just been discovered, and said, "Madame, I have never conducted Mahler, but I will do my best to give you a good accompaniment. Any way you want this played, I will be happy to oblige."

Those compliments were all because of Bruno Walter, because I had been close to the fountainhead, so to speak. He had given me the gift of Mahler. As bitterly disappointed as I was not to be able to record *Lied von der Erde* with him, in my heart I prayed that when my three-year RCA contract ran out, we would have the chance to record the rest of the Mahler works together. But not long after I last sang with him, he died.

I was rehearsing with the San Francisco Symphony one morning in 1962 when the manager came up to me and said, "Did you hear the news? It was on the radio: Bruno Walter just passed away." It was as if I had lost someone from my own family. I felt incredible sadness that I couldn't break an engagement to go to his funeral.

Even now, all these years later, every time I sing *Lied von der Erde*, no matter where I am, something strange comes over me. There's a certain point at the end of the "Farewell," when I find myself looking up toward the balcony and I can see Bruno Walter sitting there in a black raw silk rehearsal jacket that he used to wear. It was high-cut, almost like a Mao jacket, and the shirt collar he wore under it gave him a priest-like air. And as I look up, he nods with that quiet smile playing around his mouth as if to say, *"Ja, ja, mein Kind."*

EIGHTEEN

A Strong Complex Emotion

"LOVE: A STRONG complex emotion, a feeling of personal attachment, causing one to appreciate, delight in or crave the presence or possession of the object. . . ." The American composer Celius Dougherty used those words to begin a song called "Love in the Dictionary" which I sang often when I was starting out. It was simply the definition of love as it appeared in the dictionary and it went on in a very funny vein until it came to the last line: "Or in some games, as tennis, nothing." Celius Dougherty had his tongue in his cheek, but sometimes back in those days it seemed to me that my love life was a tennis score.

I was starting to give up on Eugene. Twice he had seen Paula, who by this time was nearly two years old, and he still wasn't moved. In fact, he had protested so long about not marrying me that I had gotten used to the idea of being on my own. His brother and sister-in-law had given up on his marrying me too. Finally, while I was still living in London, Murray and Libby introduced me to a friend of theirs named Bernie Winfield, who was good-looking and charming and had become quite a success in advertising. Oddly enough, he was Jewish too, but unlike Eugene, he didn't have any hang-ups about marrying outside his faith. I had told him the truth about Paula and he was very good to her. More important, he seemed to be quite taken with me. I was beginning to wonder if I should marry him when I got a long-distance call from Eugene who was taking a conducting seminar in Mexico. "I've been thinking," he said. "Maybe we should try to make a go of it after all."

I was stunned. I've never known what made him change his mind, but I had stopped writing and maybe he panicked that he was losing me. I still couldn't believe that he wouldn't think better of the idea, but when he arrived in London a few weeks later, he still wanted to get married.

On July 20, 1957, we trooped down to Marylebone town hall to do the deed and the bride wore black. I never thought of it as peculiar at the time; in my mind, I could hardly wear white. But I also had a very practical bent. I could only afford a dress that I would wear again for receptions. I chose a princess style with a big portrait collar and somebody – I'm sure it wasn't Eugene – gave me a corsage to pin on one lapel. I had a velvet band in my hair with a black feather that swooped to one side. I felt quite chic and it never occurred to me at the time that I didn't look at all like a bride.

It was a tiny wedding with only four guests: Murray and Libby, Branson Price and Luce Coast, the wife of my British manager, John. We left Paula at home with Farrell. It had been raining that morning but the sun came out by the time we emerged onto Marylebone High Street.

I had booked a table for six at the International Musicians Association, a lovely little club which was the poshest that I had ever seen. Waiters moved through the wood-panelled rooms in cutaway coats and gloves, and the whole place was enveloped in that unmistakable British upper-class hush. When the maître d'hôtel learned that ours was a wedding party, he kept saying that he wished he'd known to have prepared something special. But we just ordered from the menu: salmon and champagne, a feast in any case, although I hadn't thought to order a wedding cake.

Murray Kash stood up and made a toast. Then everybody started to nudge Eugene. "Look, this is your wedding," they said. "You have to make a speech." Finally he got up. "Well, what can I say?" he began. "This is the craziest thing I've ever done in my life." That was his toast to the bride!

Eugene and I went straight home to Paula; there was no honeymoon. As I always say, we had our honeymoon before the wedding. From that day on, for the next fifteen years, we had the most wonderful life together. Once he had made the commitment, Eugene became an absolutely adoring, devoted husband and father. It was a real love match; right until the end, whenever we were together we were always hand-in-hand. When I would get home from a tour and have to do the shopping and chores, he would insist on being with me. The torrid affair continued after the wedding. Eugene is a very romantic man and once he got married, it was as if he realized what he had been missing all his life.

He was everything a singer could dream of in a husband. Not only did he know music better than I did, but he was never jealous of my success. Wherever I sang, if he was in the vicinity, he came to hear me, and in fact he still does. He used to come backstage afterward and rave to whoever was there: "She does it to me every time. I don't know how this healthy peasant of mine pulls it off but it's just thrilling to hear her." On the way home in the car, he would tell me again how fabulous I had been. Then often, a few days after the performance, he would gently introduce a note of criticism. Once he said, "You know, your interpretation was very effective but did you ever think you might be achieving the opposite effect to what you want?" Early in my career, he detected that I would hold back on the high notes. I would sing a crescendo and then suddenly at the very top make it *subito*. It drove him wild because it created an effect that was very precious. I admitted that I did it because I wasn't sure of my upper range. "So work on the top notes," he said. "You don't need that bit of fakery." And he proved to be right. I didn't agree with Eugene every time but he was an excellent analyst and a man of impeccable musical taste. Nobody could have been more supportive of my career.

When we were first married, I imagined that every Jewish boy in the world was nostalgic for his mother's food. Little did I know that my late mother-in-law had been a terrible cook. I decided I would surprise Eugene with a nice Jewish meal. Off I went to Selfridge's book department where I explained to the saleslady that my husband came from an Orthodox family and I wanted to surprise him with a dinner that his mother might have made. "What you need," she said, "is Mrs. White's recipe book. She's the most famous kosher cook in London." At home, lying in the bathtub reading it, I came across all these recipes for mutton. That's when I realized that an English cook is an English cook, whether she's kosher or not. I detest mutton.

Finally I hit upon a recipe for garlic soup. It called for 102 cloves of garlic. I figured Mrs. White must know what she was doing, so I set out to make it with no food processors or gadgets whatsoever in an apartment which couldn't have been bigger than fourteen feet square. Well, it turned out to be absolutely bilious – curdled and ghastly, strong enough to knock out an entire army. But Eugene sat there, trying to smile as he gagged on it, saying, "No, no, I insist, darling, it's really quite good." Thank heavens I've become a better cook since then, but that was my last try at garlic soup. The apartment reeked for the next two years.

But Eugene was haunted by his mother's memory in other ways. In the first few months of our marriage, I noticed how tense he was; his stomach always seemed to be in knots. He went to Dr. Adams but there was nothing wrong physically. "It's nerves," she said. And then I knew what it was: guilt over marrying me. I realized Eugene was suffering the tortures of the damned. Finally I persuaded him to see a psychiatrist about it and after only a little while, he was a changed man. One day much later he confided to me what this doctor had told him: that he needed to mentally kill his mother.

By then I was expecting what we took to calling Opus Two. I had gotten pregnant again within a month of our wedding. I just had to look at Eugene and another baby would be on its way. They don't call me Earth Mother for nothing. It was then that I began to worry: what would happen if we had a son? I knew he wouldn't be considered Jewish because I wasn't. And I also knew that despite the fact that Eugene always insisted he wasn't religious, deep in his heart he was.

We had decided to move back to Montreal where it would be easier to raise the children and I would be closer to all the engagements starting to flood in for me from the United States. The CBC in Montreal had asked Eugene to write and host an educational TV show called *The Magic of Music*, which suited him perfectly. He had a tremendous rapport with young people and he was a born teacher. We found a house on Grove Hill Place in Notre-Dame-de-Grâce – the first of nearly a dozen houses we lived in over the years. Virtually as soon as we arrived home, I went to Rabbi Stern of Temple Emanu-El, whose services I had sung, and asked him to convert me.

These days convertees have to take lessons in Hebrew and have a *mikveh*, a ritual bath, but my conversion was simpler than that. I already knew all the Hebrew prayers from my years of singing them on High Holidays; unwittingly I had received my education in Judaism during those services. I had loved that music; some of it, like the *Kol Nidre*, the musical service on the eve of Yom Kippur, can move me to tears.

"There's not much I have to teach you," Rabbi Stern said. He performed both the conversion and our religious marriage ceremony in his study the same day. Rose and Louis Melzack, the founder of Classic Bookshops, stood up for us and this time the bride didn't wear black, but under her pink brocade dress, she was very, very pregnant.

To me, Judaism was not a religion as much as a way of life with the same family closeness that I had admired so strongly among the French Canadians I grew up with. Everything is a celebration, and so much of it revolves around the dining table. From sabbaths to Seders, I tried to recreate that same sense of family I had longed for as a child. I've brought up all my children in the Jewish religion and I was the one who taught them their prayers. Now it seems ironic that I – the person who doesn't really believe in formal religion – am held in very high regard by the Jewish community and do a lot of fund-raising for it. In fact, I've even been honoured as a Jewish mother! I'm a true defender of Israel and I've sung at its bar mitzvah, its thirteenth anniversary – and its twenty-fifth. I can't stand to listen to a bad word about the country. Sometimes when my children get into an argument about its politics, I have to leave the room.

My proficiency in Hebrew impressed Eugene's friends and family, but not his father. The old man had had a stroke by the time I met him and although he was always very polite and adored the children, he really only tolerated me. He had been a very pious man and a good jeweller, but his wife had been the shrewd one, the business head of the family. After he had repaired clocks for customers, she would act as the delivery service, carting them through the city in the boys' baby carriage. She kept the store's books and, very early on, she had bought four huge diamonds and put them away for the day when each of her sons was ready to marry.

But Eugene's father would never give him the diamond that she had set aside for his future wife. It used to exasperate Eugene but I said, "Look, some day soon I'll be able to buy my own diamonds. Jewels don't mean that much to me." Still, it meant a lot to Eugene as a symbol of acceptance. At last, when his father died, he inherited the diamond but I refused to wear it then. "Your father didn't want me to have it," I said, "and I couldn't wear it now."

Gina was born in the spring of 1958, and after that, the babies just kept coming. I had five children in nine years and I would have had six if I hadn't fallen down the stairs once while I was pregnant. I was trying to clean up some glasses left on the steps after a party and as usual I was done in by my tidiness. The next night I was sitting in the audience at Her Majesty's Theatre in Montreal and in the middle of *Hamlet*, I miscarried.

With every baby, my range increased half a note on the top and half a note on the bottom and John declared my voice also grew richer with each child. James Grayson, the founder of Westminster Records, maintained that the secret of my success was that you could hear in my voice the fact that I was a fulfilled woman. But my pregnancies became a joke in the music world. Audrey Michaels claimed I accused her of sending me orchids before a concert only when I wasn't expecting a baby – which certainly saved her money. And once when I was doing *Lied von der Erde* at the Casals Festival, Eugene and I walked into the first rehearsal holding hands. Eugene Ormandy saw us and came down from the stage. He put his hand on my stomach and pretended to be feeling for a pulse. "Now look, you two lovebirds," he wagged his finger, "no sleeping in the same bed this trip. You're booked to sing with me later this season."

But pregnancy never stopped me from singing. When André Mertens's office found out I was expecting Gina, they wanted to cancel all my bookings, but I really fought them on that. We needed the money and, besides, I've never had any trouble singing right up until a few weeks before giving birth. I feel marvellous when I'm pregnant and I probably sing better. "Pregnancy is not a sickness,"

I told Columbia Artists Management. "I will have clever clothes made and I will sing." I like to think that I was a pioneer – that I helped change managers' attitudes – because now a lot of singers carry on performing quite far into their terms. I used to joke that all my babies did 150 concerts before they were born.

But John Coast, my British manager, dropped me because I was always pregnant and Audrey Michaels never wanted the critics to get wind of the fact that I was expecting a baby for fear they would find an excuse to look for weaknesses in my performance. In 1961, after Linda was born, Audrey had been especially cagey with *The New York Times*'s Raymond Ericson because I hadn't given a recital in the city for three years. She hadn't said a word to him about it through the whole concert, but the next morning she picked up the *Times* and the headline read: "Canadian Contralto Excels in Town Hall. Sings 15 Days After Birth of 4th Child." He had seen the news on the wire-services from Montreal. Joe Scafidi, the manager of the San Francisco Symphony, also won't let me forget that I called him once when I arrived in town to sing and needed to look over a score to decide if I wanted to accept another engagement. "Joe, I need two things," I said, "a gynecologist and *The Damnation of Faust*."

Years later, when I was pregnant with Susie, I was engaged to sing Bach's Cantata No. 35 with Hermann Scherchen. He was a conductor I loved, even if he was notoriously difficult and could cut the legs right out from under a performer with his sarcasm. When I accepted the date in New York, I thought Susie would have been born by then, but she had turned around in my womb and was twenty-eight days late. I told my doctor that I really wanted to do this concert and he assured me he didn't think there was any danger of the baby arriving that weekend, but he made me promise to find a doctor who would stand by in Lincoln Center just in case. I called Audrey and said, "Do you know any obstetricians who like Bach?" She found me one and I explained the circumstances over the phone. "When are you due?" he asked. "Last month," I said.

Cantata No. 35 is horrendously difficult – *Geist und Seele*, it's called (Spirit and Soul) – with great long sweeping runs and lots of coloratura passages. It was quite a breathing exercise. At rehearsal, Scherchen, who looked just like Wagner, either played it so slowly that I thought I would expire or he did it so fast that I could barely keep up. But the performance went well and afterward I asked to meet the obstetrician to thank him. The stagehands told me he had been standing in the wings all night, chewing his nails as he watched my breathing. It turned out that even the orchestra had bets on whether or not I'd make it through without an act of God on stage.

Scherchen had scads of young children himself. He was in his seventies at this point, and he had been married three times, once to a Chinese woman. Whenever anyone asked him how many children he had, he always said, "Seven and two Chinese." He had this crazy idea that I should move to Switzerland, where he lived, and we would record together in his studio while his offspring looked after mine.

The night after I sang the Bach cantata, Eugene and I had dinner with Scherchen. But all through the meal I had a sense that he was somehow expecting me to say something and I couldn't understand what it was. When I got back to the Wellington Hotel, the concierge pulled a manila envelope out of my mail slot and handed it to me with an apology. "This came for you this morning," he said. "Somebody must have misplaced it." Inside was a signed photograph of Scherchen which read: "To Madame Forrester, the only Caruso-like voice. Always a pleasure to work with you." It was an incredible and totally uncharacteristic compliment coming from that gruff man, but by the time I went to thank him the next morning, he had already left town.

The next time he engaged me was to sing Mahler's

Kindertotenlieder (Songs on the Death of Children) during Easter week in Bologna. But when I got the contract, it stipulated that I had to be there a week ahead of time. It seemed so unnecessary and unfair when my children were out of school at home, but I assumed there must be a reason. I got to Bologna on time, but I ended up sitting in my hotel room for four days. It turned out they hadn't needed me at all. By the time Scherchen called me to rehearsal, I was livid.

"You don't look very happy," he said. "Whatever is the matter?" He was furious when I explained what had happened; he hadn't known I'd been asked to come early. "It's these Italian managers," he said, "they never trust singers to show up!" He gave the manager of the orchestra a terrible dressing-down right there in front of all the musicians. "Now," he told him, "you're going to make it up to us both by taking us out to the very finest restaurant in Bologna and buying us the most stupendous dinner to be had in this town.

When I arrived to have dinner with Scherchen again the last night after the performance, I found him sitting in the restaurant laboriously writing postcards. He explained that he was printing a different poem from *Kindertotenlieder* – which Mahler wrote just before his daughter died – to each of his own children, asking them to memorize the text before he got home. I was so moved by that gesture. We had a wonderful dinner and the next day he flew to Florence to conduct. He stepped onto the podium at rehearsal and keeled over, dead. It sent shivers through me to remember Scherchen writing out *Songs on the Death of Children* the night before his own.

Eugene and I made sure our lives revolved around the family. Everything we did when I was home, we did with the children. People would phone the house very gravely and apologetically, saying, "Oh, Madame Forrester, I'm so sorry to disturb you. I know you must be resting your voice."

"Resting my voice?" I'd say. "I've got four children crawling all over me with Play-Doh and crayons and I'm doing the washing." That was my idea of luxury when I wasn't on the road. Out there I was The Singer, but when I was home I was Mommy, and I tried to live double time. My life on the road was full of pretence and I craved to be ordinary. It was therapy for me to scrub the house and do real things with my hands. And besides, as Eugene always pointed out, the moisture was good for my voice.

Of course, it wasn't that I needed to do the cleaning or washing. I couldn't have gone on the road and left my children in any conscience unless I was sure that I had the very best help. In my experience, a working woman has to replace herself not with one woman but with two or three. You can't ask a good nanny to do the housework as well.

I had brought Farrell over to Montreal with Paula on the *Queen Elizabeth* but after a few years she retired. Then Teta came into our lives. Charlotte Györy was her real name, but she had been born in Dresden and she always called herself Teta, a European term of affection for nanny. She had suffered from an illness as a child which had stunted her growth and she couldn't have been much more than four feet tall. But as Eugene said, you had the impression Teta was a giant. When friends sent her to me, she arrived in my living room in her white uniform with a brooch at the neck and the starched nurse's cap that she always wore on Sundays. I was just home from a tour and pregnant as usual. I was exhausted and the children were running all over the house, screaming for supper. "Excuse me, I'll just get them something to eat," I said. "No," she said, "you're tired. Let me do it." And she just walked into the kitchen and from that moment on, she took over our lives.

Teta was a little general. She made my career possible. I learned so much from her and, for the ten years she was with us, she was the rock of the family. She was very Germanic and strict with the children but they adored her and she moved everywhere with us – from Montreal to

1. Clowning at a church choir picnic, c. 1946.
2. Mother, May Forrester.
3. Father. Thomas Forrester.
4. Brother Arnold and sister Jean, c. 1941, in father's vegetable garden behind the rue Fabre house.
5. Mother, shortly after her arrival in Canada from Ireland.

6. Publicity photo for first European tour.
7. Early publicity photograph. © *Maclean Hunter,*
Courtesy Chatelaine
8. Early publicity photograph, Montreal, late 1940s.
Photo by Gaby of Montreal
9. Program for American debut in New York,
November 1956.
10. Publicity photo taken in New York, 1974.
Photo by Christian Steiner

11

12

13

11. Maureen Forrester and Eugene Kash after wedding ceremony in London, England (July 20, 1957), with guests Libby and Murray Kash, Luce Coast, and Branson Price. © *Portman Press Bureau Ltd., London*

12. Just arrived in Berlin after an arduous journey with soprano friend, Anne Watson, 1955.

13. Publicity photo for a concert in Berlin, 1956. © *Curt Ullmann, Berlin*

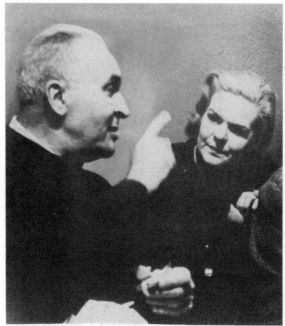

14

16

14. & 15. Bruno Walter discussing a playback at a recording session at Carnegie Hall of Mahler's *Second Symphony*.

16. Rehearsing with John Newmark in Montreal for a CBC concert, early 1950s (during a brief period as a brunette). *Photo by Jac-Guy, Collection Studio O'Allard Photography, Inc.*

17. Singing from Poulenc's song cycle *Le Travail du Peintre* for CBC television with accompanist John Newmark. *Photo by André Le Coz*

15

17

18

18. In New York with husband Eugene Kash in front of Carnegie Hall, spring 1960, before the memorable concert with Bruno Walter conducting Mahler's *Das Lied von der Erde*.

19   20

21

19. As Cornelia in a 1967 production in Buenos Aires of Handel's
Julius Caesar in which Beverly Sills played Cleopatra.
20. With Igor Markevitch (left) and Eugene at the Montreux
Festival, 1957. *Photo by Jean Waldis, Montreux.*
21. At home in Montreal, 1959. Paula practising ballet with accompaniment by her father.

22

22. Performing Mahler's *Songs of a Wayfarer* with the Bologna Symphony, 1966, with the up-and-coming conductor, Riccardo Muti. *Photo by Giuseppe Damiani*
23. "Les grands concerts" radio broadcast with John Newmark, September 1970. *Photo by Jean Pierre Karsenty*
24. Performing in *Adieu Robert Schumann*, a ballet choreographed by Brian Macdonald, music by Murray Schafer, with dancers Vincent Warren and Annette av Paul. *Photo © 1979 John Lederman*
25. Performing with Zubin Mehta during a Montreal Symphony tour of French-speaking countries, October 1966. *Photo courtesy of the Orchestre Symphonique de Montréal*

23

24

25

26

27

26. With John Boyden playing Jesus in the *St. Matthew Passion* for NBC
27. In performance at the Casals Festival, Puerto Rico. *Photo by Jack Delano*

28

29

28. Left to right: Isaac Stern, Maureen Forrester, Rudolf Serkin, Pablo Casals, and Leopold Stokowski in rehearsal for the Pierre Monteux memorial concert at Carnegie Hall, 1964.

29. The Bach Aria Group. Left to right, standing: Bernard Greenhouse, Oscar Shumsky, Norman Farrow, Maureen Forrester, Sam Baron, Robert Bloom, Lois Marshall, Richard Lewis, Bill Sheide, seated, and Yehudi Wyner at the piano.

30

31

32

33

30. Rehearsing Mozart's *Requiem* with Josef Krips in Montreal, 1954. *Photo by Dr. I.W. Schmidt*

31. Looking over the score of the Verdi *Requiem* with Alfred Wallenstein, who conducted the open-air performance at Lewisohn Stadium outside New York City. *Photo by Dr. I.W. Schmidt*

32. Being given a farewell send-off in Montreal by Mayor Jean Drapeau at City Hall before a European Jeunesses Musicales tour, 1955.

33. After the United Nations fourteenth anniversary concert. Left to right: conductor Eleazar de Carvalho, a United Nations official, Maureen Forrester, bass-baritone Kim Borg, Elisabeth Schwarzkopf, and Jan Peerce.

35

34

36

34. Caricature done for a New Zealand newspaper, c. 1968.
35. With the children's former nanny, affectionately known as
Teta, in the late 1970s.
36. 1966 family portrait with children (left to right) Daniel, Gina,
Susie, Paula and Linda, in Toronto.
37. Sitting on statuary along the walkway to the Ming tombs, on
her second trip to China.

37

38

39

40

38. A day off during the 1962 Australian tour with John Newmark at Sydney's Taronga Park Zoo. *Photo by Color Prints, Sydney*
39. A benefit performance for the Montreal Symphony. Left to right: Pete Seeger, Monique Leyrac, conductor Neil Chotem, Nana Mouskouri, Maureen Forrester, and Harry Belafonte. *Photo by Jean-Claude Adam*
40. Left to right: Composer Saul Irving Glick, Oskar Morawetz, Maureen Forrester, John Newmark, after a performance of Glick's *I Never Saw Another Butterfly.*

41

42

43

41. Hamming it up as Bloody Mary in an Edmonton production of *South Pacific* with co-star Edward Evanko.

42. Rehearsing for Gian Carlo Menotti's *The Medium.* Clockwise: baritone Gino Quilico, right (in his first opera role), Maureen Forrester, Rosemarie Landry, and Barbara Ianni.

43. Performing in the Ottawa production of Massenet's *Cendrillon* with Louis Quilico in Paris. *Photo © Daniel Cande*

44. Talking to Isaac Stern at a reception after a benefit performance, 1980. *Photo Leo Hausman of The Studio*

45. After a concert with Lois Marshall, in the mid-sixties.

46. Rehearsing with director Irving Guttman for her first major opera role, the grandmother in Gian Carlo Menotti's *The Consul.*

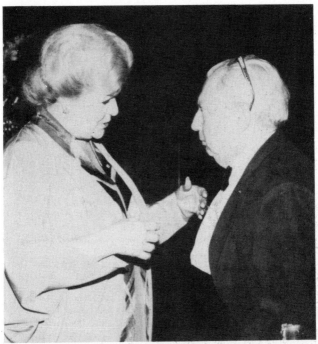

44

45   46

47   48

47. Madame Flora in Gian Carlo Menotti's *The Medium*. *Photo by Robert C. Ragsdale, FRPS*
48. As the witch in CBC's production of *Hansel and Gretel*, 1970, with Judith Forst (left) and Christine Anton. *Photo by Robert C. Ragsdale, FRPS*
49. Family Christmas, 1985. Back row: Susie, Maureen, Paula. Seated, Daniel (with Ryan on his knee), Linda, Gina (holding Galen), and Eugene. In foreground, son-in-laws Paul Dineen and Peter Berton.

49

Connecticut and then to Toronto. When I was home, the children got away with murder. My idea of being a disciplinarian once startled a reporter who heard one of the girls interrupt an interview, whining, "Mommy, Daniel hit me." "Well, punch him back," I said.

Eugene was the model father, always taking time out for the children. In the fall of 1961, we moved to Connecticut. André Mertens had a summer place in Westport, a town which I fell in love with. We bought a sprawling colonial house there on two acres of land which was almost like a park surrounded by split-rail fences. There were fruit trees and a pond which was half-covered with terrible green algae. That pond was greener than the lawn. Somebody told us to get ducks which would eat the algae but instead the ducks just swam in the clear part.

I had thought the move was a brilliant idea because, after four years, the CBC had cancelled Eugene's TV show *The Magic of Music* and we decided that it would be great for him to get back to playing violin, but this time with the best New York orchestras. It didn't matter where I lived, as long as it was near an airport. Little did we know that because of immigration rules, Eugene would have to live in the U.S. for a year before he could get a union card. He couldn't play at all when we first arrived so he became a househusband, before anybody had ever heard of liberated men doing that.

He went to all the children's school plays and concerts. Westport was rather upper crust in its own way and often he would find that he was the only parent in the audience. At Paula's country day school, the principal used to tell him how she would call to invite the other families, but people would always claim they were caught up in their bridge tournaments or their balls, and couldn't attend, although if she needed a library donated to the school, they said they'd be happy to sign a cheque for that.

Our children all played musical instruments and I used to joke that I would have my own Canadian Trapp family, but none of them liked to practise. From the time they were young, their idea of entertainment was to put on plays or charades for us. But they were never impressed with what I did. Once, interviewing one of them for a human interest story about me in the paper, a reporter clucked to Gina, "Isn't it lovely that your mother sings?" "Yes," said Gina, "but she really sings too loud."

I never made a point of having them hear me perform but I always let them know they could come to a concert if they wished. In Puerto Rico, they decided they wanted to go to one of the dress rehearsals for the Casals Festival, so Teta dressed all the girls up in pinafores and braids, and as they marched down the aisle to the front row they looked so adorable they almost stole the show. I had warned them beforehand that they mustn't make any noise or try to talk to Mommy when she was on stage. I tried not to look at them too often but every once in a while when I would glance at the front row, they were all lined up with exaggeratedly grave looks on their faces, watching a version of me they had never seen before. To them, it was just like one of their dress-up productions at home. They were as good as gold but every time Gina would catch my glance, she would want to show me how well she was following my instructions so she would clamp a hand over her mouth and give a little wave of her baby finger that was absolutely hysterical. It was all I could do to keep a straight face.

Once I had been discovered by Bruno Walter, my greatest joys in life came not through my career, but through my children. They kept my feet on the ground. People always want to talk to me about the fabulous places I've been and the fabulous people I've met, but the greatest satisfactions have come from my family life. At home, puttering in the kitchen, I'm a completely different person from the one the world knows as an entertainer; in fact, I don't even talk that much about my work. But those are the moments which feel most real to me – and make it all worthwhile.

The only frustration was not having more time with the

children. When I was away on the road, my best friend Irene Bird, who acted as my secretary and general trouble-shooter, helped keep the household running. But sometimes she would stop by the house and find the children sleeping in my clothes, wrapped in a bathrobe or a fur coat because it held the smell of Mommy. Stories like that sent pangs of guilt through me.

As I discovered, although I loved having babies, that was the cheap part; then you had the bills to pay. I wanted my children to have what I never did – lessons, clothes and weeks away at summer camp. My expenses were astronomical. People hear of my fees and they think I'm rich. But it cost me a fortune to keep the household ticking on in my absence. I used to joke that I worked for my help.

Here I was, a great success, and yet I never had any money. For years, it was one long renegotiation with the bank just to keep the rent or mortgage paid. Although Eugene was teaching and playing, I was the major bread-winner and I would have to trek down to the bank manager's office with my next year's contracts in hand to prove that I was worthy of a loan so I could keep us all afloat a while longer. Sometimes my manager would phone with a last-minute request to fill in for another singer and even if I was worn out, I would accept, thinking that it would pay for replacing the broken-down washer or the broken-down car. I would never have sung so much if we hadn't needed the money. Occasionally it would get to me and when I was alone in a hotel room somewhere, I would have a few tears to myself.

I never let on what a wrench it was to have to tear myself away from the family each time I had to fly off for engagements. Often, for the first five minutes sitting on the plane, tears would be streaming down my face at leaving my husband and babies behind, sometimes when the children were only five days old. Your body cries out for that baby when you've just given birth and the separation was torture. But then I would snap myself out of my depression and remember how lucky I was. After all, I loved singing and I had chosen this career. I would just carry on. I've never been the moaning type.

My major indulgence was to call home every day. Eugene and I lived on the phone. I always talked to each of the children as well, trying to give them the time they needed. But, as I was to discover, Paula for one never felt she got enough of me. Once, I was talking to Eugene from New York and I said, "I'm not feeling very well. I think I'm pregnant." Suddenly, over the line, we heard this high-pitched squeal of delight. That's how we found out that for years Paula had been listening in on our calls.

When we had first moved back to Montreal in 1957, we naturally had to come up with some explanation for the fact that we had a two-year-old child in tow. We told everybody, including the press, that in fact we had been secretly married in England in 1954 but that we couldn't have a religious wedding until I had converted because Eugene's family would never have approved. It became part of our family lore and the children never questioned it. Now, whenever Paula looks back on those days when she used to listen in on most of our calls and thumb through all our mail, hungry for more information about her absent Mom, she finds it hard to believe that she never once suspected the truth about how her life began.

NINETEEN

Under the Baton

EARLY IN my career, Seymour Solomon, the head of Vanguard Records, asked me to record Mahler's *Das Knaben Wunderhorn* (The Magic Horn of Youth) in Vienna, where studios had become all the rage because union costs were so much cheaper than in New York. To get there then, you had to change planes in Frankfurt and in those days the Frankfurt airport was a disaster. I was whiling away my four-hour lay-over when suddenly I noticed a commotion on the staircase. First-aid attendants with stretchers came running. It turned out that an elderly man had fallen down the marble steps and was lying in a pool of blood. Later, when I boarded the flight to Vienna, I noticed that they wheeled him onto the plane, swathed in bandages.

I had never been to Vienna before and when we landed, no one came to meet me. I thought it was strange. Then I heard a voice paging Felix Prohaska, the conductor I was to record with. Next I heard my own name paged over the loudspeaker. When I went to the phone, Solomon was on the line. "Sorry we couldn't get out to meet you, sweetheart," he said in his New York accent. "We're in the middle of a session. Say, you didn't happen to see Felix Prohaska on the plane by any chance?"

"Well, I sure hope he wasn't the guy on my flight who was wheeled out of here in bandages," I joked.

"Uh-oh," Solomon said. "I'll get back to you when you get to the hotel."

Sure enough, it had been Prohaska; as I found out later, he was famous for being accident-prone. He wasn't in great shape for days afterward, but at least his conducting arm was intact. While he was recuperating, I went to rehearse with him at his house, which had once belonged to Johann Strauss. He asked where I was from.

"Canada," I said.

"Canada," he mused. "I once knew a fellow student in Vienna from Canada. A young violinist . . . now what was his name: Nash? Dash?"

"Kash?" I ventured.

"That's it! Do you know him?"

"Know him?" I said. "I'm the mother of his children."

"Mama!" Prohaska yelled for his wife. "We've got a friend of the family here. Bring out the photo album and the schnapps!"

Felix Prohaska was just one marvellous example of that curious, awesome breed of men I've spent so much time with in my career: conductors. When I was starting out, I really didn't realize the full extent of my incredible luck to have worked with so many of the legendary maestros. Just a few years after I had been discovered by Bruno Walter, a journalist asked me how many conductors I'd sung with and I guessed about fifty. But my mother, who kept track of reviews and programs, counted them, and she corrected me: I had worked with 200. I hate to think what the number would be now – more like 2,000.

One of the reasons so many opportunities came my way was that there were so few altos around. As soon as I had scored a success with Bruno Walter, every conductor wanted to book me as his soloist and, in the four-year period after that, I sang twenty-four times with the New York Philharmonic alone under various batons.

One of the first conductors I worked with was Igor Markevitch – "le prince Igor," as orchestras used to call him because he claimed royal Russian blood. I originally sang Brahms's *Alto Rhapsody* with him at the Empire State Music Festival, but later we worked together often when he became chief conductor of the Montreal Symphony. He was a very colourful character, very old-worldly, a tiny elegant bird of a man in his forties. At one performance in Montreal, I was pregnant, and to hide the fact I wore a clever green velvet dress designed with a big shawl collar and a train. The soloist always walks out on stage ahead of the conductor and as I was sailing on ahead, I thought my dress felt a little heavier than usual. Igor Markevitch had accidentally stepped on the train and he was being dragged along in my wake, as if he were riding a magic carpet. The audience was in stitches.

The first time Eugene Ormandy asked me to sing with him was for a performance of Bach's *Christmas Oratorio*. This was a big engagement for me: to work with the mighty Philadelphia Orchestra and the great Eugene Ormandy. I was living in Connecticut at the time and had just come in from having an impacted wisdom tooth removed, with two stitches in my jaw, when I called Philadelphia to confirm that the rehearsal was the next day. "Tomorrow? Are you kidding?" the orchestra manager said. "It's today." Then Ormandy himself got on the line.

"Where are you?" he asked. When he heard I was in Connecticut, he sounded exasperated. "Oh, you singers are all alike," he said. "Undependable. You'll never get here in time for rehearsal."

I jumped in the car and drove like a maniac through New York and down the New Jersey Turnpike at top speed. I pulled up to the hall and raced inside just as he was picking up the baton for my aria. "Ta dum," I sang from the wings and strode on stage. He never got over that.

Ormandy had never heard me sing before but I must have turned him on that time. At the end of the rehearsal, he grabbed my hand, pulled me after him to his dressing room and proceeded to change his clothes, dropping his trousers right in front of me. When he saw the startled look on my face, he said, "This shouldn't upset you. You're a married woman, aren't you?" I thought it was a bit odd, but Ormandy was a darling. Although he had a very tall ego, he was a tiny dapper man with a lame leg. I certainly wasn't worried about him making advances. If I had sat on his knee, he would have collapsed.

"My dear," he said afterward, "you must be exhausted from racing here today. Now I want you to go to a hotel and get some sleep and we'll rehearse again tomorrow at 10 a.m. Have a good rest."

"Of course, Maestro, thank you for your patience," I said. Then I went out and got in the car and drove back to Connecticut because I didn't have a stitch of luggage with me. The next morning I got up at 5 a.m. and made the same harrowing drive all over again.

After the performance, Ormandy asked if I knew a modern piece by Bartók called *Bluebeard's Castle*. When I said I didn't, he suggested I look at the score because he wanted me to sing it with him to open the next year's season. This was quite a compliment. I bought the music and studied it very carefully. It was the sort of piece in which women are sighing behind doors, waiting to be murdered – very melodramatic. Later, I went back to him and said, "Mr. Ormandy, I can sing every note in that piece but I don't think you'd be pleased with how it would sound. It would be the first time I've sung the work, and for the opening of the Philadelphia season, which is such a critical event, I think you need someone who has had more experience with Bartók."

He couldn't believe that I would turn down such an opportunity but he respected me for the reasons that I gave. "You know, that is a very noble thing for a young person to say," he told me, "and I'll remember you for that." And in fact, he was as good as his word. For years, Ormandy engaged me every season.

When I first auditioned with Bruno Walter, he told me that I sang too intimately. It came from doing so much radio work; I was used to singing for myself. He suggested I ought to learn the Verdi *Requiem* to bring my voice out. But I told him that I didn't think I was the Verdi type. "Young lady, you'll live to regret that remark," he smiled and, as usual, he was right. The Verdi *Requiem* has become one of my mainstays, as thrilling to sing as any opera.

The first time I sang it was the most thrilling of all – with Sir Malcolm Sargent as part of the summer Proms series in London's Royal Albert Hall. Singing in that enormous space, where they take the 10,000 seats out in summer so even more people can crowd in, and looking at that sea of faces, I sensed what I imagine rock stars must experience performing in a jammed football stadium.

Sir Malcolm was a dear man – a little pompous and vain and conscious of being Sir Malcolm – but a delight to sing with. I had a real soft spot in my heart for him and we worked together again in Norway shortly before he died in 1967, doing his famous arrangement of Brahms's *Four Serious Songs*. On the way back from that concert, flying through Shannon Airport, he introduced me to Irish coffee and I don't remember a thing about the rest of the trip. Oblivion!

"Flash Harry" was Sir Malcolm's nickname, even with the public, because he dressed like a dandy in perfect pinstriped suits with a red carnation in the buttonhole, rather like Pierre Trudeau. After a concert, he refused to see people backstage until he had changed out of his perspiration-soaked tails. He was very fastidious. Following that first *Requiem* at Albert Hall, a lot of people had come backstage for autographs from the Dutch soprano Gré Brouwenstijn, Jon Vickers and me, and after a while the crowd had thinned. Finally, Sir Malcolm decided he was ready and he said to his valet, "Alright, you can let them in now in threes." "Oh, I'm sorry, Sir Malcolm," the valet said, "there are only two people left outside."

Another performance of the Verdi *Requiem* was also unforgettable. Alfred Wallenstein, who had been a great cellist, was conducting it in the open air in Lewisohn Stadium, an enormous football field near Jones Beach on Long Island on a hot summer night. It was the first time I'd sung the piece in New York and it had a star-studded cast: the tenor was Kurt Baum, who had been with the Met for years, the bass was Nicola Moscona and the soprano was Eleanor Steber, one of the two great soprano voices of America, along with Eileen Farrell, until Leontyne Price came along. Eleanor Steber was a real diva. At the first rehearsal, which was on an oppressively humid day in New York, she walked into the studio in an orange décolleté dress, a panama hat with matching orange ribbon and little white gloves. At a rehearsal, of course, you have to follow the score, but I could only assume she'd been gardening and wrecked her manicure, because she wouldn't take her gloves off. I kept having to lick my finger and turn her pages for her so that we could continue. That ought to have warned me.

The night of the performance I made the terrible mistake of wearing the dress I had worn for my Town Hall debut, the black Grecian wrapped number, and she turned up in a dark green gown which was virtually the same style. Well, she couldn't have that. She disappeared back into her dressing room and came out wearing a white mink stole as big as the Ritz, and she kept it on during the entire performance on that sweltering summer night.

Lewisohn Stadium is vast and the sound engineer had arranged for two microphones, one for the two men, and one for the two women, but when we arrived and tested the system, I noticed that Eleanor Steber kept turning the mike toward her own golden throat. These days that wouldn't be a problem: I could probably out-sing anybody with sheer volume because I'm accustomed to projecting my voice, but when I was younger I still sang in a very controlled way all the time – always perfect, pear-shaped tones. And was I naïve about other performers!

As the concert got underway, I noticed that Eleanor Steber would wedge her foot slightly in front of mine beneath my gown so that I was thrown off balance. I would have to lean away from her to get my footing, which left me off-mike. It's an opera tactic, but never having sung much opera, I was caught completely off guard. At intermission Nicola Moscona beckoned me aside. "Darling," he advised, "be a rock of Gibraltar. Refuse to budge." André Mertens, who could see the whole thing happening from the audience, came storming backstage in a fury. "We have to do something about this woman," he fumed. "No," I said. "I don't want to play her game. Let's wait and see what happens."

In the Verdi *Requiem*, the alto part is enormous – as much as ninety per cent of the piece – but the whole drama of the last seven minutes comes from the soprano and chorus. If the soprano is great, by the time she's finished, the audience has completely forgotten the alto. Of course, Steber had an outstanding voice, so I was resigned to that. That stifling night had been an unusually quiet one for New York, almost eerily quiet. But the minute Steber opened her mouth to sing her final aria, "Libera me," a plane roared overhead. A few seconds later, fire engine sirens screamed by the stadium and seemed to be circling the block. More planes and more sirens followed. All through her solo, there was an incredible cacophony that went on and on. It ruined her part. I sat there looking up at the sky, saying to myself, "Well, Lord, you do take care of those who misbehave."

Conductors come in all shapes and sizes and personalities, but there is more often than not one common denominator – the health of the ego. But who can blame them? What they do is a little like playing God – taking all the disparate elements of sound and combining them to create something transcendent. Even for the greatest of them the task isn't easy.

I once watched Szell nearly done in by an Italian orchestra at La Scala. Italian orchestras, like French ones, often behave at rehearsal like rebellious schoolboys. They kibitz, they lounge about and they don't make much effort to play, although they always shape up for the actual performance. For a guest conductor, it can be nerve-racking, especially for one as demanding as Szell. He got more and more furious during the rehearsal, particularly with the cellist, who seemed to be the ringleader. "You know," Szell finally announced, "I don't have to stay. I can catch the next plane home." The cellist just gave one of those inimitable nonchalant Italian shrugs. "Be our guest," he said, calling Szell's bluff. Of course, the concert went on.

While Szell was known for his furies, Sir Thomas Beecham had a reputation for capriciousness. When he had come to Montreal in the war years during his stint with the Seattle Symphony, he was giving a summer festival concert out in the suburb of St. Laurent when a locomotive blew its whistle on the railway tracks not far from the church which was used as an auditorium. He stopped conducting and waited for the whole train to chug by before picking up his baton again. People say that even his posture through that pause telegraphed the message: "Barbaric country!"

When he travelled on to Toronto for another engagement, he had an encounter that he loved to relate. Sir Thomas liked his little nip, and on the afternoon of the concert he had slipped into a liquor store where at that time, under Ontario's laws, you had to have a permit to buy a bottle. When the clerk asked him his profession, he replied that he was a conductor. The clerk wrote on the form "TTC" – Toronto Transit Commission. He assumed Sir Thomas drove a streetcar.

Beecham was a short, mischievous man, but he had a powerful presence. Waiting to audition for him the first time, I was standing at the far end of the huge Maida Vale radio studio in London and I had my back to the door. Suddenly I could feel eyes on me with such force that I thought they were boring into my skull. Sir Thomas was the equivalent of half a block away in this enormous room but his eyes could draw a bead on whoever they settled upon. When he looked at you, you turned around.

That audition was for a recording he was scheduled to do of four songs by Delius, the composer he had championed and written a book about. After I had sung for him, he turned to his wife Betty, a pianist, who was with him. "Well, lady," he said, "I don't think we could do any better, do you?" After he had chosen me for the alto voice, I flew back to France where I was then on tour, and learned my part, even though I wasn't mad about the piece. Then halfway through memorizing it, I received a letter from him. He had changed his mind and decided to record Delius's *Songs of Sunset* instead.

When I flew to London for the recording session, Sir Thomas was in a playful mood. The piece called for orchestra, chorus and two soloists, and the huge BBC symphony and choir were all in place. But he decided to begin by rehearsing only the harpsichord and strings. We all had to stand around and wait for hours. This was to be a one-day session, but it was dragging out interminably. Suddenly, with half the piece still left to record, Sir Thomas put down his baton, bowed to the orchestra and the rest of us and said, "Ladies and gentlemen, thank you very much. I'll see you in eighteen months," and walked out.

It turned out that he was famous for never finishing a record. Because of Britain's tax laws, he had to stay out of the country a certain number of months a year and, on that occasion, as on so many others, he claimed that his deadline was up that day and he had to get back to France. But, in fact, he used that excuse as a way of demonstrating his pique with English record companies. His family's fortune had built much of Britain's music industry and sustained it through the war years. But after the war, Sir Thomas found himself increasingly passed over by record companies on the look-out for hot new talent. His way of getting back at them was to hit them where it hurt – in their accounts. He would half-record everything so they could never release it. It seemed an odd way to wreak revenge, but it apparently brought him some satisfaction.

We never did get to finish that session and not long afterward, Sir Thomas died. But eventually a recording of him conducting *Songs of Sunset*, listing me as a soloist, appeared on the market. The critics raved that it was stupendous, but when I listened to it, I was sure that was not Sir Thomas playing, and one thing I had absolutely no doubt about: that was not my voice I was hearing. I can only assume that the record company wanted to recoup its investment and re-did the work with a new cast. Although I could have caused a scandal protesting, it was such a delicate matter that I didn't want to raise a fuss. But the voice which is supposed to be Maureen Forrester's on that record is, I believe, actually that of a young mezzo who was then just starting out in her career. I only hope she got paid, because if it's who I think it is, she ought to have gotten her name on the credits as well: Janet Baker.

Sir John Barbirolli was another British legend I often worked with – a brisk, wizened genius who in his later years always took his teeth out to conduct. The first work I sang with him was an Elgar oratorio called *The Dream of Gerontius*, which I knew from having done it years before with the Elgar choir in Montreal. The British adore it, but North Americans find it a bit tedious. It's a lovely piece, but never-ending. About three-quarters of the way through, you notice that people in the audience are starting to look at their watches. I had a beautiful part, singing Angel to Richard Lewis's Gerontius. All through the rehearsal, every time I would sing a certain word like "dance," Barbirolli would stop and say in his thick Manchester dialect, "It's not *dance*, it's *dahnse*. You are *so* American!" He did it because he loved to provoke me. "I'm not American," I would protest, "I'm Canadian!"

Sir John was known for never going to receptions after concerts. In fact, I discovered later that, while I was putting in my obligatory appearances, he would go back to his apartment-hotel, have a few drinks and then, well past midnight, slip into the kitchen and whip up some marvellous pasta concoction for himself and his wife, Lady Evelyn, a noted oboist. How I would have preferred to be invited to that feast.

Once, however, when we were performing the Verdi *Requiem* in Houston, where he was principal conductor, Sir John made an exception to his after-concert party rule. The reception was being given by the orchestra board at the Petroleum Club and, in self-defence, he asked me to accompany him. I was sitting next to the president of the orchestra, a wealthy oilman, and toying with my food because I'd unwittingly eaten dinner beforehand. As usual, I was trying to make conversation. Sir John was by then quite an old man, at least in his seventies, and he was cutting back on his concerts. "How wonderful that you were able to convince Sir John to come to Houston," I said to the president. "Who else have you invited to conduct this year?" "Honey, I'm the wrong person to ask that question," he drawled. "I don't go to the concerts. I just pay for 'em."

One conductor I sang with many times and felt a special affection for was William Steinberg, a German-born Jew who had been Klemperer's assistant, then had fled to Palestine before the war, finally coming to the United States. He had an unusual style: he conducted in figure-eights which were always slightly ahead of the beat and which took some getting used to. The first thing I sang with him was the Verdi *Requiem* at the Vancouver Festival, together with Lois Marshall, Jon Vickers and George London, the bass-baritone from Montreal who died a few years ago. It was a dream Canadian cast.

Jon and I repeated the Verdi *Requiem* with Steinberg nearly ten years later at Lincoln Center but this time the soprano was Martina Arroyo, a great gregarious spirit who loves to regale people with stories as much as I do. She can party till dawn, which I can't, but then she doesn't get up until afternoon. Once when Martina and I were both singing in San Francisco we kept running into each other at 3 a.m. in a hamburger joint to which we both had become addicted called Hippo. I would be on my way home to bed but Martina would merely be taking a break in her nocturnal schedule. When we sang that Verdi *Requiem* with Steinberg in New York, it was near the end of his life. He had a disease which left his whole body almost petrified and his hands could barely gesture, they were so rigid. It wasn't important for me because I had worked with him so often that I knew what he wanted, but it was very difficult for musicians who weren't used to him.

The last time I sang for Steinberg was at what turned out to be his second to last concert, a performance of *Lied von der Erde* with the Pittsburgh Symphony where he had been musical director for years. When he shuffled on stage, it broke my heart. I had the feeling of seeing some furious creature trapped inside the prison of his own skin. When he played the "Farewell," it was as if you could hear the man weeping from inside. He was dead within months, but I always felt that his body had died long before his spirit.

Oddly, I was never in awe of those great men of music. Maybe that's why I got along so well with them. I never fawned or flattered. But once in the Boston airport waiting for a connection, I spotted Pierre Monteux, a huge warm walrus of a man who was the conductor's conductor, the inspiration for so many young maestros. He had played for Diaghilev's Ballets Russes in Paris and was the conductor for the debut of Stravinsky's *Rite of Spring* in 1913 when the audiences at the Théâtre des Champs-Élysées rioted over the piece. I had met him once at RCA's offices and he had said something about working together, but I wasn't sure that he would remember me. I couldn't resist going over to speak to him. "Oh, Maestro, I just wanted to say hello and tell you how much I admire your work. We met at RCA Victor. I'm a singer."

Pierre Monteux glanced up at me. "You know," he said, "you look like a singer."

I never did get to work with him; soon after that he died. But I was asked to sing at his memorial concert at Carnegie Hall in 1964. It was an engagement with the London Symphony that Monteux was originally supposed to have conducted himself, but when he died all his friends decided to use it as an opportunity to honour him. The concert was the hottest ticket in New York at the time because it featured such an amazing collection of talent. Pablo Casals flew in from Hungary to conduct one of the *Brandenburg Concertos* and Rudolf Serkin and Isaac Stern played the piano and violin solos. Leopold Stokowski led Beethoven's *Fantasy in C Minor* with Serkin and I sang the "Erbarme Dich" aria from the *St. Matthew Passion* with Casals at the baton and Isaac doing the violin obbligato. What a night! Even the audience was star-studded: among those in front-row seats were Aaron Copland, Eugene Istomin and Emil Gilels.

That evening someone told a wonderful story about Monteux. One day when he was on tour in the Deep South with the San Francisco Symphony, which he led, he was very late in stopping for lunch on the road. He told his driver to pull over at a quaint cottage restaurant and the orchestra manager went in to make the arrangements, but the owner didn't want to serve them. It turned out that it was a segregated restaurant, all-black. The orchestra manager finally persuaded the owner that it would be alright; they would take the blame. Nobody would be able to accuse him of anything if the great Pierre Monteux had insisted on eating there. After lunch, as they were leaving, the owner came up to Monteux to apologize for being so difficult at first. "I didn't know you were somebody," he said. "My good man," said Monteux, "*everybody* is somebody."

The only sad thing about working with all these great old men of music when I was still so young was that I watched so many of them die. Most of them were already at the end of their careers by the time I met them and it was like making a last connection with a vanishing era. It wasn't that I struck up everlasting friendships with them. The music world isn't like that. Often our lives brushed only for a moment on stage and then we'd both be gone to our next engagements in the next city. But with the great ones I could always feel the magic. There's no doubt when you're working with genius.

Still, genius shows no matter the age of a person. Seventeen years ago when I arrived in Bologna to do Mahler's *Songs of a Wayfarer*, I called my Italian manager, Emi Erede, in Milan to ask about the performance. She said that the scheduled conductor had fallen ill and that an up-and-coming young Italian was filling in. He was twenty-two. "Twenty-two to do a Mahler work?" I exclaimed, sure that someone so green could never fathom the depths of that rich, emotional cycle.

I went off to rehearsal very sceptical. But I was stunned when I heard the sensitivity and intelligence that this young man brought to the piece. His reading so meshed with mine that it was as if we had been performing it together all of our lives. When I came back to New York from that trip, I raved about him to whoever would listen and called Columbia Artists Management, pleading with them to take him on. But they weren't interested. "We don't need any more talented young Italian protégés," they brushed me off. When I kept insisting, they acted as if I'd gone crazy. But of course we now know who was crazy. That young man has become one of the world's leading conductors and recently we repeated *Lieder eines Fahrenden Gesellen* together in Philadelphia where he is permanent director of one of the great orchestras in America. His name, of course, is Riccardo Muti.

Another young maestro who was a joy to work with from the first was Lorin Maazel. He had been a child wonder on the violin before becoming a conductor and I often wondered if there was something in that experience which made his style so similar to that of another conductor who had been a *Wunderkind* too: George Szell. They were both cool and analytical, with very definite ideas about how a piece ought to be done. I've sung *Kindertotenlieder* often with Maazel and it's very satisfying: it brings back the memory of working with Szell. Perhaps because he was thrown into such a serious world so young and really exploited by managers as a child, Lorin was very aloof and proper when I initially met him. I found him difficult to talk to. One day when I was recording in Vienna, I was walking across the lobby of the Imperial Hotel when I heard a voice behind me calling out in this broad New York accent, "Hey, Forrester, how the hell are you?" I spun around and who should be leaning out of a phone booth but Lorin Maazel. He had a new wife and he'd become a changed person.

As I was beginning my career in the fifties, the new young lion was Leonard Bernstein, who had just been named joint director of the New York Philharmonic with Dimitri Mitropoulos. It was quite an honour to be asked to sing the *Missa Solemnis* with him in New York and I found him great fun to work with. He's very theatrical and warm. He lavishes hugs and kisses on everyone he meets. I've sung with him a number of times since and he's always the same – sensitive, emotional and exuberant. But I can't pretend that I've ever really gotten to know Lenny and I wonder how many people do. He has a façade that's very hard to penetrate. In fact, he's very introverted and, like so many people, he camouflages the anguish that lies inside with all that gregariousness.

Critics detect traces of Mahler in his compositions and Lenny conducts Mahler like nobody else. He plays the last movement of the *Third Symphony* so slowly that sometimes when I listen to him, I'm afraid it's going to come to a full stop. It drives some Mahler aficionados wild because it's so emotional, but it appeals to my sense of melodrama. I find it absolutely gripping. Although I've done the piece with many conductors, I'll never forget the way he conducted it at Robert Kennedy's memorial service. It was so moving, I thought: God, that's what I would like played at my own funeral. Bruno Walter's Mahler was completely different – more lyrical and spiritual, almost mystical. When he picked up the baton, he had an overall vision in mind; he knew exactly where he was going in the piece and how the final notes would sound before he had even started the overture. But Lenny is a conductor who lives in the moment. You have the impression that whatever mood he is in will determine the interpretation of the day. When he's finished a performance, it's as if he has wrung the last drop of blood and guts from that music. With Lenny, it's emotional gangbusters all the time and he can wear you out. Of course, he wears himself out too and he drives himself non-stop. It was one thing when he was a young man, but now I wish he could relax sometimes. He's so emotional that I'm afraid he's going to burn himself out.

Once when I was in Jerusalem for the Israel Festival, Lenny was there rehearsing the Mahler *Third* with another alto. She was a young Israeli with a wonderful voice, but he decided he didn't like the colour of it for some reason and he wanted to replace her. He asked me if I would take on the part. "No," I said, "I could never do that." After all, he had heard her sing, he'd known who he was hiring, and even more important, she was in her home town. "For you, it's only one performance," I said. "But for this girl it could be a question of her future in her own country. It could destroy her. You've got to think of how it could decimate somebody's self-confidence." In the end, he came to agree with me and kept her on.

But once I did step in when he asked. I had been singing with Seiji Ozawa at the Tanglewood Festival, the summer home of the Boston Symphony in Lenox, Massachusetts, and I was barely in the door back home when the phone rang: the Tanglewood management wondered if I would turn around and come back. Lenny was not happy with his alto in the *Missa Solemnis*. This time he wanted to replace two singers, the alto and the soprano, so Phyllis Curtin and I flew in to do it for him.

But sometimes I think conductors should think more carefully before engaging a singer. It's not as if they're getting an unknown commodity: either they've auditioned the artist or they know the voice from records. It doesn't seem fair to me that some conductor who decides on a last-minute whim that he'd like a different colour in a piece can ruin a young singer's career.

Seiji Ozawa, who had been Lenny's assistant at the New York Philharmonic, took the musical world by storm in much the same way that Bernstein had. He was a genuine superstar when he arrived to lead the Toronto Symphony at only thirty – dashing and brilliant with a cryptic, maverick air. He was still working on his English when I first sang with him and we were doing Harry Somers's *Five Songs for Dark Voice*, which Harry had written for me. I would say, "Can I have it like this?" and he would smile and nod, saying, "Ya, ya," and then, when the orchestra started playing, I realized he hadn't understood a word I'd said.

But he's a quick study and within two years his English was excellent. I adored working with him, but some of the Toronto music establishment never did adjust to having an *enfant terrible* in their midst. What irked them most was that Seiji wouldn't dress up after a concert and go to the receptions. When he did show up, it would often be in blue-jeans and sneakers which, in the sixties, made him the darling of the media, but some of the old guard were outraged. The truth was that Seiji never did want to be invited to those receptions and he didn't want to *have* to go. What he really wanted to do after a concert was gather together a gang his own age and go home to play rock music and cook a great Japanese meal.

210 Out of Character

For a while, Seiji was intent on seeming very western-
ized, but in the years since he left Toronto for San Francisco and has married and had children, he has become
more conscious of his Japanese roots. He now lives half
the time in Japan and has insisted that his children be
educated there. Musicians tell me that he has also become
more aloof and demanding, screaming at the orchestra
management when he doesn't like things, which was not at
all his style in the days when he was in Toronto.

Without a doubt, the most unusual conductor I've ever
worked with was a man whose name is virtually unknown.
Several years ago, my manager at the time, Harold Shaw,
called and told me that he had received a bizarre offer. A
millionaire named Gilbert Kaplan who had had a lifelong
dream of conducting the Mahler *Second* had hired the
American Symphony for a closed concert for some of his
banker friends in New York and he wanted me as a soloist.
I thought I had never heard anything so ridiculous in my
life. The Mahler *Second* is one of the most difficult pieces
of music ever written, and I had just finished singing it
with Zubin Mehta and the New York Philharmonic for the
umpteenth time. "I'm not going to do it with some amateur," I said. But Harold kept trying to persuade me.
Kaplan was willing to pay my $10,000 fee and he had
hired the Westminster Choir from Princeton, New Jersey,
the same one I had sung it with that first time I performed
the *Second* with Bruno Walter. "Look," Harold said, "it's
a private concert, the embarrassment will be behind
closed doors, and all your friends, even the Bronfmans,
will be there." But I was adamant. There was no way I
would do it.

In the end, a few critics sneaked into the concert and
they gave Gilbert Kaplan raves. The next year, when he
was on the board of the American Symphony, he decided
to conduct the piece in public as a fund-raiser. Again, he
asked me to sing it; this time he called me himself. Finally,

because it was a benefit for a symphony in trouble, I thought, Well, why not?

It turned out that Gilbert Kaplan was an American who had heard the Mahler *Second* at the age of twenty-four when he sat in on a rehearsal of Stokowski and the American Symphony, and he became obsessed with it. He was a genius who had gone on to found his own New York-based magazine, *Institutional Investor*, which every financial whiz in the world receives. In fact, you don't even subscribe to it, it's sent to you free if they feel you are worthy. He was a millionaire by the time he was thirty and, once he makes up his mind to do something, he throws himself into it totally. His wife Lena is a Swedish beauty and every Christmas they go back to her home in Sweden to spend the holidays with her family. But as Lena tells it, although the Swedes are very careful to speak English to visitors, after a while her family would always forget Gilbert was there and start speaking Swedish among themselves. One Christmas this was going on as usual, everybody nattering away in Swedish around Gilbert, and one brother said, "Well, Gilbert is great, but why in the hell does he wear his hair so long?" And another chimed in, "Yes, and why would a man in his position wear those terrible red socks?" Suddenly Gilbert rose and made a speech – in perfect Swedish. "By the way, if you must know, my dear brother-in-law," he added, "I wear my red socks for the same reason I wear my hair long: because I want to." Well, any man who would spend a year to learn Swedish in secret you can't help but like. It's easy to see that once Gilbert Kaplan had become obsessed with conducting the Mahler *Second*, there was no stopping him, even though he had never conducted in his life.

He played a little piano, but Gilbert played a little piano like I play a little piano: it's the sort of thing I wouldn't want to do in public. But he hired a conductor to teach him to read the score and learn a conductor's movements. Then, whenever he heard that anyone was playing the piece, no matter where in the world, he would hop into his private plane and fly there to sit with him for hours discussing it. I had heard of him wherever I sang in Europe. It certainly took a lot of chutzpah on his part.

The concert with the American Orchestra in New York was sold out. It was a gala evening and the crème de la crème of New York was there. For me, the performance was a revelation, not an embarrassment at all. Gilbert not only conducted the *Second*, he did it from memory, and the *Resurrection Symphony* is an hour and twenty minutes long. At times, his rendering of it was quite moving. In fact, the performance was awe-inspiring in its own way because it made you wonder whether anyone with intelligence and determination could conduct whatever work he set his mind to. I sang the *Second* with him again in December 1984 when he did it with the London Symphony. And again, every move he made was right. He knows every recording of that piece which has ever been done and he has succeeded in achieving a homogenized sound which reflects them all. He's conducted it with other orchestras since, and I always have the feeling watching him that he is like a fine-honed instrument, almost like a computer. He knows all the notes and there is nothing left out, but if you look at his face while he's conducting, you see that every movement is calculated. He's not simply living and breathing the music. And that is what makes all the difference.

Still, it was more of a pleasure to work with Gilbert Kaplan than with a few of the young conductors I've occasionally run into. Sometimes I arrive in a small town with a bright, bushy-tailed young maestro who thinks he knows all the answers. Nobody can tell him anything. And I sit listening to the tempo, which is way off, and an interpretation that I frankly consider outlandish, and I have to bite my tongue. The conductor is always the boss. But though I often think that to have started my career with geniuses like Bruno Walter and Fritz Reiner and

George Szell was a blessing, it was also in a way a curse. Having begun with the greatest conductors of the century has left me with no patience now for the young know-it-alls.

While I always like to say that I was never star-struck by the great names in conducting, I have to admit there was one who did dazzle me. Two years after I had been discovered by Bruno Walter, André Mertens called with a booking which thrilled me: to sing the alto aria in the American première of Prokofiev's *Alexander Nevsky* at the 1959 Empire State Music Festival with Leopold Stokowski. It was a special honour because Stokowski prided himself on having introduced the work to U.S. audiences over NBC radio during the war. Because it was the first time I had ever sung in Russian, I went to a language teacher in Montreal who used to give lessons to the diplomatic corps. To sing in Russian, the voice comes from two inches deeper and two inches farther out – or at least, that's how I visualize it.

When I got to New York, I was excited about the prospect of my first piano rehearsal: it was to be at Stokowski's apartment on Fifth Avenue. When I arrived, I thought at first that a woman had answered the door. The person standing there had a halo of the wildest curly white hair erupting around the head. But it was the maestro himself.

He was married to Gloria Vanderbilt at the time, so of course the apartment was palatial. There seemed to be photographs of his children and the great moments of his life studding every surface, but neither Gloria nor the children were in sight. Stokowski played the grand piano himself for our rehearsal and we got along very well. He seemed happy with my interpretation, but every once in a while, he would stop and say, "Very good, but now . . . more . . . more Russian!"

The next day we all drove up through the Hudson River Valley to Bear Mountain, the festival site. The composer Heitor Villa-Lobos, who had a work being played at the concert, was there. He was short, heavy-set and very Hispanic-looking under a wide-brimmed fedora which gave him the air of an aged Brazilian gaucho. He was very old and looking quite frail in Bear Mountain's draining humidity. Villa-Lobos motioned me over to the bench where he was sitting by a fountain and told me he had heard me sing. "And now you must do my one-act opera," he said. "It would be perfect for your voice." He never gave me the title and at the time I was too excited to be singing with Stokowski to think to ask, but later I could have kicked myself for not getting the name of that opera from him, because within months Villa-Lobos died. I've never been able to locate it, and most musicians haven't even heard of such a piece. I was so casual about the opportunities coming my way in those days.

When Stokowski was ready for me to rehearse, I left Villa-Lobos and joined the orchestra on the outdoor stage. He was a very dramatic conductor; every gesture he made had flair and he used to have his orchestras sit in a very unorthodox way – all the brass on one side and all the strings on the other – to get the sound he wanted. Some purists were absolutely appalled at that and dismissed Stokowski as a mere showman.

My part in *Alexander Nevsky* was a stunning aria about Mother Russia searching for her child among the dead on the battlefield – a very moving, tragic piece. I was sitting beside Stokowski in front of the orchestra during that rehearsal when suddenly I started to smile. He stopped. "Why are you smiling?" he asked, puzzled and a little miffed.

"Maestro, I've just realized that my fantasies have come true," I said. "Ever since I saw *One Hundred Men and a Girl* as a child, I've dreamed of sitting here singing with Leopold Stokowski and a symphony orchestra."

TWENTY

On the Road

ON TOUR WITH the Bordeaux Orchestra for a series of concerts in France, I suddenly realized half an hour out on the autoroute that I had forgotten the special bra for my low-backed gown. Now, I cannot sing without a bra; there is a *lot* of fall-out. At every little provincial town we came to, the driver of the VIP Peugeot, who was chauffeuring the conductor Roberto Benzi and me, stopped so I could run into the local lingerie shop. But the salesclerks just rolled their eyes when I told them my size. "Oh, Madame," they said, "you have to go to Germany for that." Finally, in desperation, I found a yard goods store and bought a metre of fabric and elastic. I stitched, glued and knotted myself into this self-designed contraption. It worked so well that after the concert they had to cut me out of it. That's the glamorous life of a singer on the road!

Once when I forgot the entire bodice of a dress, Lois Marshall had to wrap me in one of her long silk scarves for a performance. Improvise, I always say. I'll never forget the shock of a portrait painter who was seated next to me at the wedding of the daughter of my friends Jackie and Paul Desmarais at Montreal's Museum of Fine Arts. The painter mentioned that her sandals kept falling off, so while we were waiting for the bride to arrive, I persuaded her to take them off and give them to me. She was speechless as I took a pair of scissors out of my purse and fixed her shoes right there during the ceremony. But on the road you learn that you have to be prepared for any emergency.

For the past thirty years, ninety per cent of my existence has been spent on tour. Musicians are a company of vagabonds; if we want to work, we have to keep on the move. It can be a very solitary life. That's why some artists hire a retinue to follow them everywhere; they can't stand the loneliness. But I've never had a companion besides my accompanist and when I'm singing with orchestras, I'm always travelling solo. I don't even have anyone to make my plane and hotel arrangements because I find that I'm better at it and quicker to figure out the connections than any travel agent.

Musicians don't even see much of one another on the road – just a night playing here or there and then it's on to the next engagement, the next town. But a closeness develops, a kind of fraternity. A few years ago when I was performing *The Medium* in Toronto, I arrived at the Mac-Millan Theatre one night and the manager said, "Oh, Rudolf Serkin was playing here last week and he left you a note." "Sorry I didn't get to kiss you in person, sweetheart. I wish you well," it read. And what had he written it on? Toilet paper!

Serkin was one of the kindest men on this earth. I once sang at his Marlborough Festival in Vermont. After we had finished Brahms's *Two Songs for Contralto with Viola and Piano*, he came up to me at intermission and apologized that his wife Irene and his daughter Judy hadn't come backstage to tell me how much they had liked our performance. "Why should you apologize?" I asked. "Because they were so moved, they ran off into the woods to cry," he said. From a lot of people, that would sound like so much public relations, but from the Serkins you believed it. They were that kind of people.

My most delightful recollection of Serkin comes from a concert in which I wasn't even singing with him. I was sitting in the audience at the opening night of the festival in Saratoga, the summer home of the Philadelphia Orchestra, where I was to perform the following evening. Serkin was playing a Beethoven concerto with Eugene Ormandy and the orchestra, and in the second movement, a power failure put out the lights. Serkin and the orchestra played on beautifully in the dark. When the lights came up again, Ormandy was overheard muttering, "I always knew they didn't need me."

Life on the road breeds so many crazy stories. In the first years after he had signed me, André Mertens booked me into recital tours all over the United States, which Columbia Artists Management arranged in a series called Community Concerts. For musicians who hadn't had the benefit of a tour such as the one I had done with Jeunesses Musicales, it provided experience and exposure. One of the first concerts was in Vernal, Utah, a town where they extract oil out of the sand. A committee met John Newmark and me at the airport, and in the car on the way to the hotel, John asked them if they had arranged for a page-turner as he had requested. "Oh yes," they assured him, "we've found a wonderful little girl who plays the violin." She came to rehearsal and sat beside John on the piano bench. He explained to her that whenever he nodded, she should stand up and then when he nodded a second time, it was the moment to turn the page.

The night of the concert she was very nervous. She arrived wearing a little dress with a skirt which was stiff like a tutu and when she sat down on the bench beside John, the net stuck straight out and covered the lower end of the keyboard. From the audience it looked a little obscene as John, who is so proper, groped for the bass notes. Finally the moment came for her to get up and turn the first page. John smiled at her and nodded and she just smiled back. He nodded again but she just sat there smiling at him the whole time. She never turned a page during the entire concert.

Later that night there was a reception at a local hotel. As I was walking in, a man dressed in a lumberjack's shirt was coming out. "Are you the singer?" he demanded. I admitted I was. "Well, honey," he smacked me on the back, "I've never been to a concert before, but I tell you, if I never go to another, I sure got my money's worth tonight."

We went on to El Paso, Texas, where the local impresario was a fascinating character called Ma Short. She was eighty-nine years old and she lived on the top floor of what used to be the Hilton Hotel, smoking stogies in a room that was piled so high with newspapers it was a firetrap. When I met her, I was curious about this business that I was starting out in and I asked her what had made her engage me.

"Sweetheart," she drawled, taking the cigar out of her mouth, "I read *The New York Times* every day of my life and anything that's good enough for New York City is good enough for El Paso."

One minute I would be booked into a Community Concert in El Paso, the next into a grand concert hall in Italy. My first recital in Milan seemed to be dying on its feet. I was singing my heart out but all the women in the audience were just sitting there in their hats and gloves, stone-faced, offering the most tepid applause. At intermission I said to my accompanist, an American named Donald Nold, "My God, this is a disaster." Just then a little old man came backstage, oohing and aahing over me. He introduced himself as a professor of voice at the conservatory. He could see that, despite his praise, I was upset. "Ah, Signora," he said. "I can tell that you think the old ladies out in the audience don't like you. But don't worry about them, they don't know what they like. They come to me at the intermission of every concert and ask me whether it's good. This time I told them it's magnificent. You'll notice a difference in the reception now." In the second half, sure enough, they gave me bravos and standing ovations.

In Italy, they often have an annoying practice of paying singers at intermission. There you are, stuck with either trying to hide your next month's bread and butter in your dressing room while you go out and sing the second half, or stuffing the cash into your girdle, hoping the audience won't notice the bulge. In a country where the lira is so badly devalued and the bills are so big, it's no wonder that you see singers wearing gowns which are looser and looser.

Once I was doing the *Missa Solemnis* with Hermann Scherchen in the cathedral at Monreale, a historic Sicilian town outside Palermo, and there had been a full house. They hadn't paid me at intermission as usual. Afterward, I gathered up my things and was leaving by the side door to be driven back to my hotel when this little character walked up to me in a pinstriped suit and an Al Capone hat pulled over one eye, a big cigar dangling out of his mouth. "Forrestieri?" he said.

"*Si*," I replied warily, just in case anybody was thinking about a kidnapping.

"*Vieni qui*," he beckoned me to the bumper of a car outside the door. And standing there, with the audience still streaming out all around us, he started peeling off lira notes from a huge bundle and handing them over to me.

I was incensed and when I got back to my hotel, I called my Italian manager in Milan. "Emi, you will not believe the rudeness of what has just happened to me. I was paid over the bumper of a car in the street like some hooker."

There was silence on the other end of the line. "But you got paid, darling?" she said anxiously.

"Oh, yes, of course," I said, "that's not the point."

"Darling," she said, "be grateful. You don't know how lucky you are."

Getting to a concert has always been half the battle. One winter when I was still living in Montreal, I was booked to give a recital in Boston. But the night before, a blizzard hit the East Coast and the authorities closed Dorval Airport. I couldn't take the chance that it would stay closed the next day so John Newmark and I jumped into the car and drove almost all night through a snowstorm which had grounded even trains. When we pulled up at Jordan Hall for the concert, we were only fifteen minutes late. On another occasion, my plane was fogged in at the Pittsburgh airport and in order to get to a concert in Toronto's St. Lawrence Centre, I rented a private jet. It ended up costing me more than my recital fee.

I sometimes feel I spend half my life in the air and I've been in countless near-misses. Once, when I was pregnant with Gina, John and I were on our way from Montreal to Toronto where we had to make a connection to Rapid City, South Dakota, for a concert. Suddenly I realized that the plane had been circling for some time. Eventually the pilot's voice came over the intercom. "Now, don't worry, folks," he said. "We're having a little problem – we've put the landing gear down and only one wheel has dropped – but we're going to circle over Lake Ontario and try to use up most of our fuel to get rid of some weight." Most of the passengers went into a panic, but for some reason I wasn't scared. All I was worried about was missing our connection to perform that night. I put on the new mink I had just bought for padding and the stewardesses piled cushions around us, but when they asked us to bend over and put our heads down for landing, I got a case of the giggles. I was eight and a half months pregnant and, believe me, nothing would bend. I put my head down and said to John, who was white, "See you later, alligator," a note of levity he did not appreciate at all.

Below, rescue crews were standing by along with ambulances and fire engines and they had sprayed the runway with anti-inflammable foam. But in fact when we came down, the single wheel broke off and we belly-flopped without crashing. When the doors opened, we could step right off the plane onto the tarmac without needing stairs. Everybody was shaken but my only concern was that my new mink had gotten covered in the sticky white runway foam. The press converged on us and I begged them not to report that I was on the plane until the next morning. "I don't want to upset my husband," I said. "He's got a violin concert to play tonight."

Perugia, Pittsburgh, Vienna, Vancouver, Warsaw and Walla-Walla. Often it was a blur of boarding passes to me. The only way I can figure out when anything in my past occurred is to calculate which of my children I was pregnant with at the time. Sometimes the constant movement made me a little crazy. Once when I had sung with the Concertgebouw Orchestra in Amsterdam, I found out I had three days off before the next performance. It had been raining wherever I went in Europe for what seemed like months. I went down to the concierge of the hotel and asked where the sun was shining within an hour's flight from there. He checked the weather reports. "Copenhagen," he said. "Book me a flight," I told him. I discovered Copenhagen and Georg Jensen silver both on that trip. The year must have been 1961 because I was pregnant with Linda at the time.

Every spring for years I sang at the Vienna Festival and at the same time recorded Handel's operas for the Westminster label there. The first year we did *Rodelinda*, then later *Xerxes, Theodora* and *Hercules*, which I sang with Louis Quilico. They were operas and oratorios that were almost never performed, and invariably I ended up singing the male roles: Bertarido, the decadent king in *Rodelinda*, or Xerxes himself. When I went there, I always stayed at the Imperial Hotel, the city's finest. I was a firm believer in indulging myself on the road. Eugene always said that if you couldn't live better on tour than you did at home then you shouldn't be making the trip. In the Imperial's coffee shop there was an old, sad-eyed waiter who would remember me every year. *"Frau Kammersängerin,"* he called me – Madame Chamber Singer – the highest honour a singer can win in Vienna, where they love titles. This waiter would never let me order a thing from the menu. "You will have *Suppe*," he would say.

"Oh, is the soup good tonight?" I would ask.

"Singers should have soup," he would say. "And next you will have the wiener schnitzel."

One evening when they had finished recording my part of the recitative in *Hercules* early, I found myself with an unexpected night off. I was in the mood for a reward for good behaviour so I dressed up in my best, donned a fur stole and went off to the opera, only to find out that even standing room had been sold out. Instead, I decided that for a change I would have dinner at the poshest dining room of the hotel. It was almost empty because everyone was at the Opera House, but when I got to the door, this incredibly haughty maître d'hôtel swore that every table was reserved. He had clearly taken one look at me and decided I was a boring North American tourist. But I insisted on being seated, and finally he put me at a table, the worst in the room. I hate airs in anyone and in my experience all the greatest people have always been the most unaffected. I was so furious with this man that I decided to teach him a lesson about pre-judging his clientele. I ordered caviar with vodka, but told the waiter to bring me the whole tin of caviar and the whole bottle of iced vodka, so I could sample as much as I wanted – money was no object. Then I ordered pheasant under glass with a Château Mouton-Rothschild and finished off with Sachertorte. I mean, if this lesson was going to cost me, at least I wasn't going to suffer. By the time I had finished, the entire staff was falling all over me, but especially the maître d'. As I swept out after overtipping everybody, he said, "Ah, and will we be seeing you again tomorrow night, *Hoheit*?" which translates literally as "Your Highness."

"No," I sniffed, "I didn't care for it very much, thank you." The next evening I went back to my expert on singers' nutrition at the coffee shop.

Vienna is a wonderful town to visit, but I would never have liked to live in that city where so many great musicians flourished. For foreign singers coming there to work, it can be a cut-throat town. There are horrendous stories about what has happened to visiting stars at the Vienna State Opera House. I never sang there myself, but, according to friends of mine, the Viennese would flatter them to their faces and then stab them in the back. Once I flew into the city, did a concert and flew out again without the impresario as much as sending anyone to greet me or to see if I needed anything. I couldn't believe the rudeness.

Still, going there as a tourist I loved the art museums, which I try to visit in whatever city I find myself. It gets me out of my hotel room, where I can sometimes go mad with nothing to do but stare at the four walls or the television set. Hotel rooms and more hotel rooms. Sometimes that seems to be all I see for months on end. The first thing I do when I check into a hotel is to go out and buy flowers. If I'm in a city long or doing an opera, like most musicians I usually rent one of those apartment-hotel efficiency units which have to be the most depressingly decorated places in the world, next to a prison cell. The furniture is inevitably plastic, the glasses are old jam jars and the dishes are Melmac. I end up going out and buying cushions and posters and a coffeemaker and a little Teflon pan to make it feel more homey. Before I know it, I've got a whole trunk of housewares and the world's largest collection of travelling Teflon.

But I'm not as domestic on the road as some singers I know. The soprano Evelyn Lear and her husband Thomas Stewart, the bass-baritone, never go anywhere without one suitcase which holds their portable kitchen. And bass-baritone Paul Plishka, who is a wonderful cook, has his wife accompany him to wherever he's booked to sing for a long run. They cram their car to the roof with a Cuisinart, a coffee grinder, a coffeemaker, electric frypans, kettles, knives and who knows what else. It's the nesting instinct that takes over, even in this company of gypsies. When Lois Marshall was on the road, she spent a lot of time in her room, because her lameness made it awkward for her to get out. I never asked what kind of housekeeping utensils she had packed in her suitcases, but when we travelled together in the Bach Aria Group, I don't know how many times I put out my back carrying her luggage in from the parking lot.

The Bach Aria Group was quite a travelling group itself. It had been created by a wealthy American musicologist from Princeton named William Scheide, who had dedicated his life to popularizing Bach. His idea was to select arias, duets and quartets from the 215 cantatas Bach wrote so the public could hear them in recital backed by just a chamber quintet instead of the huge choruses written into the opening and closing of the works. The original group consisted of very big stars: Eileen Farrell, Jan Peerce, Norman Farrow, the bass who came from London, Ontario, and Carol Smith, who sang the alto part. But in 1958, when Carol Smith was away in Europe, Scheide asked me to fill in for her. It was a very prestigious invitation.

I had imagined that all these famous singers must be very grand. But as I walked down the hall to my first rehearsal, which was in the studio of pianist Paul Ulanowsky's New York apartment, I could hear a woman's voice saying in a distinct New York twang, "Jesus Christ, this is bloody difficult music."

Scheide was trying to cajole her. "Now, now, as you sing it, just think of your Lord on the cross."

"Hell," she said, "you've had me nailed to the damn thing for years."

That was my introduction to the great Eileen Farrell. She is a terrific, jovial woman with a build not unlike mine. She didn't have an ounce of pretence. Her vocabulary could resemble a sailor's, but somehow on Eileen it sounded hilarious.

Jan Peerce, who had begun life as a violinist under his real name, Pinky Perelmuth, was an absolute sweetheart, like everybody's favourite uncle. He was never a snob, despite his fame and fortune, and he had such a personal voice that every time he sang, he could touch an audience. He had become a star as soon as he recorded "The Bluebird of Happiness" and he used to regale us with tales of his career and singing with Toscanini.

Once in 1960, we did a gala performance of Beethoven's *Ninth* together for the United Nations' fourteenth anniversary, along with Elisabeth Schwarzkopf and Kim Borg, the baritone whose Berlin debut I had heard the night before Paula's birth. Before we walked onto the dais of the General Assembly, the New York Philharmonic manager had instructed us to enter by following the lines painted on the floor. I always walk out on stage with my head high, smiling at the audience, and I completely forgot his directions. I ended up wandering off all by myself at the front of the stage and the audience started to giggle. I turned scarlet but Jan Peerce just leaned over and whispered in my ear, "Some people will do anything for a laugh."

He and his wife Alice often invited Eugene and me to their home in New Rochelle, outside New York City, where they kept a strict kosher household. They weren't the type to make a big point of that fact, but years later when I was in Vienna and I heard they were coming to town, I searched all over to find them a good kosher restaurant. They never forgot that. At the end of his life, Jan Peerce was left with only peripheral vision, so he had to stand sideways on the stage to read the music, but he never turned in a bad performance. He was one star who deserved every ounce of praise he ever won.

Gradually, the Bach Aria Group went through several evolutions and by the time I was invited to join as a full-time member, only Norman Farrow was left of the original quartet. Lois Marshall was by then the soprano, Richard Lewis was the tenor and the quintet was made up of some of the most respected musicians – Ulanowsky on piano, Sam Baron on flute, the famous oboist Robert Bloom (who had been in the NBC orchestra under Toscanini), Oscar Shumsky on violin and Bernard Greenhouse, who was my best pal in the group, playing cello.

We performed about fifteen concerts a year together,

three in New York and the rest on tour, usually at universities. We drove from place to place and Scheide, who felt he was the father of the group, used to want us to travel in wagon-train fashion, one after another. I don't like travelling in groups. I'm a very organized person and I can pick up and be out of anywhere in five minutes once I decide to go. I hated having to cool my heels for hours waiting for other people, so I insisted on driving one of the cars myself. When Scheide handed out his little maps, saying he would lead the way, I just kind of disappeared and took a shortcut, arriving before everyone else. It used to drive him crazy.

But once my independence backfired on me. We had landed in Memphis late one evening and we had to drive from there to the small town where we were to perform. I had four of the musicians in my car and when I saw a police van, I stopped and asked directions to the motel where Scheide had booked us. The instructions the officer gave me seemed to lead us on a circuitous route, and when we finally got there, I understood why. The policeman was waiting in the lobby, all set to arrest me. He thought I was a hooker on a spree with my four customers.

The music we did was exciting to perform because it was so difficult. Bach requires tremendous discipline. Brahms can be a balm for the voice, but Bach wrote for it as if it were an instrument. He gives you very little time to breathe and there's no way you can fake those cantatas. Lois and I sang a duet from one, Cantata No. 78 – "We Hasten with Weak but Eager Steps" – which was a tour de force. We usually did it as an encore and it would bring people to their feet, screaming bravos. It was so fast with so little time to breathe that at the end we would be gasping, but obviously having had a great time doing it. The audience loved it because people don't usually think of Bach as fun, but I always said, "Listen, any man who had twenty-six children had to have a sense of humour."

When we sang, people were often surprised by the power in Lois's voice. They would look at this tiny doll-like figure and think how fragile she was, but in fact Lois was as strong as an ox. I once threw a surprise fortieth-birthday party for her in Toronto and when she went to blow out the forty candles on the huge cake, she filled her lungs and blew so hard she drove them right into the bottom layer. We couldn't eat a bite of that birthday cake, which looked as if it had been machine-gunned with wax.

The Bach Aria Group was fun because we were all so gregarious. But when you put nine musicians together, you've got nine temperaments to cope with. And were some of those egos sensitive! People always say singers are difficult, but in my experience, it was the instrumentalists who were more preoccupied with their billings and their place on the program. Sometimes I felt like the group's housemother and after nine years, I got tired of that role. Finally I quit because I also thought we were beginning to sound a bit stale.

My first Australian tour in 1962 was the longest I've ever done – three months away from home. In eleven weeks, I sang thirty-seven concerts, and half of each one was broadcast over their national radio network so the amount of repertoire I had to learn for the trip was staggering. At the reception after every recital, without fail, the organizers would serve an Australian delicacy called a pavlova, a sinfully sweet mountain of three layers of meringue, whipped cream and passion fruit. It must have contained at least 1,000 calories a serving. I loved it the first time I tried it, but after thirty-seven pavlovas, I was ready to give my life for a night free from that brand of passion.

In Sydney, the Opera House was just being built and as a publicity stunt I was asked to pose on the site in a hard hat and to sing a duet with an opera-loving construction worker named Bill McGinley who knew an aria from *Samson and Delilah*.

As a treat for us, the city had also arranged a car to take John Newmark and myself through Sydney's Taronga

Park Zoo. John had just had a very elegant houndstooth suit made for the tour and he was wearing it that day. In the koala park, one of our hosts decided we had to have our photos taken so she shoved a bear into John's arms. They're adorable nocturnal creatures, but with the longest claws you've ever seen, and this one kept digging his talons deeper and deeper into John's new tailoring. Apparently koalas, like camels, don't urinate very frequently, but having been awakened to all the excitement and flashbulbs, John's little friend was convinced that this was the occasion. John felt a large damp patch growing on the front of his jacket and it just reeked from the koala diet of eucalyptus leaves. As soon as we left the zoo, he took the jacket straight to the dry cleaners. "What on earth is it?" the clerk said. Nobody would believe John when he said, "Koala pee."

We were glad of the hilarity because the Cuban Missile Crisis had just exploded. The headlines in Australia were screaming with the threat of apocalypse. I panicked, afraid that a war would break out and I would be separated from the children. I vowed never to be away for so long again.

On the road, you feel so helpless when things are happening to the people you love back home. Ever since he had returned from the war, my brother Arnold had been battling for serenity – and sobriety. During his depressions and drinking bouts, he had driven over a cliff twice in a truck and had separated from his wife Nan and their two children several times. A priest in Trois-Rivières had taken him in hand for a while and straightened him out, but Arnold started drinking again. His life had become such a tortured one, in and out of psychiatric clinics and hospitals. I always thought his wife Nan was such a strong, solid woman to have tolerated a husband who was loving, but a misfit somehow. All his life Arnold had been too sweet, too sensitive for the real world.

A few years after my Australian tour, I was in New Zealand rehearsing the Verdi *Requiem* when the concert house manager handed me a telegram: Arnold had died. An overwhelming sadness washed over me as I thought of that wasted life. With the difference in hours, I realized that I couldn't get back to Quebec in time for the funeral, but it seemed curiously appropriate to be singing the *Requiem* that night. I've always felt that the audience doesn't want to know an artist's problems, and I try to keep mine out of my performances, but when I sang that night, the tears in my eyes were as real as the mourning in my voice. People in the audience later said they sensed this was no ordinary concert.

I tried never to accept engagements which would take me away from the family on special occasions, but on one New Year's Eve I made an exception. I had been asked to sing Beethoven's *Ninth Symphony* in Berlin with three of the most famous singers in the world at the time – Ernst Haefliger, Irmgard Seefried and Dietrich Fischer-Dieskau – all of us under the baton of the great Hungarian conductor Ferenc Fricsay. Just as the *Messiah* is a Christmas ritual in most countries, Beethoven's *Ninth* is a New Year's tradition in Berlin.

Between the performances, we went to one party after another. At one of them, we all gathered around a bowl of ice water for another Berlin New Year's ritual. It involved dropping tiny pieces of lead, melted down in a spoon over a candle, into the bowl where the shape they took supposedly predicted a person's future for the coming year. But in casting his fortune, Ernst missed the bowl and dropped molten lead down the front of my leg where it seared right through to what felt like the bone. Some New Year's prediction!

I sang often in Berlin with Fricsay, who had been conductor of the RIAS orchestra since the end of the war. He was a marvellous elegant man in his fifties who had spent many of his recent years in hospital having operation after operation. One day in 1963, he invited me to lunch at the home of his friend Mrs. Fish, an extraordinary, spirited Canadian-born woman who was the last living grandchild of Anna, the tutor to the King of Siam, on whom the musical *The King and I* was based. As the three of us were chatting, Fricsay complained how tired he was. "Ach, I have to go for another operation," he said. "But the trouble is there's nothing left to remove." It seemed he had been right. Not long after that, he died.

On another occasion, I had just finished recording Mahler's five *Rückert-Lieder* with Fricsay and the RIAS orchestra and had flown back to Montreal. I took a taxi from the airport to Roslyn Avenue, where I had bought us our first house, a lovely stone bungalow with a studio over the garage where Eugene could practise and teach violin. As the cab pulled up in front, Teta ran down the walk to greet me, wringing her hands. "Oh, Frau Forrester, Paula is so sick," she said. "I don't know what to do."

I bolted in the door and upstairs to find this little creature lying in bed so emaciated that her skin seemed pulled back taut from her teeth like a cadaver's. She said she wanted to go to the bathroom, so I carried her there. I saw that her urine was brown. I called our pediatrician, Dr. Dick Goldbloom, who told me to meet him at the emergency room right away. Then Eugene and I bundled Paula in a blanket, jumped in a cab and raced to the Montreal Children's Hospital. It turned out that she had caught scarlet fever at nursery school and it had then become infectious hepatitis. As if that weren't enough, she had picked up a case of chicken pox in the hospital and brought it home to all the other children. For a while I was petrified that she might not pull through. But a month later, by the time the danger had passed, I had to fly off again for an engagement. Friends asked why I didn't cancel, but I couldn't tell them that I couldn't afford to. I had to travel to keep our bills paid. I felt so guilty, torn in two at times like that, but thankful at least that I had made it home at such a critical moment.

But the tour that caused me the most anguish was in 1973, when I was in Bordeaux singing Rossini's *Petite Messe Solonnelle* with two Israeli pianists and a chorus.

The French telephone workers were on strike at the time, but my infallible sixth sense told me that something was wrong at home and I kept trying to get a line to Toronto. Finally I went to the Canadian Consulate which put me through on their phones. When Eugene answered, I asked if everything was alright.

"Now, don't get excited," he said, "it's nothing serious. But the doctor says Paula has to have her kidney removed."

Nothing serious! I went into a tailspin. I made him promise that he wouldn't go ahead with an operation until I got home. But when I arrived, the verdict was still the same. One of Paula's kidneys had shrivelled into a useless prune and was infecting the other good one. The surgeon operated before Christmas and by New Year's she was sitting up in a chair. Everything turned out happily in the end.

But at times like those, I was almost ready to curse this profession which had given me a travelling salesman's life. I only thanked my lucky stars that, while I had been agonizing over Paula an ocean away in Bordeaux, I hadn't been scheduled to sing Mahler's *Songs on the Death of Children*.

TWENTY-ONE

Master Class

SINGING is like weight-lifting: you literally heave the sound into place. The muscles you use – sucking in the rear end, expanding the rib cage and swelling out the back to fill the chest cavity with air just like a bellows – often give singers the same inverted-pyramid silhouettes that bodybuilders have. Once when I was backstage at an American arts centre waiting for my part in a concert to begin, two performers from an adjacent auditorium in the complex were also cooling their heels in the same area before the show started. They were big bruisers in bikinis and cave-man skins from the wrestling match next door. We struck up a conversation and it wasn't long before we were discussing each other's professions. The funny thing was that we finally agreed our work came down to the same basics: showmanship and muscle control. We ended up forming a real mutual admiration society and that encounter confirmed a theory that I've often shared with students of mine – that singers are really a breed of athlete.

It's a very physical profession and, if you use all the right muscles, it takes a lot of exertion. After a performance, my hair is often soaked at the back of my neck. I throw off so much body heat that the underarms of my silk gowns eventually get eaten through with perspiration, as if they'd been nibbled by moths. I can lose three pounds during a concert.

Because I believe that much of the secret of vocal technique is physical, it's easy for me to see at a glance what other singers are doing wrong. Some people think that makes me a good teacher and I'm often asked to give a master class wherever I'm singing. I try to do as many as I can, but, in my opinion, I have one major fault, which means I shouldn't finish my career teaching as a lot of singers do: I have no patience for hearing people make the same mistake over and over again.

I had given some master classes which the National Film Board turned into a movie and distributed on several continents. When Joe Castaldo, who was head of the Philadelphia Music Academy, saw the film in 1966, he phoned and asked me to take over his voice department. "Oh, Joe, I'm not really an administrator," I declined diplomatically. "And besides, I have a husband and children. I can't just pick up and move like that." The next thing I knew, Joe had phoned Eugene, offered him a job too, teaching violin, and we were all moving to Philadelphia.

For Eugene, it was perfect timing since his term as manager of the National Youth Orchestra in Toronto was winding down and he already knew Philadelphia from having studied there as a boy. It was also his introduction to teaching, which it seemed he was destined to do; he's a walking encyclopaedia of music and he loves turning young people on to the art which has been his whole life.

Off we went with five children, assorted dogs, cats, gerbils, fourteen tons of books and music and the nanny who had by then replaced Teta. Through an agent, I found an enormous house for rent in Haverford, on Philadelphia's Main Line. We weren't in it long before the owners reclaimed it, but we much preferred the house we promptly moved to around the corner. It was really more like an estate: five acres of land with its own tennis court, swimming pool, a separate coach house by the garage and, surrounding it, vast woods sprinkled with statuary. The backyard alone was literally as big as a football field. From the road, the place looked like the White House.

The main difference was that instead of a portico, it had a huge awning which later became distinguished by a large hole: one day when Gina and Linda had snuck up on the roof for a secret smoke, Gina toppled right through the canvas. It was a miracle she wasn't killed.

In spite of all that external grandeur, however, inside the house was a bit of a wreck. The carpets were stained, the linoleum was rotting and the walls were painted a dun-blue or elephant-grey which was terribly depressing. I tore up the carpeting, laid acres of linoleum by hand and had the whole interior painted a bright, airy off-white. It was a transformation. But four years later when we left Philadelphia, the owners made me pay for what they considered the destruction of their house: they demanded that I re-paint the whole thing that gloomy elephant-grey.

The City of Brotherly Love, people call Philadelphia, but obviously they didn't have our neighbourhood in mind. When I insisted that my children go to a local public school, all our Main Line neighbours refused to talk to us. Actually, we had three strikes against us: first of all, we were Jewish; second, we didn't send our children to private schools; and third, horror of horrors, the children would bring their black friends home from public school. But for our family, those years in Philadelphia were an eye-opening education. The children had a wonderful time and made lasting friends. Daniel joined a choir there which was so good it later toured Europe. And I realized I didn't have to worry about their values, when they quickly made clear that, no matter how rich our neighbours were, they had no time for human beings like that. Some of the people on our street were such snobs that I once got a call inquiring if I wanted to contribute to the Red Cross and when I agreed, asking whether I ought to drop the money off at my neighbour's house, she sniffed, "That won't be necessary. We'll send the maid over for it."

While we were in Philadelphia, I hurt my back and the doctor ordered me to bed for weeks. He said my spine was such a mess that it was a wonder I was still walking around, and he gave me some pain-killers. After swallowing several capsules, I began to feel that I was floating on the ceiling, looking down at my body lying on the bed. I've never taken drugs of any kind and that hallucination absolutely horrified me. I reached over to the bedside table, grabbed that bottle of pills, crawled to the bathroom and flushed them all down the toilet. "I would rather have the pain," I told the doctor. "I will not take a drug that makes me lose control like that."

But it was impossible for me to stay in bed doing nothing. Since I was in agony, and couldn't manage the drive into Philadelphia to teach, I convinced the school to send my pupils out to the house where they could take their lessons and then swim. The Music Academy recruited students from the worst ghetto in the city so its enrolment was at least forty per cent black. The neighbours went into shock when the academy bus pulled into our driveway and disgorged all these black youngsters. They went so far as to call the police, complaining that the bus driver was revving his motor, sending fumes into their houses.

I loved my teaching stint in Philadelphia, but I was conscious that some singers are abysmal teachers. Once Rudolf Bing had asked Zinka Milanov, a great Metropolitan Opera star whose *pianissimo* was one of the most beautiful in the world, if she would come to the Met studio and give the students some special hints. She came up at the intermission of rehearsals for *La Gioconda* which they were also studying at the time. "Alright, all you little Giocondas out there," she purred, and they all leaned forward for her pearls of wisdom. "Look, look, look," she said. "Listen, listen, listen; learn, learn, learn!"

Birgit Nilsson is known for imparting more practical advice. When Lisa Della Casa, a great beauty from Switzerland, was cast in *Tristan und Isolde* for the first time, she went to Nilsson, who had made the role famous, for advice. "Oh my God, darling," Nilsson said, "the most important thing you must remember is to buy a good pair of shoes. The first act is an hour and a half long and you're on your feet the whole time."

In fact, knowing how to stand is one of the secrets of singing. You can't stand with your feet planted together. You have to relax your knees and position yourself as if you're ready to pivot. If you sing in a rigid stance and go to make a big sound, you can fall over backwards. When it came to knowing tricks like that, my years as a student basketball player came in handy.

Unlike some singers, I'm not afraid to pass on to others what I've learned. Once I walked into a *Falstaff* rehearsal at the Met that James Levine was conducting with the Italian mezzo Ebe Stignani and he had to apologize for asking me to leave. She wouldn't allow anyone of her voice category to watch her rehearse, not even her understudies, in case they stole her secrets.

I learned a lot watching the great singers of our time. Rehearsing at the Met, I was fascinated by Nilsson whose voice is the biggest I have ever heard, but it pours out with such deceptive ease that it sounds like liquid steel. Watching her, I realized that while most people sing out, she brings the sound in and rolls it around before releasing it again. It's a brilliant technique which keeps her from ever losing control or running out of breath. Listening to her, I had the impression that she was born with two extra speakers in her body.

The most important thing I feel I can give to students is confidence in their own powers of interpretation. "The notes are on the paper in front of you," I tell them. "There's no great secret to singing them. The secret is to pick them up off the paper and make them come alive. Everyone might not agree with how you go about it, but at least it's *you*, not a carbon copy of some record you've heard. It's your own interpretation which sets you apart from the next singer."

I can tell immediately, from a look in the eyes, if a student understands the words of a song. "You must never sing a piece you can't believe in," I always say. "Every line must mean something to you." I consider it the highest compliment when people come backstage and tell me that I could make the telephone book come to life.

I also tell my classes to treat every performance as if it were the most important concert of their career. I always believe that there is someone sitting in the back row, no matter how modest the hall, who will stay a fan for life if only I can touch that person with my performance. I still have followers today who heard me first at my Town Hall debut thirty years ago and who show up at every concert I give in New York or Washington or Los Angeles; in fact, they're constantly surprising me by waiting at the airport, even when I think I'm arriving unannounced. Some of them are just as faithful to Marilyn Horne or Martina Arroyo; they're almost lifetime fans.

Indeed, you never know who'll be listening. When I first sang for George Szell, I asked him what had prompted him to choose me as his alto. He said that he had been driving outside Boston when he heard a broadcast of me singing *Kindertotenlieder* and he said to himself: that's the voice I want for *Lied von der Erde*. There are no unimportant performances.

On stage, it's important to keep an interested look on your face when you're not singing, even if you've heard the piece a hundred times in the last month. I always try to look engrossed, despite the fact that I'm sometimes sitting there planning a great menu in my head.

When I was younger, I used to close my eyes a lot as I sang to stay in the mood of a piece. But later I realized that was a mistake because I created an impression of singing for myself; I was pulling a blind down and cutting out the audience. Now I sing to faces and I find I can make people respond just by looking at them. I play to reactions, which is why I hate it when the house is dark.

I also learned early that it's essential to look good on stage – special enough so people feel that if they've made the effort to come out and hear you, they aren't being served up the woman next door. You have to try and convey a bit of magic. Some young singers want to show off their slim figures, so they wear gowns that are too tight. But as soon as you start singing and pressing those muscles out, all the bulges start to show. I still shudder when I see pictures of myself in my jersey phase. I ought to have been arrested for wearing those clinging gowns.

Elisabeth Schwarzkopf was a singer who understood the importance of image. I sang with her several times in New York, but I didn't know her well because she was a star in the generation ahead of mine. She was married to Walter Legge, the recording genius who was head of Angel-EMI records and who was famous for driving her and other musicians mercilessly. There used to be a saying in the business: Walter Legge would do himself and the world a favour if he dropped dead. But he coaxed tremendous recordings out of her. The more he would berate her, the more she would sing like a goddess. People who knew her told me that when she arrived at a concert hall to rehearse she wasn't interested in checking out the sound system or acoustics. What she worried about was the lights. She would stand on the stage with mirrors until she made sure the lighting man had the spotlights trained flatteringly on her. Some people might call that vanity but I call it professionalism. In this business, part of the secret is knowing how to put yourself on display.

In Philadelphia I had two outstanding students. One was Florence Quivar, a black mezzo who was the star of the school. The first year I taught, when she auditioned for me, I told her she had one of the most beautiful voices I had ever heard. "But," I added, warning her not to take what I was going to say the wrong way, "you sing too black." It wasn't the colour of her skin that I was talking about; it was the colour of her voice – that dark plummy sound which can get boring if that's the way you sing everything. She didn't like that critique at all and turned down the chance to study with me then. But the next year she came back and learned more avidly than any student I have ever seen. She reminded me of myself when I was young, hungry to soak up every lesson. It's no surprise to me that Florence ended up singing at the Met and building a very big career, which is still flourishing.

The other student who made an impression on me was Bonita Glenn, a black lyric soprano who later sang as a *fest* soprano – a singer under permanent contract – in the opera house of a Swiss town named St. Garlan. There she had the most incredible encounter. She was standing at a crosswalk in the town one day when a man strode past, then turned on his heel and started walking back toward her. "Excuse me for talking to you like this," he said, "but I can't stand it. You're the most beautiful woman I've ever seen and although I'm a married man, I swear some day I'm going to marry you." It may sound amazing, but he did just that.

As a student Bonita showed such promise that when she graduated I decided to take her on a brief tour with me. Everywhere I went, I arranged for her to audition and she won an engagement. But I was amused to watch her on that trip. As soon as we would arrive at a hotel, she would order room service – steaks, shrimp, wine – nothing but the best. The bills were enormous, but I never said a word. Later, when she went on the road alone, she wrote to me asking how I ever could have allowed her to carry on like that. But I wanted her to learn by experience that just because someone is well-known and commands high fees doesn't mean that she can live as if she's rich. By the time a singer has paid her manager twenty per cent, her accompanist, both their plane fares and hotel bills, not to mention the cost of her music and gowns, she may be left with a quarter of what she has earned. When you're starting out, you have to get smart fast – make sure your manager books you on consecutive dates in the same area to cut down on travel costs and doesn't charge you for printing up a useless number of publicity brochures and posters.

Some managers sit on singers' fees for months, collecting interest on them. For young musicians, economic reality is a shock: you're brought up to be an artist and suddenly you find out that you're also in a business.

In fact, now when schools ask me to give a master class, I sometimes try to talk them out of it. Someone like myself breezes in once, listens to a young person sing and points out what is wrong, but isn't there later to make sure the correction is made. A teacher who drops in like that can end up doing more harm than good. Or every student sings his or her best number for me and the class turns into an exercise in flattery. Instead, I would rather talk to them about the business of singing so they don't run out with their first cheque and buy a mink coat. I learned that lesson myself the hard way.

When I finally had what I considered my first windfall in Montreal, I decided I had to look like a star. I took myself down to a furrier whose windows I had stared into longingly for years. I walked in wanting a nice warm beaver coat, which would have cost me $1,500, but by the time I came out, the owner had talked me into letting him make me a mink for $5,000. Within a year of wearing that coat, I noticed the skins were beginning to split. I brought it into Creed's fur salon in Toronto, where I happened to be performing at the time, and the chief furrier practically threw me out of the store, as if my coat might contaminate the rest of his stock. He told me that my mink was irreparable because it had been made with ancient, dried-out pelts. When I thought of what else I could have done with that $5,000, I wept. I went back to Montreal and didn't make a fuss. I just told that man he had not only lost a customer, he had lost one of his best advertisements. "Wherever I go, even in interviews, I'm going to tell people what you did to a naïve young girl." In fact, I didn't need to wreak my revenge. The store went bankrupt shortly afterward.

It's also important for a young singer not to develop a

reputation for unreliability. In all my years of performing, I've only cancelled twice. At a certain point, my back hurt so badly that I found I couldn't put my weight on one side at all and off stage I had to walk with a cane. To get through a concert I stood on one leg the whole time and no one even noticed that, under my long gown, I was perched up on the stage like a flamingo. Another winter, I broke my arm in two places while ice-skating with the children and when I sang a week later, I had the cast in a black nylon stocking under flowing black sleeves. When a woman came backstage to congratulate me, she touched my sleeve, then her face froze. "Oh my God," she turned and gasped to her friend, "she's got a wooden arm."

The business side of singing doesn't end when the concert is over. It means going to the reception too. A lot of younger artists and Europeans pride themselves on never attending receptions but I believe they cut their chances of being re-engaged. It's important for the audience to meet you and feel that you're approachable. An example of that was unwittingly provided by a British baritone who once came to Montreal to perform in *Rigoletto*. After the opera, he turned up at the reception, which was an elegant affair with magnificent French food and wine. Almost as soon as he got in the door, he demanded a beer. The hosts apologized profusely for not having any, but he uttered a profanity, turned on his heel and left. The symphony board and conductor were mortified and that man has never sung in Montreal again.

Receptions can often be more tiring than the concerts because you're still on stage. But I like people and I've found a lot of friends – and recipes – by going to them. Not long after my touring began, I realized from the stories told at concert societies across the continent that Jan Peerce kept a card file, noting every recital and reception he had attended, right down to the exact menu served. When he came through town again, he would phone and say, "Mrs. Smith, I just wanted to call and tell

you what fond memories I have of your city and that
lovely Apple Brown Betty you made for the party afterward." Can you imagine any board member resisting a
compliment like that? Jan Peerce was a singer who built a
career not only on his wonderful voice, but because he
understood the value of good public relations.

In my own career, after André Mertens died, I gradually
became dissatisfied with the attention I was receiving from
Columbia Artists Management. It particularly bothered
me that, after a certain point, they weren't winning me
more prestigious bookings. My recitals were always in
Town Hall, never in Carnegie Hall which was a notch up
the ladder. I felt that they were taking me for granted
because I was always so amiable, like a dutiful daughter. I
would go into their offices for an appointment and be kept
waiting in the anteroom for hours while Renata Tebaldi
sat inside with her poodle in her lap playing the temperamental diva. She had a tiny little girl's speaking voice and
whenever a manager would tell her that some demand of
hers was completely out of the question, she would begin
to pout, "But I have no husband to look after me." I was
so self-sufficient that I never got that kind of attention.
   Over the years at receptions, I had often met Sol
Hurok, the legendary impresario, who was very flattering
to me and offered to take over my career. I considered it a
great compliment because Sol Hurok wasn't just a manager, he was like an artistic czar, but I felt I owed my
loyalty to André. After André's death, however, I switched
to Hurok's agency, where Harold Shaw was in charge of
the concert division. They arranged for my first recital in
Carnegie Hall, but Hurok was already old and sickly by
then and he died not long afterward. An entertainment
conglomerate took over the agency, which Harold Shaw
wanted no part of, so he struck out on his own and has
remained my manager ever since. We're such old friends

now that if I call and say, "Harold, I've just bought a new house, I need $10,000 right away," the cheque is in my hands the next day. As I've learned, not all managers are the same.

Still, I believe some singers these days have carried their obsession with business too far. The astronomical fees that superstars like Luciano Pavarotti and Placido Domingo command are crippling the concert business. Producers know they can't make any profit on such high-priced names unless they book them into a place like Madison Square Garden. But who wants to hear all the best music in hockey rinks? An impresario can't possibly cover fees like theirs as part of an ordinary concert series, so what he often does is use their names as loss leaders to sell subscriptions and then he pays the rest of the artists in the series less. Every musician down the line has to make a sacrifice.

Personally, I like both men. I sang a Verdi *Requiem* with Placido in San Francisco and he's a prince of a human being; he doesn't strut or posture and he's a terrific gentleman. I'm full of admiration when I think how he paid his dues, hired as a young man to sing in a Tel Aviv opera company. He had to sing Verdi in Hebrew before he went to New York and had to relearn every opera in Italian.

Although I've never sung with Pavarotti, I met him backstage, also in San Francisco, when we were rehearsing different operas, and he was gregarious and charming. But when he came to Toronto, my secretary got a call from Walter Homburger's office at the Toronto Symphony asking if I had the score for the *Anthology of Italian Songs*. Pavarotti needed it because at the last minute he'd changed his program. What he'd originally planned to sing was a very difficult group of songs and I was incensed that people were being asked to shell out $50 a ticket to hear songs every student learns in the first year at a conservatory.

I'm the last person to criticize high fees, but after a certain point, I think there ought to be a ceiling. Past that, you're no longer talking art, you're talking egos engaged in a game of one-upmanship.

While we were in Philadelphia, my mother often came to visit and the children became very attached to her. During one of her stays, I took her out shopping in the morning, then came home and made her lunch. But she didn't want to eat much and protested that she didn't feel well. I moved her into the den to watch soap operas, dismissing the complaint as her usual indigestion. When you've spent your whole life watching your mother going into swoons over her health, you tend to be rather cavalier about these incidents. Suddenly she started vomiting and I realized that this time was different. She couldn't even lie down comfortably. I got her into the car and to a hospital ten blocks from the house. It turned out that she had suffered two massive heart attacks within a matter of hours and she was in the hospital for the next six months.

It was a shock to see my mother suddenly helpless. Worse, I felt awful about not being able to spend more time with her. I was on the road constantly, Eugene taught for the entire day in Philadelphia and the children were too young to be allowed into the hospital on their own. I realized gradually that it would be better for her to be near my sisters and her friends in Montreal. But when the doctors wouldn't allow her to fly because of her heart condition, I was stumped as to how to get her there. Finally I found a marvellous ambulance service which drove her that whole twelve-hour trip.

She recovered for a while, but progressively her health began to fail. She developed Menière's disease, a middle-ear disorder which causes loss of balance, motion sickness and the sensation that the room is constantly swimming before your eyes. You have to live on Gravol and your life becomes a nightmare. As she weakened, it became more difficult for my sisters to look after her. Finally one of them phoned and said she had located a nursing home for Mother. I drove up from an engagement to look at it and found it situated in a very posh area of Montreal; but I set one foot inside and I was sick from the smell of urine in the hallways. I was horrified to find my mother confined to her bed in a dark corner of a room with no activities all day. Right then and there I called a doctor friend of mine at the Jewish General Hospital, ordered an ambulance and moved her to his clinic. The nursing home operator kept protesting that I had no right to do it, but I was livid at what I had found. "This is my mother," I said. "I pay the bills. Just try and stop me." I couldn't stand to see that dynamo of a woman left lying in such a terrible place to die.

For the next two years, she did well and loved the geriatric centres I found for her first in Montreal, later in Toronto, when we moved back there. She was in her element again chatting with the other patients, participating in crafts and entertainment. For my mother, it was the Fairmont Taylor church socials all over again. But eventually, she began to have a series of strokes. She would make a comeback on some miracle drug the doctors administered, then slip back with another cerebral haemorrhage. I could see her dying by inches. This woman who had weighed 200 pounds and boasted a larger-than-life personality shrivelled to barely seventy-five pounds, her body crippled and bent like a little broken bird. She became almost totally blind, although she was too vain to admit it, but her mind remained as active as it had always been.

One day Eugene and I brought her a little portable hi-fi with a new record I had made. She had always complained that I never recorded any songs in English, but the cbc had just made an lp of me singing English works by Ralph Vaughan Williams and Healey Willan. We plugged the record player in beside her bed and she was delighted as she listened, recognizing so many of her favourite songs. "Lovely, lovely," she kept repeating. It was a very emotional moment for all of us and Eugene and I kept having to turn away to the window to hide our tears. Finally she drifted off to sleep and we crept out.

Hours later, as we were getting into bed, the phone rang and I knew even before I answered it that my mother had died. I was relieved that she was finally free from her pain – that her crumpled little body could relax at last in peace. But for me, it was as if an empty seat had been left at every concert I would sing from that point on – a place impossible to fill. It was my mother who had wanted the career I had, who had pushed me into it and gloried in all the reviews and triumphs. In a way, she came to live vicariously through me. At one time I know she had even imagined that she would travel the world with me and was disappointed when it became clear such a plan would never work. Often now, at a performance or an awards ceremony, I think of her and how proud she would be, although a part of me feels that she must know about them. My mother isn't very far away.

If she had been able to pursue a musical career, she would have been the kind of artist I'll never be myself. I'm the organized type who likes clean bathrooms and spotless floors. She would have worn gypsy turbans and danced on tabletops, hanging out with a bohemian crowd all night in Paris's grotty Left Bank cafés.

Right until the end, she was melodramatic. That last day as we were playing my record, her doctor had walked into the hospital room and remarked to her that it must be wonderful to hear me sing like that. "You used to sing yourself, Mrs. Forrester, didn't you?" the doctor asked.

"Oh yes," my mother said. "Music has been my whole life."

They were the last words she spoke.

TWENTY-TWO

Touring Company

WHEN PAULA, Gina, Daniel and Linda were young, Eugene would make up bedtime stories for them about three little girls named Florabelle, Dorabelle and Isobelle who were always off having exotic adventures with their father all over the world. Coincidentally, these little girls always happened to be embroiled in their latest escapade in exactly the country where I was singing at the time. By kindergarten my children all knew that Venice had streets of water where people rode in gondolas and spoke Italian and that Moscow had winters as cold and snowy as Canada's, although the natives there spoke Russian and couldn't say what they thought about the government. From those stories, my children developed a better sense of geography than a lot of adults I know, but most important of all, it was a brilliant way of helping them share their mother's life on the road.

Still, as they grew older I realized that if I was going to share it in more ways than in bedtime stories, I would have to take them on tour with me. Every summer or whenever they had holidays and I was invited to sing at a music festival for more than a week, no matter how little the booking paid, I accepted so I could take the children along and make a family outing of it. The logistics were mind-boggling, but the fun we had more than made up for the complications. In summertime, they loved exploring the town around the Tanglewood Festival in the Berkshires, with its endless lawns and ice cream shops. To them, the Aspen Festival didn't mean music; it meant trail rides in the mountains and rafting down the Colorado River.

Sharing trips with the children often cemented my bonds with other artists. During one Easter vacation, we turned a booking I had to sing with Zubin Mehta and the Los Angeles Philharmonic into a trip to Disneyland. On that visit, Zubin invited us all to an Easter Sunday lunch at his house where his wife Nancy had arranged an egg hunt on the lawn and then surprised our assembled offspring by opening up her apron and producing a chirping baby chick for each one of the children.

Not every outing resulted in rave reviews. When Susie was three, I decided I hadn't been spending enough time with her so I took her with me on a little tour through the States that I was booked to do with the Bach Aria Group. We were driving from town to town and I knew I could find baby-sitters on the campuses where we were to sing. Remembering my own travels with my grandfather, I thought she would find it a terrific adventure. But as the days wore on, she grew quieter and quieter. Then she started saying things like, "I miss the dog," and "Gee Mommy, what do you think the other kids are doing right now?" Finally she got so homesick that Eugene had to fly to Chicago to pick her up and bring her back to Philadelphia.

For years our family never took holidays where I didn't have an engagement. Every summer from 1960 to 1966, Eugene and I took them to the Casals Festival in Puerto Rico where they met not only Casals but Artur Rubinstein, Rudolf Serkin and Isaac Stern. People would say to them, "My, my, what a glamorous life you have travelling around with your mother," but my children would just shrug. After six summers at the Casals Festival, their most vivid memory of the whole thing was the peacocks running free in the gardens of the Caribe Hilton.

I first sang at the festival after an invitation from Alexander Schneider, the mad Russian violinist who had founded it three years earlier. Sasha, everybody called him, and he dubbed me *Snegourochka* – which means Snow Maiden – or *Putscula Smutscula* which means absolutely nothing. Sasha is quite a ladykiller and looks not unlike Eugene. In fact, he never got over the fact that a blonde to whom he had been giving the eye for hours during a concert came backstage later and insisted it was Eugene she wanted to meet.

Sasha was a great friend and admirer of Casals, who had been living in the southwest of France since his self-imposed exile from Spain after Franco had come to power. Sasha lured him out of retirement with the idea of a cello festival to be held in Casals's tiny peaceful village of Prades in the Pyrenees, which proved to be very successful. Later, in 1955, after learning that Casals yearned to move to Puerto Rico, Sasha created a larger festival in his name in San Juan, with the help of the island's Governor, Luis Muñoz Marín, who was also a famous poet. In fact, it was the natural site for it, since Casals's mother had been Puerto Rican, as was his last wife, Martita, a beautiful one-time cello student who was years younger than he was. Indeed, if you looked at the paintings of Casals's mother in his living room, you realized that Martita was the spitting image of her.

For our family, the festival was a marvellous vacation. After the first year, Eugene played violin in the orchestra which boasted some of the finest musicians in the world who were also there on busmen's holidays. And when we weren't working, we romped with the children on the beaches, where Paula first learned to swim, or explored the island. Whenever I hear people talking derogatorily about Puerto Ricans, I won't listen. Even if some of them were forced to live in terrible hovels, I noticed that mothers would periodically round up their children for a bath and out they would march from their shanty, dressed in spanking clean shirts. There were a lot of squatters but, no matter how flimsy their shack, there would always be a bit of corrugated tin or cardboard for a roof even if there wasn't much in the way of walls. It seemed that in Puerto Rico, once a squatter's house had a roof on it, the government couldn't throw the inhabitants out.

The people of Puerto Rico were so gentle and courteous, capable of incredible kindness. *"¡Qué linda es!"* they would exclaim over Gina or Paula during the first years. "Isn't she pretty?" Later, when we realized that our next daughter had been conceived on the island, we named her Linda in tribute to Puerto Rico.

Not many Puerto Ricans could afford tickets to the festival so Luis Muñoz Marín arranged for television sets to be rigged up in the public squares and boulevards of San Juan. Crowds would cluster around them on the hot humid summer nights to watch the performances, sipping Coca-Cola and beer. In the early years of the festival, the people of the island were in awe of the musicians who came to play. One day I was walking downtown when a distinguished old gentleman in a panama suit and straw hat came up to me and kissed my hand. Then he pointed at me and put both his hands over his heart. It was such a beautiful gesture to show that my performance had touched him.

Don Pablo, the people of Puerto Rico called Casals, but we affectionately dubbed him The Old Man. By the time I sang with him, he was already eighty-four and appeared to be absolutely doddering. But Casals was very deceptive. He walked so haltingly, clutching Martita's arm, and he wheezed for breath sucking on his pipe. You watched him shuffle his way up the aisle of the University of Puerto Rico theatre, where most of the concerts were held, and you thought: My God, he's never going to make it through the performance. To conduct, he sat in a tall swivel chair because he had a problem with balance. Then he would pick up his baton and, as soon as he put down the first beat, he would begin bouncing in that chair. The instant the music started, he sprang to life.

One year he also played the cello at the festival and,

quite frankly, I had wondered if he would be able to carry it off. But his bow didn't quiver a centimetre, and as I watched him, I realized that his hands reminded me of Charlie Chaplin's: they were small and delicate with not a line on them. Casals had the hands of a child.

Backstage, he kept an enormous tattered armchair in which he liked to sit and receive people who came to congratulate him after a performance. One night I watched as he kept almost toppling over in it and Martita kept propping him up again. My God, I thought to myself, I hope nothing serious is happening to him. And then I noticed that he collapsed sideways every time a pair of good-looking legs walked by. He had a constitution of iron, that man, and he could eat like a horse. At eighty-four, he would sit in a restaurant with one hand on Martita's knee the whole time.

Casals and I worked well together in the same way that Bruno Walter and I had – with very few words spoken. With Casals, you were either on his wave length or not. But I'll never forget the first time I sang for him. He was to conduct Brahms's *Alto Rhapsody* and before the opening rehearsal, Sasha, who was the concertmaster in the orchestra, came up to me with an anxious look on his face. "You know," he confided, "The Old Man is very emotional about this piece. The last time he conducted the *Alto Rhapsody* was years ago for his former wife Susan Metcalfe. He's worried that he may not be able to get through it without breaking down."

Well, Casals started into the prelude and, although he was famous for doing things slowly, by the time he got to the alto solo, which is slow anyway, it was almost funereal. We paused for a moment and I turned to Sasha. "This is so slow it's going to die," I whispered.

"You tell him," he said. "I can't."

Finally I hit upon a way of doing it. During the break, I decided that I would say, "Maestro, I realize that I'm dragging and that when we get to the *adagio* it's going to be so slow that it will destroy the piece. It's my fault and

I'm sorry." Casals started to shuffle toward me, leaning on Martita and pulling at his pipe, and before I could open my mouth with my spiel, he put his hand on my arm. "At last," he said, "a singer who can sing at my tempo."

He was so shrewd that he had figured out what I was going to say and killed it with a compliment. When it came time for the performance, however, he speeded up the tempo. He had gotten the message, unspoken.

In 1962, he asked me to sing in his oratorio *El Pessebre* (The Manger), which he had written as his personal hymn for world peace. It was based upon a nativity poem which Joan Alavedra wrote for his daughter in Catalan, a very difficult language which is as different from Spanish as Finnish is from the rest of the Scandinavian tongues. Some of the performances were in English, but when we were to record it in the original later in New York, I asked Alavedra to coach me in pronunciation. To me, it sounded like Russian with the same lazy "l" lolling on the tongue, but I was very nervous about doing it because all the others in the cast were Spanish-speaking singers. Oddly enough, Alavedra told me that, for that very reason, my Catalan turned out to be the best of all. I can only credit it to the fact that I'm a born mimic of sounds.

Some of the musicians who played *El Pessebre* were humouring Casals when they performed it. They thought it was corny, old-fashioned music, derivative of Wagner and Brahms. But The Old Man was very attached to the piece and he would get weepy leading it, so you couldn't help wanting to do it well for him. When we premièred it in New York a month later with Robert Shaw's Cleveland Orchestra Chorus, the performance was incredibly emotional. Casals hadn't appeared in the city for four years and he was eighty-five by then, looking more feeble than ever. But there was nothing feeble about his performance. He got swept along by his own fervour until you would see him rise right up out of his chair. The audience gave him six curtain calls and a ten-minute standing ovation, and he kissed everyone in sight who crowded around him on the stage afterward, including most of the orchestra members.

At another Casals festival I premièred a lost Domenico Scarlatti manuscript called "Salve Regina," a hymn to the Madonna, which Sasha had found and which was terribly difficult to sing; as far as I was concerned, it could have stayed lost. That year a National Film Board crew accompanied our family to San Juan. Here I was, trying to concentrate on this impossible piece while a three-ring circus of children, nanny, husband and cameras was trailing me everywhere, even to cocktail parties.

At the Casals Festival, I met many of the great musicians I went on to work with later. One of them, Artur Rubinstein, was playing in a different night's program than I was, but I heard afterward from friends that in an interview he had referred to me as "the singer with the Stradivarius in her throat." Some time after that I saw him again in Biffi Scala, the elegant restaurant in the La Scala opera house, where he left his group to come over to my table. "Ah, my dear, I noticed that you are singing *Kindertotenlieder* tomorrow," he said. "I haven't heard that piece since I was in Petrograd in 1904. If I weren't playing myself, I would be there to hear you."

I never knew whether to believe him or not because he was such a charmer – and he was extra charming when someone was young, blonde and voluptuous. Artur Rubinstein knew how to flatter a woman so she felt like a schoolgirl again.

He later asked me to sing at a testimonial dinner for him in New York. It was an early version of a celebrity roast. He and Stokowski traded stories about each other which had the room in stitches. First Rubinstein stood up and told an anecdote about travelling on a train in South America and finding himself in the dining car where a man stared at him all through his meal. "I knew the poor man had recognized me," he said, "but I was hoping he wouldn't come over and make a spectacle of himself."

Rubinstein could really ham a story up. "Finally the fellow came over to my table and was terribly apologetic. 'I do beg your pardon, sir,' he said, 'I realize this is a terrible thing to ask but could I beg you for an autograph for my grandchildren?' 'Well, certainly,' I said and took a napkin and scrawled my signature for him. He was ecstatic. 'I'll never be able to tell you how grateful I am, Mr. Stokowski,' he said."

Then Stokowski took the microphone to respond. He told a story about having a headache one day after playing a concert in Chicago. He asked his driver to stop at a drugstore so he could buy a pain-killer. There were two pharmacists behind the counter and he explained that his head was throbbing; then, realizing that one of the men had recognized him, he felt compelled to add that he had been working very hard. "Oh, yes, I understand, Mr. Rubinstein," the pharmacist said. His colleague looked aghast at his friend for making such a gaffe. "That's not Rubinstein," the other pharmacist corrected him, "That's Tchaikovsky."

The organizers of the testimonial had asked Rubinstein which performers he wanted and he chose Carol Burnett and myself. I sang an aria from Gluck's *Orfeo ed Euridice* and some folk songs, which went very well, but I didn't think I was nearly as entertaining as Carol Burnett, who did one of the most hysterical sketches I have ever seen. This was a difficult audience, the most distinguished men of music gathered in one room, and she was terribly nervous backstage. She had left the *Garry Moore Show* by then and had just started on her own as a comedian.

She began her number by relating how she used to love to sing when she was a little girl in school in California. One day she was supposed to perform a duet with her girlfriend for parents' day but her chum fell ill with the measles. The teacher stood up in front of the assembly and explained to everyone that, like a good sport, Carol had bravely agreed to carry on alone. And then she started to sing. What she sang was half a duet – only the

alto line – the harmony without the melody. It wouldn't
have been funny to an ordinary audience but in a room
full of musicians it brought down the house.

Isaac Stern was another friend I met at the Casals Festival. My first thought when I saw him was, Isn't he adorable! He was so cuddly and round. Like a lot of short
people, he always wears his glasses pushed up on his forehead as if he thinks it makes him look taller. Isaac is one
of my favourite people in the world – a very powerful
personality, and a doer. He wears open-necked shirts and
because he's constantly on the phone, you always get the
feeling that he's a tycoon in the middle of closing a mil-
lion-dollar deal. You walk into the studio for rehearsal and
he'll wave, "Hi, honey," with the receiver glued to one ear.
But the rehearsal invariably starts half an hour late because Isaac has forty more calls to make and he's got
Teddy Kollek on the line from Jerusalem.

Isaac and Sasha Schneider and I played so often together at the Israel Festival that people used to call us the
Stern Gang. In a way, Isaac and I are alike: we're gregarious and noisy and we both adore food. We're always defending the downtrodden and hustling money, but never
for ourselves. Isaac is responsible for saving Carnegie Hall
from the wreckers and he's constantly helping young musicians or arranging some benefit or other. One year when
I was organizing a fund-raising concert as chairman of the
Canadian-Israeli Cultural Foundation, I called him, and
his wife wasn't going to let me talk to him. "I bet you
want him to do a freebie," she teased. "You just remind
Isaac how many freebies I've done for him," I said. And of
course he came and it was a tremendous success: we raised
$320,000 in one night.

My first trip to Israel was in 1962 and over the next nine
months I went back three times. It was just the beginning
of a long relationship. In Israel, people treated me like an
honorary citizen and it's the only country where I've ever

felt that I had found a second home. It was not only because the country was Jewish but because the Israelis were passionate about music. In those days, the population still consisted mainly of older Eastern Europeans and every concert would be sold out twelve times over with spectators hanging from the rafters. People literally had to wait until somebody died to get a subscription to the Israel Philharmonic. Whenever you performed there, the organizers would beg you to squeeze in an extra concert because the enthusiasm was so great. On the street, passersby would stop to offer you opinions about a concert and my hairdresser there once thought nothing of saying to me, "Tell the conductor he's playing the second movement of the Brahms too slow."

The first year there I sang with a Romanian conductor named Sergiu Celibidache. I hadn't heard of him at the time because he almost never conducted in North America. He was so temperamental that he demanded at least ten rehearsals before a performance, which nobody could afford. After we had done the *Alto Rhapsody*, the organizers asked me for one more recital, as usual, because there was such a demand to hear this hot young singer who was acquiring a reputation in the United States. I suggested a group of arias from *Orfeo*, but the orchestra couldn't find the score for it anywhere. I was preparing to choose something else when Celibidache said, "It's alright, I'll write it out." Amazing! He knew the entire orchestration for a six-minute aria in his head.

I made a number of teaching films in Israel and the government put me up at the Mishkonot, the row of apartments in the Old City of Jerusalem that Mayor Teddy Kollek had built for visiting artists. Saul Bellow was staying in one at the same time and although I never got to meet him, I found out later it was during this period that he was writing *O Jerusalem*.

I loved the casualness of Israel. In those days everybody called everybody else by his or her first name. Cabinet ministers were Avi or Ben and everybody addressed the

Prime Minister as Golda. Golda Meir would come to all the festivals and Israeli security would have to clear two rows in front of her and two behind. She hated that because she was basically a woman of the people. I went to her home twice and although she must have had servants hidden away somewhere, you never had a sense of it. It was as if you were visiting your best friend's grandmother for cookies and tea. She was a woman of super charisma. She must have been very attractive as a young girl because although she never wore make-up, you couldn't take your eyes off her. She smoked non-stop and talked in a very low, masculine voice. When she invited us over, it was clear that she loved music and she was always wanting to chat about how ticket sales were going. She seemed concerned about every person she met.

The most moving concert I ever sang in Israel was a performance of Srul Irving Glick's *I Never Saw Another Butterfly*. He wrote the cycle of songs from a book based on the graffiti and children's workbooks which the liberators had found in the Nazi death camp of Terezin after the end of the war. It was such a powerful piece. In the book, at the end of each entry is the name of the child who wrote it, which Glick included on his scores. On one piece that had inspired him, he wrote: "By Peter Fruschel, perished 1944."

Before I arrived in Israel for the concert, Avi Shoshani, the orchestra manager, called me and said, "Maureen, great news! I put the names of those kids in the music through the computer at the Museum of the Diaspora and Peter Fruschel did not perish. It turned out that he lived and went back to Czechoslovakia after the war, then emigrated to Israel where he took a Hebrew name and he now works as a psychiatrist helping people who were in the camps."

When I got to Tel Aviv, Avi arranged for me to have lunch with Peter Fruschel and his twelve-year-old son and I gave him the record we had already made of the songs in Canada. It turned out that he didn't even remember hav-

ing scribbled anything on paper in captivity, but he came
to the concert and wept. The piece that Glick had created
from his journal never failed to have an impact on an
audience. "We got used to standing in lines," it goes. "We
got used to getting slapped, to seeing piled-up coffins; we
got used to it." As the list of things grows, the music
becomes louder and louder until the piece ends, "We got
used to seeing thousands of unhappy souls come here . . .
and thousands of unhappy souls go away." At that point
seven chimes sound, like the bells they used to ring in the
camps when the ovens were going.

Wherever I sang those songs, there was an ovation, but
in Israel the reaction was different than anywhere else.
You would see people put their hands over their mouths as
if the memories were bringing floods of nausea. Then they
would stand and clap wildly, but you sensed a silence in
the applause and, all over the concert hall, you could hear
the sound of sobbing.

When Susie was five, I took her along to Tel Aviv.
During a rehearsal with the Israel Philharmonic in Mann
Auditorium, I sat her in the twelfth row with her crayons
and a big drawing pad. All the musicians got a tremendous kick out of her. At a break, the first violinist went
down to talk to her. "Your daughter is going to draw my
picture," he winked when he came back. When we got
home that night, I noticed she had a lot of Israeli pounds
clanking in her pocket. "Susie, where did you get all this
money?" I asked. "All the men gave it to me for drawing
their pictures," she said. That's when I knew I would
never have to worry about my youngest daughter, the
artist.

I had always wanted to take all my children to Israel
and in 1967 I finally managed it. It wasn't exactly a direct
route. That year I had engagements lined up from London
to Dubrovnik so Eugene and I decided to turn it into a
blow-out family vacation. When people heard our itinerary, they would look at me as if I'd lost my mind. The
chaos started even before we left Philadelphia. Maria, the

housekeeper who was supposed to come along and help, disappeared just as I was in the middle of packing. I discovered she was pregnant and was off saying goodbye to all her boyfriends. It made me so furious I fired her; I thought that if she was off playing the coquette in Philadelphia, what would she be up to on the Continent with five children in her care? I didn't need another child along.

We flew to London where I was recording Handel's *Jephtha* with the Irish soprano Heather Harper. While I was busy in the day, Eugene took the children off to see the Tower of London and the changing of the guard. We stayed in Branson's old flat, where I had first lived with Paula, and Farrell, who had retired to the English countryside, came into town to visit us and brought each of the girls tiny evening bags – part of her unflagging determination to turn them into proper ladies. For me, it seemed things had come full circle to a happy ending.

From London, we went on to the Salzburg Festival in Austria where I was to sing Pergolesi's *Stabat Mater* with the Berlin Philharmonic and Claudio Abbado. The other soloist was Gundula Janowitz, a German soprano I had sung with once before in Bonn. She was a very big star in Europe but too haughty for my taste. When she found that she didn't have the breath control to sing her whole line without a break, she had asked if I would break mine as well so she wouldn't be left looking bad. Gundula Janowitz reminded me of what my life might have been like had I stayed in Europe. There she was, swanning about Salzburg like a queen, and there was I, worried about keeping five children's underwear washed in hotel bathrooms.

Zubin Mehta was also conducting at Salzburg and he had with him his two children Zarina and Mirwan. With Claudio's two, plus my brood, we made up our own mob scene. We all stayed at the Bristol Hotel and took our meals together at a big round table where I would play den mother. The last night there we ate an enormous dinner and were struggling from the table when Zubin motioned us back. "Wait, you can't go yet," he said. And in came a parade of waiters with tambourines bearing trays of palacsinta, Hungarian crêpes stuffed with cottage cheese and drenched in chocolate sauce, which he had ordered as a special treat. Nobody wanted to hurt his feelings but by the time we had finished them, we could hardly heave ourselves out of our chairs.

On one of our days off, Zubin decided we should go on a tour of an old Austrian salt mine. When we got there, we discovered Susie was too young to be allowed in. I sent everybody on without me and stayed outside in the sunlight, thinking the wait wouldn't be more than half an hour. Three hours later, they finally reappeared. They'd had to don white overalls and go whooshing down long underground leather slides with their legs wrapped around each other in a human chain, constantly going deeper and deeper. There was no turning back. Eugene thought he would never get out. When I heard about it, I blessed Susie for being under age.

From there, our whole entourage went on to Dubrovnik where I was singing with the Bach Aria Group. Zubin talked the Yugoslav government into giving us a motorboat to see the coastline in the brilliant sunshine but that night, as I began a Bach cantata in the open-air courtyard of an old castle with the lines "Open my sinful eyes . . . ," the heavens opened and rain came down in a deluge. The whole audience ran for cover.

Finally we were to go on to Israel. But when we got to Athens airport for our connection to Tel Aviv, El Al informed us there had been a hijacking, one of the first. It meant we had a wait of at least eight hours. The airport was crowded and stifling, and I hate to waste time, so we hired a little sightseeing bus and on that layover, we toured the whole city from the Parthenon to Piraeus.

At last we landed in Tel Aviv, where the children had a wonderful time. After performing there, I sang *El Pessebre* again with Casals at Caesarea in Herod's great old

Roman amphitheatre by the sea. It was beautiful, but Paula fell ill with a terrible fever. I kept running down from rehearsal to the dressing room to see her, but her shivering grew worse and worse. Finally, while I was singing upstairs, Eugene and the doctor had to rush her to a hospital where she stayed overnight.

My last engagement was in Spain with the Bach Aria Group, then we flew from Bilbao to Paris, where we were to catch the plane home to Philadelphia. In the three hours before our flight took off for the United States, I packed the children in a cab and gave them a quick tour of the Eiffel Tower, the Arc de Triomphe and Montmartre.

It had been an exhausting odyssey, and when we got home I had three months of laundry to do before turning around and taking off again the next morning to sing in Buenos Aires. But the children agreed it was the trip of a lifetime and it gave them all an appetite for travel. At different points in their lives, they all turned into gypsies.

Through all those experiences my children were never impressed with the glamour of a performer's life. Still, something must have rubbed off. In one way or another, they're all artists. Paula writes well and Gina wants to make films after her two children are older, Susie is studying fashion design and Daniel has just left theatre school in England to join the Stratford Festival Young Company, which makes me very proud. Some day I'd love to do a show with him. Linda has already made a name for herself with the Second City troupe in Toronto and has just acted in her first TV movie. From the time she was eleven, there was no doubt in any of our minds that Linda would become an actress. She used to corral my mother into watching her one-woman shows, and she was so melodramatic we dubbed her Sarah Heartburn. Eventually she studied at the American Academy in Pasadena, where she had so much free time she used to hang out with bag ladies and a collection of weird characters who seemed to be drawn to her like a magnet. Now, they've all resurfaced in her Second City sketches. But she claims she also draws her inspiration for those sketches from sources closer to home.

In one improvisation session, she created a female character who was sitting in her living room ostensibly visiting with a friend. As the friend is chatting away, the woman keeps jumping up emptying ashtrays, straightening pictures and checking the end tables for dust, all the while humming to herself. "The Obsessive Cleaner," Linda titled the sketch, and no one in our family seems to have any problem figuring out who it's based upon.

TWENTY-THREE

Never the Bride

EUGENE AND I would be out for dinner with friends and he would notice a faraway look come over my face. "You just think she's here with us," he would say to them, "but in fact she's in the middle of *Lied von der Erde*, which she's singing in four days."

It would be true. Whenever I didn't have enough hours alone, or the conversation wasn't involving me, I would close myself off and go over a piece I was worried about learning. Luckily, I've always been able to memorize in the midst of commotion. For most of my career, I would learn repertoire on planes or trains or at home with the children playing rock music and shrieking in the basement. For a certain period when we were living in Toronto and they were in their teens, I secretly rented a studio downtown just so I could have some quiet to learn new works. I never told anybody about it, not even Eugene. But to this day, as soon as my children hear me humming, they say, "There goes Mother, absent again."

In fact, when I'm memorizing a modern composition and I get to the point where I want to test my grasp of it, I'll turn on the radio to the most hyperactive rock station I can find and try to sing it against that background. If I can pull that off, I know I can hold my own against an orchestration which runs in counterpoint to my melody line.

But I'm impatient and my concentration span isn't all

that long. When I'm learning an opera role, I can't sit for more than half an hour at the piano before I find myself washing the windows or dusting the paintings. It's always easy to tell when I'm memorizing opera; the house is even cleaner than usual. Then, when I think I know my part, I go for a walk downtown. While the traffic is streaming around me, horns are honking and people are rushing by, I'm going through the whole scene in my head. I may be nodding to people on the sidewalk when they say hello, but mentally I'm on stage making sure nothing that occurs can distract me. I'm sure people pass me on the street and say, "My God, that woman looks demented."

Singers – what a peculiar breed we are! People ask me if I've ever had a crush on one of the stars I've sung with, whom other women routinely swoon over. Well, of course, there are some who are simply gorgeous, like Simon Estes, who makes me wish I were thirty years younger, but I could never imagine falling in love with another singer. I live with my own voice; I don't want to live with somebody else's.

All singers have substantial egos but good tenors have a special brand. *Helden* or "heroic" tenors like Jon Vickers are very rare; they come along about once in a generation, which makes them such superstars. When I was performing in *Cendrillon* in Paris, my son Daniel came over to visit me and one night Louis Quilico heard him through the hotel walls while he was singing in the bathtub. The next day Louis told me that he thought Daniel was going to be a *Heldentenor*. "Take him out and drown him," I said. "He'll grow up to be insufferable!"

George London used to tell a story about walking backstage at the Metropolitan Opera and finding Richard Tucker pacing agitatedly. "What's the matter, Dick?" he'd asked.

"Oh, you wouldn't understand," Tucker said. "It's just that it's such a burden."

"What's a burden?" George persisted.

"Oh, being the world's greatest tenor," he said. "Every performance has to be perfect."

But this man who had a reputation for being a consummate egotist was always an absolute angel to me. The first time I sang with him was early in my career when we recorded the Verdi *Requiem* together in Philadelphia and I was slightly star-struck by such a great name. But afterward whenever he came to Canada on his way up north fishing, he would call me and say, "Maureen, how are you and Eugene and the children? Are you happy, dear? Is there anything I can do for you?" Not many performers are that thoughtful.

I don't socialize a lot with other singers because I don't like sitting around discussing technique. When I'm not singing, music is the last thing I want to talk about; I'd rather hear about a good play or a good recipe. Unlike a lot of singers, I can cut music right out of my life. To my mind, most musicians live with blinkers on and I can't stand people who get too precious about their voices. But then I've been lucky; I never had to work at singing.

Whenever I was on the road with the Bach Aria Group, the first thing I would ask when we checked into a hotel was where Lois Marshall's room was. I made sure I got one at the other end of the building because she used to practise three hours a day in the bathroom, starting at 7 a.m. You could hear her ten floors away, either above or below. It used to drive me insane.

For a few years after I had stopped taking lessons from Diamant, I still went back to him for coaching in new works. But since those student days I've never believed in too much practice myself because I think it takes the bloom off the voice. Before a performance, if I find I'm raspy, I do a scale exercise that Diamant taught me which works like a massage on the vocal cords, or I'll sing a little Bach. If I know I have a difficult technical passage which needs the top of the voice, I'll sing for five minutes before going to the concert to open up that part. But especially on the day of a recital I don't like to vocalize so much that the freshness is gone for the performance.

One of the rare times I've ever practised before singing for a conductor was when, early in my career, I went to rehearse Beethoven's *Ninth* with Herbert von Karajan and the New York Philharmonic. It was soon after his first controversial visit to the United States in 1955, when pickets greeted his appearances with stormy protests over the fact that he had been a member of the Nazi party and had played in Aachen and Berlin all through the war. Even though my part in that piece wouldn't show off my voice, I didn't want von Karajan to find fault with me. He had a reputation for being extremely imperious and, in fact, I found that he could be a terrifying figure at times. Still, to my mind he was never difficult to work with. He got what he wanted from an orchestra, which is what we all strive for, and I adored watching him conduct: he was famous for closing his eyes and almost going into a trance.

Often a student will audition for me with a fairly good voice and tremendous drive, but there's something that I can't quite put my finger on which tells me he or she will never make it. Almost invariably those pupils are the ones who say they practise and practise. One of the reasons I'm against students locking themselves away from life in an ivory tower to concentrate on their vocal cords is that I don't believe music should come that hard.

But of course, as an alto, it's easy for me to say that. Altos, like bass-baritones, sing in their natural speaking voices while sopranos and tenors have to work harder to force theirs up one octave into those artificial upper strata. That's why so many sopranos are temperamental; they're constantly on edge about whether they'll make their high notes. They also know they have short professional lives because after a while the voice just won't go into the upper reaches as it used to. Altos never have superstar careers like a Callas or a Joan Sutherland; the lower voices aren't capable of knocking out an audience with the same kind of show-stopping pyrotechnics that a soprano can, hitting notes that soar into the stratosphere. But we make up for that in longevity. We may gradually lose our top notes but we can slip into lower roles. Altos can go on singing forever, which may be one reason why we're inevitably easygoing types. If I had been a soprano, I would never have made my career as a singer. For every alto, there are a hundred sopranos, and I wouldn't have been happy unless I could have been one of the best. In such cut-throat competition, it wouldn't have suited me to end up as an also-ran. Altos are very friendly with one another and we're always recommending one another for engagements. The amiable peasant-girl nature just seems to go along with our category of voice. "Thrilling" or "charismatic" is how critics describe sopranos. But what do they say about altos? "Great diction," "a lot of warmth" and "charming personality." Who ever heard of a contralto who was a prima donna?

I didn't personally meet any of the great altos of the past. Bruno Walter used to tell me my voice reminded him of Kerstin Thorborg, a Swedish mezzo with whom he recorded a classic *Lied von der Erde* in 1936. Over the years, others used to compare my range and style to that of Ernestine Schumann-Heink, who was famous as both a concert and opera singer during the early years of the century. She was typical of the alto breed – good-natured and a born earth mother who had oodles of babies she used to nurse in the wings during performances. Some of her children were born in America and some in Germany, but tragically, when the First World War broke out, they found themselves on opposite sides, much to her great sadness.

Schumann-Heink was an enormous woman with a real Wagnerian build, and there's a famous story about a director at the Met who was explaining to her how to exit. "When you've finished, turn and go off sideways," he said. "Darling," she replied, "I have no sideways."

After my Town Hall debut, the critics had started a debate about whether I was really a contralto or a mezzo-soprano. To me it was ridiculous. I can sing some things in the mezzo range, but most works written for it are too high for me. My voice gets tired singing them and that's what tells me that I'm out of my range. I can lighten my voice to a young girl's brightness, which I learned to do as a way of varying texture, because I didn't always want to sing one colour; if you do, it becomes boring, like background music, after a while. But the middle of the voice – the real meat of the voice – is what determines your range and mine makes clear that I'm an alto.

One singer who makes me sad because she doesn't sing in the true range of her voice is Shirley Verrett. I first met her when she came backstage after a performance in the concert hall at the Metropolitan Museum in New York. This absolutely stunning black girl walked toward me and I said, "My dear, I don't know who you are, but if you're not an actress or a performer you've missed your calling." There was a star quality shining out of her bearing. She is one of the world's great mezzos, but she insists on singing those high dramatic roles which don't suit her. Like most singers, she doesn't believe that she can be a success unless she sings soprano and lands all the leading roles.

It's true that there aren't many star turns for the lower voices. Altos always get to play the other woman – the aunt or the nurse. I've sung mothers, maids, witches, bitches and mediums, but, as I always point out to directors, never the bride. It's as if composers don't think we're capable of passion. Some musicologists have dubbed altos the "unsung singers," and many of our roles were originally written for castrati. But considering what good-natured people we are, it's strange that composers always write such gloomy things for us to sing – songs about losing our lovers or children. In music, we're always the bereaved ones.

That's one reason why I loved singing Hugo Wolf's *Italienisches Liederbuch*, a forty-six song cycle, half for alto, half for baritone, where the man's songs are all soft and pleading and the woman's incredibly coquettish and bitchy. It was such a terrific change of pace for me. The night that Shirley Verrett first heard me, I was performing it with the great French baritone Gérard Souzay, a high-strung, sensitive man, who used to spend hours preparing for a role. My God, did he prepare. He would withdraw into a corner and almost meditate. My idea of getting ready for a part is to make sure that my lipstick is on straight. We were perfectly paired for our musical roles – he so fastidious and I so flamboyant. There was a news-paper strike on in New York at the time, so no reviews of the concert ever appeared, which was a shame because everyone who heard us agreed that there was something magical about the chemistry that night. Later Souzay sent me a signed photograph on which he had drawn a heart. "Weren't we wonderful?" he wrote in it.

After another performance of ten of those songs, the composer Samuel Barber came backstage. "My dear," he said, "I know of your reputation for Mahler and Brahms, but I never knew you had such a sense of humour. I want to write a cycle for you." I loved his music and would have adored to have a personal composition, but soon after-ward he died.

Now, whenever a composer asks to write something for me, I say, "*Please* write me a happy piece. I'm a happy woman with a zany sense of humour. Don't write me any more sad music." I told that to the Canadian composer Oskar Morawetz, who called me soon afterward, terribly enthusiastic. "Maureen, I've found something terrific: Robert Louis Stevenson's children's poems, including the one which begins, 'I have a little shadow that goes in and out with me. . . .'"

I was thrilled, but when we rehearsed *A Child's Garden of Verses*, every time I would add a jaunty note, Oskar would say, "Oh no, Maureen, not like that." Finally I said to him, "Oskar, what kind of children have you got?" Of course, he was the composer and he's a wonderful orches-trator, so I did the songs as he wanted them. But as John Kraglund wrote in the *Globe and Mail*, "Miss Forrester explained that she wanted some happy music. Unfortunately she got *Kindertotenlieder*."

Most alto works are – ~~as the title~~ of Harry Somers's cycle for me puts it – dark songs for dark voice. Singers see sound in colours and they can plan the shading they want in advance. Reviewers used to call me "the girl with the golden voice" but mine is a warmer colour than that, more like bronze, while Marian Anderson had a voice the colour of molasses. Most sopranos are bright red or shining orange, although young coloraturas such as Kiri Te Kanawa are hot pink. Beverly Sills has a silver voice and Pavarotti's is similar, but with fireworks exploding through it. Birgit Nilsson's voice is like steel, with a strength and coolness to it. Callas's soprano was not bright red; you could hear suffering in her voice. In the end when Onassis broke her heart, it became tragic and even more purple.

To my mind, the press was unfair to Callas. From what I've heard, although she was often eaten up with her own problems, as we've all read, her temperament was exaggerated. Once when I was singing at La Scala, the manager said to me, "You remind me of Callas – I don't mean that you sound like her or you look like her, but you've come prepared." She apparently was a very organized woman who had no patience with people who didn't work as hard as she did. If they hadn't learned their parts, she would close her score and say, "I'll come back when you're ready."

I only saw her once, when she came to sing with the Montreal Symphony. She walked on stage in a black dress with a blood-red stole and even if you didn't like her voice, you couldn't take your eyes off her. She seemed to float. Later I realized that it was because she was myopic; she drifted out in what seemed like a dream state because she couldn't see anything. But the look on her face would keep an audience mesmerized.

The voice that I consider the greatest of this era didn't belong to an alto but to a soprano – Kirsten Flagstad. To my mind, she had the one true Wagnerian voice, that rich homogenized sound which had not only the volume of a Birgit Nilsson but a velour on it as well. It was pure gold from top to bottom, the most perfectly produced voice imaginable. She sang until she was in her sixties and I never heard her utter anything less than a superlative sound.

I was in Oslo for a concert with Sir Malcolm Sargent when the King of Norway died. Fortunately we'd planned to do Sir Malcolm's famous orchestration of Brahms's *Four Serious Songs*, and the concert was turned into a memorial service. During a radio interview at the time, I mentioned that I was a fan of one of the country's own heroines, Kirsten Flagstad. "Let me play something for you," the announcer said. He put on a record she had made of hymns, just everyday garden-variety hymns, which she'd done in the most simple and touching way, as if she were singing them in church. To me, that record summed up what an uncomplicated person she was, unlike some singers who are obsessed with status and stardom and expend so much of their energy throwing their weight around. The interviewer told me that the radio station signed off every night with Flagstad singing one of those hymns and it seemed to me such a beautiful, fitting tribute to a great artist.

When you're a young singer, all you concentrate on is making perfect pear-shaped sounds, and I was no different. But after a few years, there came a point in my career when I realized I was dull. The sounds I produced were beautiful, but whatever I sang – medium loud, medium soft, soft soft – it was all the same. I started listening more carefully to myself and I thought: Sweetheart, your voice neither excites nor disturbs. It's seamless, like wallpaper, and just as boring. So I took myself in hand and taught myself how to act when I sing. I realized it wasn't enough just to make pretty sounds; I had to make the words come alive – to analyze a text like an Olivier or a John Colicos. This isn't something a teacher can teach; it's something you have to coax out of yourself. I learned to create different colours, to sound old or like a child, and I stopped being afraid to distort my face to create an effect.

That realization came with getting older and acquiring some life experience the hard way. As a young girl, I'd had a fairly easy-going existence, but then I found myself with a secret life which I had to cope with all alone. It made me not only a stronger person, but a stronger singer too. The difficult situations in life are what make you grow. After being desperately in love with the father of your child and finding he won't make a commitment, when you suddenly come across a piece of music like Schubert's *Du Liebst Mich Nicht* (You Don't Love Me), you can throw your heart and soul into it in a way you never could before. You have to have a strain of sadness in your own life to touch an audience's heart.

Still, I need a stage to bring out my emotions. At a table with friends, I can find it impossible to express my feelings, but singing in front of 7,000 in a stadium, I can emote through someone else's text with abandon.

As soon as I taught myself to act out the words, my reviews began to change and my career really took off. I became an actress, not just a singer, which is why I still work so much today. Even as my voice is losing its power, I can make up for what I lack in strength by colouring the text. It was a good lesson for me to learn early, rather than resting on my laurels. I realized that singing is a never-ending struggle to improve, to use whatever you have – or whatever you have left!

In 1958, when I debuted with the Bach Aria Group in New York, the backstage at Town Hall was jammed with friends and well-wishers, including Glenn Gould. Then someone led a familiar figure toward me, a tall, dark, queenly presence in a gold turban – Marian Anderson, the reigning contralto of the day. In person she was as soft-spoken and gracious as I had heard. Even though she was nearing the end of her career at that point, for me it was like talking to God.

A few years later I saw her again in a concert at Montreal's St. Denis Theatre. The organizers sat me in the second row, a place of honour for one contralto listening to another. But it was an excruciating experience because by then Marian Anderson was losing her pitch; her accompanist kept having to transpose keys, playing lower and lower until he ran out of notes. Despite that, the audience gave her a standing ovation. I went backstage later to tell her how beautiful it had been, but of course it wasn't. For anybody musical, that concert was heart-breaking. No matter what people say about jealousies in this business, no singer wants to be present at the demise of a great voice. Shortly after that she retired from the concert stage.

Still, no matter how different we might sound, I've never hidden my delight when people mention me in the same breath with Marian Anderson. As much as I ever had role models, she was one of mine, and not only because she had a beautiful voice. She was a woman who stood for something; she was never temperamental or the type to live a life which would end up chronicled in the gossip columns. Despite the hurdles and personal pain that racial prejudice put in her path, she surmounted them all with a philosophical grace and quiet dignity. The press termed her America's Musical Ambassadress and when she travelled abroad, you knew that she represented what was finest in her country. I would be happy if some day people remember me as well as they do Marian Anderson.

TWENTY-FOUR

Singing Diplomacy

THE INVITATION was as flattering as it was puzzling: in 1961 the External Affairs department in Ottawa called to tell me that the Kremlin had invited me on a tour of the Soviet Union. I couldn't figure out how such an offer had come about. But later I discovered that David Oistrakh, the famous Russian violinist, had heard me sing in Carnegie Hall during one of his trips to the United States and had recommended that the Soviet Ministry of Culture invite me to Moscow. Glenn Gould and Lois Marshall had already made visits there, but a trip to the Soviet Union was still quite a rarity in those days of the Cold War. After I had accepted, I realized that only I would have had the luck to be invited in the middle of December. I've never been so cold in my life.

John Newmark refused to go with me because he had lived under the Nazis and regarded communism as a variation on the same totalitarian theme. Instead, I asked Donald Nold, an American pianist who had often accompanied me in Europe. I had just moved our family to Connecticut about three minutes before taking off on the Russian tour and I had already made three trips to Israel that year, so by the time I left for the Soviet Union, I wasn't exactly regarding the undertaking as a holiday.

When Donald and I landed in Moscow, officials were waiting at the airport to greet us, including the interpreter assigned to us for the whole tour, a Russian beauty named Nina. In the Soviet Union your interpreter goes everywhere with you, and you know that everything you say and do will be duly reported by her. She took us to our hotel, the Budapest, which had the usual woman who acted as the keeper of the keys checking us on and off the floor. It was full of Russians and East Bloc citizens, and in the restaurant downstairs where we had to take every meal, I couldn't believe the quantities of alcohol they consumed. I watched in shock as two men downed two quart-sized bottles of apple-jack and a twelve-ounce bottle of vodka between them, then started into red wine. They ended up absolutely polluted, falling around the dance floor entangled in bear hugs. Mind you, you almost had to drink to take your mind off the food: night after night we seemed to find ourselves staring down at the same bony chickens and mounds of grainy potatoes. By the end of the trip, I was ready to kill for a fresh vegetable. When we took our places at the table, the waiters always placed little flags in front of us, a Canadian one for me, a Stars and Stripes for Donald. It was a way of making sure that everyone in the dining room knew we were foreigners and after a few days we begged them to take our flags away.

The first concert was in the Conservatoire hall and it went very well. I sang *Frauenliebe und Leben*, some Bach and a Franck piece. Since I always like to pay the courtesy of singing an encore in the native language of each country I visit, before the Russian tour I had gone back to Professor Peltnev at the University of Montreal, who had helped me learn *Alexander Nevsky*, to master Gretchaninov's famous lullaby. But what did the Soviet audiences yell for as an encore? "Ave Maria," for which I didn't have the music.

There's nothing like an audience in the Soviet Union. They treat their artists like gods. At the end of the concert, they rose in a standing ovation and then the whole Conservatoire seemed to throng forward toward the stage, looking up at me as if I were some kind of Madonna and trying to touch the hem of my gown. I've never known a rush quite like that one.

From Moscow, we flew to Leningrad. Everywhere we went, Nina shadowed me so closely I could barely go to the bathroom alone, so it was astonishing when she suddenly disappeared as we walked into the hotel lobby. Then a man came toward me with a big grin on his face. "Ah, Madame Forrester," he said, "I see your picture here. You live in Canada?"

"I'm Canadian," I said, "but I don't live in Montreal anymore. I've moved to the United States."

"Ah, I lived in Toronto," he said. "See, I still have my working card. My wife and son are still there. Oh, Madame, I want to ask you a big favour. Will you take Christmas presents to my son?"

"I'm very busy now," I said. "Could you come back and have coffee with me tomorrow?"

I felt it was some sort of trap. When Nina came back I very pointedly told her what had happened. "I don't know what's in this present of his and I don't think my government would be very happy about my doing it," I said. "Besides, I live in Connecticut now. Don't you think I had better tell him to look for someone else who can take his gift directly?"

"Very good idea," Nina said. The man never returned and no one bothered me again. It was as if it had been some test: from that moment on, Nina relaxed her surveillance of us.

After Leningrad, we flew on to Tiflis in Georgia, Stalin's home, then to Yerevan, the capital of Armenia. Travelling on small planes outside the major Russian cities had a flavour all its own. As soon as we approached the destination, suddenly all the passengers would scramble to their feet, grab their packages and rush toward the door. *"Nyet, nyet,"* the stewardesses would try to shoo them back to their seats, but these men wouldn't pay any attention. They would stay planted resolutely around the exit through the entire landing operation and I often wondered if, from the ground, those flimsy planes looked as if they were listing to one side.

It was exciting to see corners of the Soviet Union that the average tourist never glimpses. In the hotel lobby in Yerevan I was sitting reading a copy of *Time* magazine for about the fortieth time, because no one had warned me to bring reading material, let alone shoe polish, detergent or toilet paper; I already knew the magazine by heart. Suddenly a young man spoke to me in perfect English with a New York twang. "Are you American?" he demanded eagerly. It turned out that he had been born in New York of Armenian parents who had never been happy in America and had immigrated back to the Soviet Union. He himself had never been able to fit in there because of his upbringing in the States and yet he knew the authorities would never let him leave Russia. He was starved for something to read in English and leaped at my offer of the battered copy of *Time*. But before he took it, he cautioned me to wait. He went to the newsstand and bought me a copy of a Soviet women's magazine, then had me slip *Time* inside for the exchange.

In Yerevan, there wasn't another woman in the dining room and I felt I stuck out like the proverbial sore thumb, so finally I told Donald I was going up to bed early. The next morning when I met him for breakfast, he looked shaken. He told me that after I had left the dining room, he had drunk some more, then gone outside the hotel for a walk. He had barely turned the corner when three men surrounded him and robbed him. He started to holler and a huge Russian policeman appeared from nowhere and nabbed the culprits, forcing them to strip so he could see what they had stolen. It had caused a huge commotion and finally the policeman had delivered him back to the hotel manager, who had told the officer it was all Donald's fault because he had been drunk. Donald was very nervous about what might happen to us. You can become very paranoid in Iron Curtain countries and the last thing we wanted on an External Affairs tour was a diplomatic incident.

I suggested we tell Nina right away at breakfast. Her response was immediately to deny that such a thing was possible in the Soviet Union. Like the hotel manager, she tried to put the whole blame on Donald. "Soviet citizens don't steal," she kept insisting. She marshalled us out on our planned sightseeing tour and we hadn't been on the street for more than five minutes when, standing in line to buy stamps, Nina had her purse stolen.

From Yerevan, we flew on to Baku, the capital of Azerbaijan. The city was more southerly and its waterfront was a jungle of oil derricks looming out of the Caspian Sea. It was as if we had arrived in the Soviet Middle East: the people had a completely different character than the Muscovites – darker, more Mediterranean, and lusty. A woman from the local party cultural committee met us at the plane. As I walked down the steps, she announced that twenty-five years earlier, a buxom blonde like myself would have been kidnapped the instant she set foot in Baku. "Is a good thing you come now," she said. "Before, you would have been stolen." That was my welcome to Azerbaijan.

As we drove into town, she asked what we would like to do before we began our concert schedule the following day. Wherever I've travelled I've bought paintings, so I asked to see the local gallery and meet some artists. I imagined an impromptu visit to an atelier. Instead, they closed the city's art museum and threw a formal reception just for me. They had assembled thirteen artists for the occasion and I was frustrated that I couldn't speak more Russian because their faces were fascinating and vibrant. But glancing around the museum, I quickly saw that their idea of modern art resembled the sort of "Carry On Canada" political posters I remembered the government in Ottawa turning out to spur production during the Second World War. Every painting seemed to feature hammers and sickles or oil rigs. Oh my God, I thought to myself, this is going to be a disaster. How do I get out of this?

When they asked me what I'd like to see first, I tried a diversionary tactic and claimed an interest in historic art. In fact, the ancient works were in the style of Persian miniatures, truly beautiful. But inevitably we ended up in the contemporary section and the party spokesman, a nervous little man, asked what I thought of their current painting. Now I always try to be diplomatic but I have a dreadful time not being honest. "Well, it's very well done," I said. "But it's about twenty-five years behind the times." There was dead silence, but I could see all the artists' eyes light up behind him. They had pretended they couldn't understand English, but they had just showed me they did.

"What do you mean?" he asked, miffed.

"Well, you know, artists are now painting a bit less realistic and more abstract in Europe and North America," I went on. "Art has moved into another phase now. I suppose it's a matter of taste."

"The people here don't like that sort of thing," he harrumphed.

Now that I saw the artists were behind me, I couldn't resist a little political dig. "Oh, but artists shouldn't have to cater to likes or dislikes," I said. "They have to express themselves freely. A true artist doesn't paint by demand."

Since the atmosphere was getting more uncomfortable, I tried to switch the subject. I asked if any of the painters there had ever studied outside Russia. I was introduced to one bearded young man who had spent time in Paris, but the party spokesman made a point of telling me that he had never even dabbled in abstract art in France. The arrival of the refreshments finally broke the tension and we all ended up having a crazy time. The artists taught me some wild folk dance and I taught them the cha-cha.

On another free night there, I told my one-woman welcoming committee that I would love to go to the opera.

"Don't go," she warned me. "People here don't like opera; they like folk dancing, other things. Going to opera is a big mistake." But I insisted because they were playing *Tosca*, one of my favourites. When Donald and I arrived, they gave us the commissar's box right up front. *Tosca* does not have a big cast but, believe me, there were more people on the stage than there were in the audience that night. The stars were two retired singers who had come back for the performance – and needn't have bothered; the marvellous soprano aria was such a disaster that Donald and I had to bury our faces in the curtains of our box to muffle our hoots of laughter. Tears were running down our cheeks. This was the Marx Brothers at the opera. The next morning, our hostess met us at rehearsal. "Don't tell me!" she said. "I don't even want to hear about it. I warned you."

The day after the concert, she took us to our plane. It was a tiny airport where you could stroll right out onto the tarmac and as we approached the aircraft, I saw a man on a bicycle riding like a bat out of hell across the fields and up the roadway toward us. It was the bearded artist who had studied in Paris, come to bid us goodbye. He gave me a big hug. "Come back to Baku," he said to me in French. "Next time I paint you abstract painting."

We returned to Moscow for one last concert in the great Tchaikovsky hall. Donald wanted to rehearse but for days we had asked for a piano and none showed up. Nina always had a new excuse. Finally, the day before the concert, I said to her, "Nina, we *have* to have a piano. The concert is sold out." Then I pointed to my throat in a silent mime as if I were trying to sing but had lost my voice. "You wouldn't!" Nina said. Russia is like anywhere else in the world; in half an hour we got a piano.

The night before the concert, in the Budapest dining room, we were seated next to a large table of naval officers. One of them was dark and handsome with the most remarkable, sensitive face. He kept smiling at us and after their drunken party had broken up, he stayed on at the table. "You Forrester?" he asked, obviously recognizing me from the drawing on posters for the concert which were all over town.

"Yes," I said, "my name is Forrester. What's yours?"

"Ilya," he said.

"Ah, but Ilya is a first name like Maureen. What's your last name?"

"Is not very difficult," he said. "Is the same in the whole world: Goldman."

"Are you Jewish?" I exclaimed.

He shrugged. "My parents killed in war. My brother and I brought up in military school, both navy. I have no religion."

I asked him if he had any children and he said that he had a son. I was thinking of my own children then back home getting ready for Hanukkah, which was only a few days away. "Will you see your boy on Hanukkah?" I asked.

"Hanukkah?" He seemed puzzled by the notion. I explained the origin of the holiday to him and the tradition of giving children coins – Hanukkah *gelt*. He had been so sweet to us that we invited him to the concert the next night, and to join us for dinner afterward. The recital was a success and later, as we came through the revolving door into the hotel lobby, we saw him there, waiting. But as soon as he glimpsed Nina with us, he took off like a frightened rabbit. We didn't see Ilya again that night. The next morning as we were checking out of the hotel, he suddenly appeared beside me in the lobby.

"Concert very beautiful," he said. After I had thanked him, he was about to go when he turned back suddenly and grabbed my hand. He pressed a new coin into it. "For Hanukkah," he said, and vanished.

Wherever I have travelled, I've been touched by gestures of magnanimity. Music has bridged all the barriers of language and gaps of culture and class. I've watched it bring out a largeness of spirit in people which has made the universe shrink to Marshall McLuhan's global village. Through music, worlds have opened to me that I never could have dreamed of entering in my girlhood fantasies. But of all the privileged glimpses I've had, one of the most fascinating was a peek behind the scenes into the house that Mao built.

In 1978 Walter Homburger invited me to accompany the Toronto Symphony on a trip to the People's Republic of China. The Chinese had long been exposed to Western music, but during the Cultural Revolution, certain works had been banned there as decadent. A few years before Walter's invitation, the Vancouver Symphony had asked me to go on a trip to Peking, but our planned program of Romantic music, including my solo in Berlioz's *Nuits d'été*, had been rejected by the Chinese as counter-revolutionary. In the end, for a variety of reasons, that trip never did come off. By 1978, however, although the Peking Orchestra still hadn't been allowed to play Beethoven and only had a repertoire of three pieces approved in the previous three years, a lot of the constraints had been relaxed. But just to be on the safe side, I decided to sing something that had its roots in music of the people – Mahler's cycle based on German folk poetry, *Das Knaben Wunderhorn*.

The day we arrived in Peking, it was snowing slightly and the winds were raging in from the Gobi Desert. It was so cold that we couldn't resist the old cliché that we had brought our own Canadian weather with us.

Visits such as ours were still new to China then and our welcoming ceremony was the height of formality. At least fifty Chinese dignitaries greeted us at the airport. Then, when it came time to allot us cars for the drive into the city, they followed a strict pecking order – but not our pecking order at all. In the first car they put the president of the orchestra; I was assigned to the second as the soloist; then Walter Homburger, the general manager, followed in the third; and last of all came Andrew Davis, the conductor. In China, the conductor is far from the most important person in the orchestra.

From the airport to the centre of Peking, there is a long highway lined with trees which reminded me of the roads in the south of France with their endless *allées* framed in poplars. In Peking, the streets were jammed with thousands of bicycles, and since a law obliged the drivers of cars to honk their horns whenever they passed a cyclist, there was non-stop cacophony.

The government installed us in one of the older hotels where everything was decorated in a colourless "greige." External Affairs had advised us beforehand not to wear too much jewellery or overly bright colours so as not to contrast too glaringly with the monochromatic colours of the revolution, but it would have taken an all-out effort not to stand out from that decor. Every room had a table with a thermos of hot water, a canister of tea, a cup with a lid to brew the tea and a package of cigarettes with matches. Mao had smoked so everyone was supposed to.

Some of the orchestra members found their rooms overrun with cockroaches and the ubiquitous beetles became the running joke of the tour. I didn't notice any myself, but while we were there, Andrew Davis was celebrating his birthday, so Corkie Monohan, a double bass player who later became Andrew's wife, trapped one of them and we painted it with nail polish to make it resemble a jewelled brooch. Then we wrapped it in a box and presented it to him as a present.

The food was fascinating, with menus of snake and wild dog, among other exotica. I did notice there was a distinct absence of pets in the streets. I didn't always know what I was eating and sometimes I was afraid to ask. At every formal banquet, there was a toast with *mao tai*, an alcohol which is not unlike slivovitz. The first time I tried it, I thought it tasted like paint remover, but after a while it grew on me. Everywhere we went, the Chinese were so generous and gracious. They wouldn't let us pay for our laundry to be done or even for my visit to the hairdresser.

Before we had left, External Affairs had suggested that it would be wonderful if I could do an encore in Chinese. "Now wait a minute," I said. "I sing in twenty-five languages but Chinese is not one of them. I have no idea what the sounds mean." Singing Chinese is extremely difficult because the sound originates much higher in the body than in any Western music; as I visualize it, it comes out between the eyes. For a classical singer, that high metallic tone is completely foreign. Still, I agreed to try if they could find an instructor to teach me a very slow one-verse lullaby and sing it into a tape-recorder for me to take along on the trip.

They sent me Abe Mannheim, the librarian of the Vancouver Symphony, who had lived in China for some years and who taught me a song called "Nanni-wan." I wasn't too sure what I was learning, but I consoled myself with the thought that I could brush up on it when I got to Peking. On the first day there, I arrived at rehearsal and found we were such a curiosity that a crowd of 5,000 had turned out to watch us, mainly young people in khaki uniforms. The whole rehearsal was also being filmed by the Chinese television news. Before a number began, an announcer called out the name of the piece from the stage. When he finally announced "Nanni-wan," the audience went berserk. It was one of the country's most popular songs.

I sang the first verse and the crowd went wild. The second verse produced the same reaction. But when I was almost through the third verse, I began to hear titters and I realized that something was terribly wrong. I had been assigned a charming interpreter, Mr. Duan, and when he came backstage later, he complimented me on my Chinese. "Well, I don't really know any Chinese," I admitted. "I learned the sounds by rote, but I'm embarrassed because I have a feeling that I didn't get them quite right. What was I saying out there?"

He explained to me that Nanni-wan was the name of a village, a beautiful site with trees and flowers which the workers had planted and where their sheep grazed in the fields. "The first verse was perfect," he said.

"What about the second verse?" I said.

The second verse, he told me, described how Nanni-wan had gotten old and no one lived there anymore; it had become empty, barren and dusty. "The second verse was more than perfect," he said.

"More than perfect?" I began to get the drift of Mr. Duan's diplomacy. "Tell me about the third verse."

"Well, in the third verse, you mix up words a little," he said. "Song says, 'Then came the revolution and Regiment 395 arrived and brought in the workers. So learn the lesson of Nanni-wan, because they made it bloom again.'"

"And what did I say?" I asked nervously.

"You said, 'Then came the revolution and Regiment 395 arrived and brought in the workers, so learn the lesson of Nanni-wan: now it is deserted and forlorn, there are no people there at all!'"

My gaffe became a national joke, but apparently it endeared me to the Chinese. Everywhere we travelled in the country after that, in the street or in hotel elevators, people would come up to me and touch my arm with a sweet shy little smile and giggle, "Oh, Nanni-wan!" At every concert, they demanded it again as my encore. A few years ago, before Trudeau retired, he invited me to a reception in Ottawa in honour of the visiting Chinese Prime Minister. As soon as the Prime Minister saw me, he walked over. "Ah, Forrester," he greeted me, "you are very famous in China."

"Yes, Mr. Prime Minister," I said. "By your mistakes shall you be known." He couldn't suppress his laughter.

By then I had already gone back to China a second time. In the spring of 1982, the People's Republic had invited me on a cultural exchange to both give recitals and classes. They asked me to bring another singer along, so I thought of the Quebec bass-baritone Claude Corbeil, who has a great jovial personality. We chose Claude Savard as our accompanist. Our itinerary was to take us from the

Peking Conservatory to those in Shenyang and Harbin, with the National Film Board following gamely along to record the trip for a short documentary which later ran on the CBC entitled *Singing: A Joy in Any Language*.

Driving in from the airport to Peking, I immediately noticed the changes which had taken place in only four years. The avenue of trees I remembered had mush-roomed into a forest, thanks to a reforestation program which asks every citizen to plant one tree a year. When the Chinese decide to do something, they go all out.

In China, people were fascinated by a voice as low as mine, particularly since their tradition requires them to sing in a high-pitched series of squawks. The whole of Chinese opera is still performed in an archaic language, which is a sort of falsetto on springs. But once the Chinese decided to promote singing in the Western style, there was no lack of marvellous voices; when you can hand-pick the best from a billion singers, you end up with a lot of talent. The government really indulges the musicians it chooses for training. Singers live free of charge, are much better fed than the average citizen and don't have to do anything all day but study. As in Russia, they're totally govern-ment-supported. Some Western countries might take les-sons from the Chinese on how to treat their artists. In Canada I still occasionally run into people who inquire about what it is I *really* do for a living.

Claude's and my Chinese students were like sponges, they learned so fast. But to surmount an 800-year-old tradition which is totally at odds with ours, some of them needed coaching on a very basic level. I had to teach them to open up their entire bodies and not to sing only on the throat muscles. I also kept having to interrupt lessons on breathing and interpretation to correct basic pronuncia-tion. I hope before the next trip I make to China to teach, the government will pave the way by giving the students some lessons in German, French and Italian in advance. To get around the language barrier in our recitals, Claude and I chose a crazy finale, Rossini's "Duet for Cats." The audiences couldn't believe that two ordinarily soulful singers would carry on a dialogue of musical meows. But cats sound the same in every country and ours were the hit of the tour.

The students became very attached to me and even after I had given my last class and, I thought, said my good-byes, the officials from the Ministry of Culture insisted on taking me back to the conservatory for another farewell from my pupils. They had prepared a little ceremony and one girl was singing *Kindertotenlieder* in my honour. But the instant she opened her mouth, the interpretation was so wrong-headed that I had to interrupt her. "Wait a minute! Stop!" I said. "You have a beautiful voice but you don't understand the poem at all. This is about a parent who has lost a child, it's not a romantic little ballad. You can't sing it that way." I ended up giving another three-hour lesson at my own goodbye party.

On the way to the airport at dawn the next morning, a mist was rising through the *allée* of trees along the road. It gave the landscape a surreal look, and sprinkled among the woods were elderly Chinese in their straw peasant hats taking their morning exercises – striking the controlled poses of Tai-chi. They looked like herons and flamingoes moving through the fog in slow motion. It was such a stunning image.

I had told Chinese officials on that trip that it wasn't fair for a foreign visitor like myself to come and teach for only two weeks, then fly off again. "You plant a seed and then you're not there to see that it takes root and grows correctly," I said.

Recently I was invited to dinner by the Chinese ambassador in Ottawa. I had thought it would be a large formal dinner, but I was the only guest at this sumptuous meal which seemed to have a dozen courses. As we were sitting sipping our *mao tais* and exchanging the ritual pleasantries which always begin any conversation in China, the ambassador told me that he had just returned from Peking and that he brought me a message from his Prime

Minister: the government wanted me to come back to China to teach for six months. Six months was out of the question, although some day I might return for an extended period – as long as they guarantee that I don't have to take another tour of the Great Wall and the Ming tombs. But as the ambassador saw me groping for words to respond to such a staggering invitation, his eyes twinkled in a mischievous smile.

"The Prime Minister told me to tell you," he said, "that your seedlings are waiting."

TWENTY-FIVE

No Diva

FOR YEARS, interviewers used to ask why I didn't sing opera. To many of them, that seemed the natural outlet for a classical singer. I would patiently explain that it was a pure case of egotism. In a concert, I could run through a whole gamut of emotions on stage for ninety minutes, using my voice to best advantage, and I didn't have to share the audience with anybody. Opera composers almost never wrote works to show off the stuff of altos and if they did, it was usually a ten-minute supporting role. After all, I've never been the Carmen type.

It also didn't take me long to realize that concert singers could earn more money than most opera stars. I could fly into town, sing a performance and be gone again to my next engagement the following day with my fee in my pocket. When you're doing an opera, it's not unusual to rehearse for three weeks, but you're only paid for the performances themselves. I couldn't afford to spend that much time running through a ten-minute part as some soprano's mother-in-law when I had five children to feed at home.

Most singers start out in opera and, as they grow older and their voices diminish, they end their careers as concert artists performing in smaller halls. But I've gone about the whole process backwards. I'm singing more and more opera now that I've hit the downside of my career. In retrospect, I realize the amazing part is not that it took me so long to come to opera, but that – after some of the horrendous experiences I had – I'm still singing it at all. For a while, every time I stepped onto an opera company stage, it seemed like an invitation to disaster.

My introductions to the form were ordinary enough, but nothing that made me want to continue. Pauline Donalda, who had been one of Canada's most famous opera stars and had sung with Caruso, had given me tiny roles in her Montreal Opera Guild productions when I was twenty-three: one solo line as a sewing girl in Charpentier's *Louise*, then the innkeeper's folk song in *Boris Godunov*. They whetted my appetite for the stage, but not for more bit parts like that. By then I had just made my recital debut in Montreal and had tasted what it was like to have the whole show to myself.

Soon after that, Irving Guttman, who was just starting his career as a director, was responsible for talking me into my first major opera role. A group of us, including Irving, had gone to the Montreal Forum to see Blanche Thebom sing Delilah and she was so sexy that when we came out Irving started tearing off his shirt right there on the street. "Maureen, we've got to do an opera together," he kept declaiming while the rest of us were in stitches over his dramatics. But within a year Irving was good to his word, staging Gian Carlo Menotti's *The Consul* in Cornwall, Ontario. He talked me into playing the grandmother, a rich role with a wonderful lullaby to sing. My only concern was that, at twenty-five, I wouldn't look the part. But when my picture appeared on the front page of the Cornwall paper the day after the opening, I saw that I needn't have worried. I looked like some eighty-year-old hag who didn't have a tooth in her head. No matter what opera role I've sung since, I've never had one that would inspire anybody to exit tearing off his shirt.

It was nearly another ten years before I succumbed to the temptation of opera again. In 1962 Nicholas Goldschmidt persuaded me to sing in a production of Gluck's *Orpheus and Eurydice* with the Canadian Opera Company at O'Keefe Centre. As often happened, I got to play the male role – the one that was first sung by a castrato – Orpheus, who is the lead. It was a propitious part for my formal opera debut, but when Nicholas approached me about it, his first question was, "How are your legs?" He wanted to give them the once-over because Orpheus spends the whole opera wearing only a tunic. The production was stunning, almost ahead of its time: Hanya Holm's choreography featured dancers who whirled through Hades in a blaze of scarlet streamers and lights which exploded from raised platforms, floating surrealistically behind us. My part went well enough and the famous aria "Che Farò Senza Euridice," which I had often sung in recitals, earned enthusiastic reviews. But personally, I felt too young to carry such a heavy leading role. I had never really acted before and I had to navigate it all on instinct while singing very difficult music.

I had also never sung before on a stage as enormous as O'Keefe Centre's and I didn't have the experience then of throwing my voice into such a cavernous upholstered expanse. The Canadian Opera Company cheats now and subtly mikes the O'Keefe but it didn't then and I still argue that for a young company like ours, the O'Keefe Centre, even lightly miked, absolutely kills the voice. You're forcing the sound all the time. At that point in my life, I was vocally unequipped to deal with the O'Keefe, and I knew in my heart of hearts that I hadn't been world-shaking as Orpheus. In fact, my New York managers had invited the woman who ran the Chicago Opera Company to hear me and it was obvious that I hadn't impressed her either. I never heard from her again.

In the early years of my career, André Mertens was constantly pushing me to try out for a role at the Metropolitan Opera. He argued that if my brochure listed an appearance at the Met, it would boost my fees by thousands of dollars. But something in me had always resisted. At first I didn't think my voice was big enough for the Met's 4,000-seat hall, then later, as I became more successful, I wasn't interested in the also-ran roles which inevitably fell to contraltos and which would earn only two lines from the critics. I could sing a concert in New York and get a rave review to myself every time.

Finally I gave in and, against my better judgment, agreed to audition for the Met. If I had been smart I would have been preparing a stunning role that I wanted to sing and which was meant for my kind of voice – something like Delilah. But I never saw myself as Delilah any more than I did as Carmen. All the parts I seemed to sing best were those of decadent kings.

In fact, I may have had a subconscious fear of opera because it was an unknown world which I didn't have anyone to guide me through. I had heard horrendous stories of how people had been forced to sing the wrong thing while they were on contract at the Met and had crucified their voices; it had finished their careers. I became so convinced that I would never impress anybody singing opera that, although it was totally unlike me, I didn't even bother to prepare well for the audition. No wonder, with a defeatist attitude like that, my first try-out at the Met was an absolute bust.

La Scala had also offered me a chance to sing whatever role I wished, but Italian opera seemed even more forbidding. There were too many good voices there. To be a success in Italy I realized I would have had to sing either an ancient opera that was so totally unknown it was a curiosity, or a modern one, which would win attention for its novelty.

For a long time I avoided opera, happy with my career as it was. But gradually my confidence – and my voice – grew. Finally in 1966 André Mertens persuaded me once more that I simply had to make my New York opera debut before it was too late. In fact, some critics believed it was an unwritten rule that if a singer hadn't performed on the stage of a first-class opera house by the age of thirty, he or she would never make it, and I was already thirty-six by then. That year, Julius Rudel, for whom I had sung at the

Caramoor Festival, offered me the role of Cornelia in a New York City Opera production of Handel's *Julius Caesar*, which he had designed expressly for Beverly Sills. It was to be a gala occasion, not only because it was the 1966 season opener at Lincoln Centre, but because *Julius Caesar* had almost never been performed. Like all of Handel's operas it was extremely difficult and very long, a real test of endurance. But Beverly and Julius had already established an annual tradition of resurrecting some obscure opera which would make both their careers shine and the whole New York musical world was holding its breath for this one.

Cornelia, the widow of Pompey, was the second most important female role next to Beverly's Cleopatra and the part had some really very beautiful arias. When Julius offered it to me, André Mertens was overjoyed at the prospect of such a vehicle. My public relations agent, Audrey Michaels, worked overtime drumming up publicity for me and I received an enormous splash in all the papers. In fact, I got so much hype that I could see it was getting on Beverly's nerves. I came into rehearsal one day and she said, "*Well*, that was quite a spread you got in *The New York Times*!"

"Look," I said, "it's not so much because of me, even though this is my debut. It's because I've got a public relations agent. You should get one yourself."

She promptly followed my advice. Of course, the timing couldn't have been better. It was that production of *Julius Caesar* which catapulted Beverly Sills to real superstardom.

Beverly had agreed to sing Cleopatra's role only if Julius Rudel left in the big aria in the second act. Then she had ordered the most remarkable coloratura decorations to show off the best part of her voice, spinning it out in long cadenzas in the very high stratas. In Handel, such a thing is stylistically possible. You can sing an aria through straight, then come back and do it with embellishments in a *da capo* which make it almost improvisational, like jazz.

It's like putting icing on a cake. I was so naïve and inexperienced that I never even thought of doing the same. In fact, if I had known how stunning Beverly's role was I would never have accepted the part as my New York debut. Although my reviews were good, Cornelia wasn't headline-making material.

In fact, for me that production represented a triumph over adversity. José Varona, who is usually such a marvellous designer, had a conception of my character that he had taken from a Roman statue. Now that's a nice idea but Roman statues don't have to clamber up and down stairs saddled with two tons of costume and wig. My headdress was covered in thousands of tiny corkscrew curls which looked as if they had been carved straight out of stone – and felt the same. It is an understatement to say that I hated it. But worse, I didn't have the courage to say so. Because it was my debut, I didn't dare make a fuss. The costume itself must have weighed forty pounds. The skirt was covered in huge leather appliqués of palm leaves sprayed with gold paint that turned it into an enormous immovable object. I looked like a giant overdressed pumpkin.

At the end of the second act I had a lovely duet with Beverly Wolff, who played my son Sextus, during which I had to walk up a stairway of scaffolding to a little platform where he was in jail. In the dress rehearsal, I suddenly realized that my skirt was twice as wide as the ladder. I had to climb up those rungs at an angle, hauling forty pounds of gown behind and trying to make it seem effortless. I tell you, I felt defeated in that opera before I had even started.

On opening night, Peter Ustinov, who is a real opera buff, was sitting out front in a box. In one of the early scenes, I was supposed to faint dead away. Well, you just try and faint in that costume. I put my hand to my head, sang, "Woe is me," but when I collapsed, my body disappeared into this skirt which stayed upright with a life of its own. As I went down in what was supposed to be my shining moment of melodrama, I heard Peter Ustinov let out a wild hoot of laughter.

It's a wonder I ever did another opera, but I'm a bear for punishment. A year later, Beverly and I did *Julius Caesar* again at the Teatro Colon in Buenos Aires, but this time it was a different version – the same music set in a different period with, thank heavens, different costumes. There was also a different conductor: Karl Richter, the German harpsichordist-organist who was famous for his choral works as founder of the Munich Bach Choir. He was a strange man with a very unorthodox style and he and Beverly did not hit it off at all. After she had ordered all these decorations written for her part, he didn't want her to sing them. It came down to quite a serious set-to between them. In the end, she all but told him where he could get off. "Look, I was hired here because I became famous for doing the part like this in New York," she said, "and I don't care what you say. I'm going to do it my way and if you don't like it, you can lump it." Richter was so mad at her that all through the opera, he refused to look at her. Whenever she sang, he would conduct with his head buried in the score, just beating time like a robot.

It was a hard time for Beverly, but she is a tough dame. Beverly and I became good friends during those productions. "Murine," she always calls me now. "Murine, you're so good for the eyes." And I call her "Befferly." She came up through the school of hard knocks. She had been singing a long time, ever since she was a child star on the radio, chirruping Rinso White commercials, then going through all those fat teenage years when she had to take every job that came along. She may not have had much education but she has a wonderful intuitive brand of smarts. As soon as you meet Beverly, you can tell you don't fool around with her. She knows what she does well and she capitalizes on it. She's a good actress, she moves well on the stage and she always makes sure she has a lot of control over her costumes. She has a very tiny waist, but she's heavy in the hips and thighs – just the opposite of me – so you always see her in costumes with décolletage or fussiness at the neck, then a nipped-in waist with big full skirts of tulle. She was smart to wear what showed her off to advantage. Nowadays, after years of enduring costumes that were really horrible, I've finally learned that lesson myself.

Norman Treigle played Caesar in both those productions and I picked up a lot watching him. Norman had sung with Beverly for years and together they chose roles which showcased both their talents. But as Beverly became a bigger and bigger star, she naturally had to start accepting parts without him. You could see that Norman gradually lost his confidence and he finally gave up singing and died a tragic figure. It seemed so sad that he had put all his eggs in Beverly's basket because, as good as his voice was, Norman was also a phenomenal actor. He had a gaunt, haunted face and when he made a gesture as Caesar, I noticed that he would take his time extending his arm, then at the very last moment let his wrist snap up to punctuate the high note. He could create such power with an economy of movement.

After the performance, which began at 9 p.m. in Buenos Aires, you take your make-up off and the cast emerges into an enormous foyer where the management has erected tables to keep the fans from clawing the stars to death. Then you stand there and sign autographs for at least an hour. Sometimes we wouldn't get back to the hotel until 3 a.m.

One night, Norman and his wife and Beverly and I were in the elevator on the way up to our rooms when suddenly it stopped between floors. We were trapped. Beverly let out the most blood-curdling soprano screams. Boy, did we get action fast. But the mechanics couldn't find what was wrong and had to chase all over the city to find the chief elevator technician. Beverly just kept hollering and from the corridor the hotel management kept trying to shush her up so as not to awaken the other guests.

"Look," said Beverly, "if Sills doesn't sleep, nobody does."

That same year I accepted the role of La Cieca, the blind mother in *La Gioconda*, which Lotfi Mansouri was staging with the San Francisco Opera. It was the first time I had worked with Lotfi but it wasn't his first exposure to me. It turned out that he had been in the audience the night of my Town Hall debut in New York years before. He told me that he had wept at that concert, unable to believe a young unknown just starting out could put so much feeling into such a difficult repertoire.

La Cieca was my first part as an old woman since my role in *The Consul*, and Lotfi knew I was insecure about how to approach it. "Now, I want you to be a big success," he said, "so do anything you want to feel comfortable in the role." But he made me think about what it must be like to be blind. I remembered how sightless people never really focus on anything in a room; their eyes stare straight ahead, blank. I played it that way, but it was more difficult to do than it sounds. By the end of the performance, my eyes would absolutely ache from fighting back the blinks.

One day I showed up at rehearsal even though I hadn't been scheduled, and Lotfi looked shocked. "Oh, darling, I'm so sorry, did you think you had a rehearsal this afternoon?" he asked.

"No," I said. "But I don't know the opera and I thought I'd come to learn it." Lotfi loved that so much that apparently he now tells all his students that's how a pro learns an opera. But in fact I adored the rehearsals and I learned a lot watching – not only about *La Gioconda*. Leyla Gencer, a soprano with a fabled ego and temperament, was singing Gioconda and Laura was being played by Grace Bumbry, who had studied with Lotte Lehmann and was then one of the hottest of the rising young stars. At that point, Bumbry felt she had to have all the trappings of a diva, so she was always buying herself Lamborghinis and arriving in limousines a block and a half long. She must have spent all her fees on that kind of window-dressing. When Bumbry arrived in San Francisco, the rivalry between her and Gencer was palpable. They would never look at each other in a performance or take bows together. It would have been terrible if it hadn't been so comical.

One afternoon I was sitting in the audience at rehearsal beside Gencer. Bumbry was on stage singing and she was spectacular, prowling the boards like a sinewy black cat. She had an innate sexiness when she moved. "Doesn't she look just like a gorgeous sleek panther?" I said to Leyla.

"A panther?" said Leyla. "Oh, no, darling, I think of her more as a spider." She paused. "A black widow."

Opera provides a field day for egos. But those star turns don't go down very well with me. I've never resented anyone else's success. As far as I'm concerned, you can't be the best; you can only be the best you can be. Everyone's voice is different and there's no point in wishing that your voice were like someone else's. Still, sometimes you overlook prima donna behaviour when you thrill to a really marvellous performance.

One of the most exciting productions of my life was in 1968 singing Brangäne, the handmaiden in Wagner's *Tristan und Isolde*. Zubin Mehta was conducting it for the Opera of Quebec and Jon Vickers was singing Tristan, a role that he had already become famous for in Europe. My part was meaty and long, almost all of the first act. It was originally written for a soprano, but to differentiate Brangäne from Isolde in their duets many conductors choose a heavier voice. Still, after singing it, I think they ought to cast a mezzo, not a contralto. I found the part very difficult to learn anyway and the long, long phrases require incredible breath control and support, but a lot of the high passages through the second act left me vocally exhausted. As I sang it, my rib cage actually grew in size because the sound you need to make for Wagner comes from deeper and farther back than when you're singing Verdi.

The stage director came up with a brilliant idea for my watchtower aria in the second act: Brangäne's warning that Isolde should not fall in love with Tristan because it's actually he who has been responsible for killing her betrothed. He sent me up the backstage elevator at Place des Arts into the flies, where he planted me on a catwalk five stories above the middle of the audience. It's a good thing I didn't have an attack of vertigo. I felt like I was performing a high-wire act. He had to install a remote control TV set up there so I could see Zubin conducting below. The audience couldn't figure out where the sound was coming from, but from that height my voice was magnified in a stunning wrap-around effect, as if the theatre had been studded with at least 50 speakers.

But all the derring-do which that required was worth it to me just to hear Jon sing Tristan. He had done the part so many times by then that he had made it his own. It was worked into the voice. He was superb and, if I never hear the opera again, I'll always remember that production. It was also emotional because it was the farewell performance of the Opera of Quebec, which had gone bankrupt. There were fans hanging over the pit on the last night weeping, "You can't close down!" You couldn't beg, borrow or steal a ticket to that opera.

Jon started out in his career at almost the same time I did. I had first heard him sing in a performance of the *Messiah* in Kingston, Ontario, when he was still a slim, handsome young man, freshly graduated from the Toronto Conservatory, and I was dumbfounded by his voice. But it was when he went to Europe that his career really took off. Jon is a fascinating singer who is also a brilliant actor and to my mind he has nearly always played roles which are parts of himself – characters caught in inner turmoil and anguish. He's a very complex human being, but it's thrilling to work with him. I'll never forget doing the death scene with him as the Countess in *The Queen of Spades* at the National Arts Centre in Ottawa. When he picked me up out of my chair and shook me after I had expired, I could go completely limp like a rag doll, staring unblinking out at the audience. It was exciting at last to play that scene with someone who could handle a big woman like myself and who wasn't afraid to be rough with me.

But I can't pretend that Jon and I have ever been close pals. He is rather private and doesn't socialize very much. Like a lot of *Heldentenors*, he is wrapped in a god-like aura and it doesn't always make him an easy person to be with. Once we were doing Handel's *Samson* together in Dallas and he showed up a week late for rehearsal. I suppose he figured that Lotfi Mansouri would work with the chorus and get everything ready for him, but it didn't help the rest of us who needed somebody to relate to on the stage. During that run, the soprano Patricia Wells and I found out it was Jon's birthday so we went to Neiman-Marcus and bought him a beautiful Irish sweater and a huge birthday cake. We planned to present it to him from the whole cast at the rehearsal break. In the first act, he was standing on a stairway waiting to sing "Total Eclipse," the aria he is famous for, when suddenly he announced, "Mr. Mansouri, I didn't come to rehearsal in order for you to work with the chorus. When you get ready for me, call me." And he swept out the door.

Needless to say, that didn't go over very well with the rest of the cast. We just left his present in his dressing room the next day with a note: "Sorry you didn't find it in your heart to stay last night. We had bought a birthday cake to help you celebrate but we found out that one of the choristers had a birthday too yesterday so we gave it to him instead. Too bad you couldn't make it to the party. Best wishes." Of course, Jon felt awful and was full of apologies.

By the time I sang in *Tristan*, I felt more comfortable in opera and finally, in 1974, the Met offered me a role: Erda in *Das Rheingold* and *Siegfried*, from Wagner's Ring cycle, which they were doing a month apart. Again I accepted against my better judgment. Even though Schumann-Heink had made Erda famous, it wasn't a brilliant vehicle for a Met debut. Both those roles were only four minutes long. As the Goddess of Earth, Erda is not so much a player in the drama as she is the voice of doom.

I learned the parts in a flash and the day of my first rehearsal I was terribly excited. After all, here I was singing at last at the Met in a role which suited me: as I joked, I had spent my whole life as an earth mother; I was finally getting paid for it. Dressed up in my very best, off I went to the Metropolitan Opera House. The switchboard operator who was guarding the stage door welcomed me and initiated me into the Met rituals: already awaiting me was a stack of fan mail a foot high. When you're debuting at the Met, everyone wants your autograph because later it will be worth more on the market. Collecting operatic autographs has become a full-fledged industry.

She directed me to the fourth floor, but when I got there all I found was a carpenter hammering sets together. "Honey," he said, "you're on the wrong floor, but if you want to stick around, we can use all the help we can get." Finally, I located my rehearsal coach a storey below. When he played the first chord, I realized it wasn't from *Das Rheingold*. "No," he said, "I thought we'd do *Siegfried* today." Then all he wanted to do was tell me the latest Met gossip. It all seemed rather casual to me, considering the fact that I had my first rehearsal down on the big stage in half an hour and I'd never even seen the opera in my life.

Finally, he led me downstairs. The rehearsal was more than half through, but it didn't matter. My part didn't come until after the first four and a half hours of the opera. I walked on stage and suddenly I found myself on the set of an enormous dark mountain. There were rocks and crags of cardboard everywhere. I panicked. My God, I thought, where do I make my entrance? Then somebody told me that I was to come out of the Alps above. One thing about Wagner: in case you fall asleep, he writes your theme into the music fifty bars before your appearance so you have plenty of time to get yourself in the mood. I walked backstage behind the rocks. A stagehand was standing beside a hydraulic lift reading a comic book with a flashlight. "I'm Erda. Do you know where I make my entrance?" I interrupted him.

"Oh, you must be the dame I screw up here," he said.

He winched me up high into the set and there I was, my head just peering over the top of the mountain about five blocks from the front of the stage. I was so far from the orchestra pit I could have used a pair of binoculars to see the conductor, Sixten Ehrling. I just got out the first note of "Erda's Warning" when he decided to call a break. "Now, good for you to have found your way to your place up there, Miss Forrester," somebody called to me and off they all went for coffee. When they came back, I sang my part. I waited for some tips, some stage direction, anything. "Bravo, Miss Forrester," they said and that was it. The stagehand winched me down and I left. Talk about an anti-climax.

When it came time for the dress rehearsal, I showed up in the make-up room. "Oh, we never make up Erda," they said. "You won't need it and you won't need a costume because only your head shows over the rocks. There's no spotlight on you anyway at that point; you're just an ominous voice." They gave me a sort of bathing cap to hide my blonde hair and lit me in a bilious green light. That's when I started referring to my role as that of the Jolly Green Giant.

The night of the opening, everybody came – Eugene and Irene Bird from Toronto, plus a lot of my pals from Washington and New York. There were flowers everywhere and after the performance, people streamed backstage saying, "Oh boy, aren't you glad that's over with?"

and "My, my, isn't it terrific to debut at the Met?" But I was smart enough to notice that nobody was saying I had sounded great. Finally I said to Eugene later, "Tell me honestly, how was it?"

"Well, sweetheart, let's put it this way," he said. "When you can't see someone, you're not exactly sure you can hear them either." The *New York Daily News* noted that I was "barely visible," and *The New York Times*'s Donal Henahan said I was "musically fine, but somewhat lacking in contralto power and timbre, particularly since Erda was placed deep in the stage and far from the amplification." The critic for the *New York Post* wrote that it was difficult to tell whether I was the Goddess of Earth "or a greatly enlarged amoeba." That was my triumphant debut at the Met.

I wasn't any luckier when the Met asked me back the next season to sing Ulrica, the gypsy fortune-teller in Verdi's *A Masked Ball*. It's a thankless part to do; nobody has had a big success with it since Marian Anderson sang it for her Met debut. It's very, very low, like a bass in drag, but that production with Roberta Peters and Louis Quilico was particularly ghastly for me. My costume looked like a haystack gone wrong. It was falling apart and I left a trail behind me everywhere I went. If anyone ever wanted to locate the fortune-teller in that enormous theatre, all he had to do was follow the straw.

It's every singer's dream to sing at the Metropolitan Opera but I can honestly say that I've had more satisfaction singing with smaller companies in San Francisco or Santa Fe or Toronto. It's not a case of sour grapes. At the Met, one performer may do opening night but another often does the next night and still another does the recording. When we recorded *Siegfried*, Birgit Nilsson, who hadn't sung any of the performances, stepped in for the broadcast. At the Met the cast is always changing like that because some star either has to go off to another engagement or suddenly falls sick. The trouble is that the newcomers never have the chance to rehearse with the rest of the cast or relate to them. That's what has made prompting such an institution at the Met. A new baritone flies in, doesn't know the staging, and can't remember what they told him about it that afternoon, so what does he do? He spends the entire performance planted in front of the prompter's box where a voice sings every line a bar ahead of the music. It becomes very distracting to other performers. It's not acting anymore, it's just a concert performance with sets.

The smaller companies don't have prompters and the cast plays the whole production through together till the end of the run. In fact, it was far from the Met that I learned what opera is really supposed to be about – ensemble performances, a camaraderie of musicians.

Now, at this stage of my life, I love to do opera. For me, it's magical – like a child's game of dress-up. You get to put on extravagant costumes and emote in exotic settings, play-acting out your most bizarre fantasies. But it's no accident that I've now turned to singing more operatic roles. One morning when I was on the road for a concert tour, I woke up in yet another hotel room which looked like all the others of its kind and I wasn't even sure what town I was in. I thought to myself: this is really a lonely life for someone who loves being with people so much. Although appearing with orchestras is more lucrative, I'm now having a better time in that portion of each year I spend as a member of opera casts, kibitzing all day and often joining the other singers for dinner at night. In fact, it's why I love the rehearsals of an opera even more than the performances. For me, it's almost a let-down when opening night comes and we go our separate ways once we leave the theatre. After the solitary existence of a concert singer, to be part of an opera is like being part of a family again.

TWENTY-SIX

Bewitched, Bothered and Airborne

ON ONE OF the rare afternoons when I was around the house not long after we had moved back to Toronto in 1971, Linda brought a friend home from school. The little girl just stood in the doorway and stared at me. "Show her how you can fly, Mommy," Linda begged. "Just once around the living room." At a certain point, it seemed that every child in Canada, including my own son and daughters, believed that I could become airborne on a broomstick.

That was due to the wonder of television's technical wizardry. But it was also thanks to the inspiration of the conductor Mario Bernardi, who phoned me on a whim one day in 1970, when we were still living in Philadelphia. "I just wondered if I could ask you something," he had said, sounding unusually nervous. "We want to stage Humperdinck's *Hansel and Gretel* for the CBC and we'd like to offer you a role." I yawned, sure that he was going to suggest the small bland part of the mother, which didn't interest me. I was trying to think how to refuse diplomatically when he said, "Now, I hope you won't be offended, but we were wondering if you'd like to play the witch." The witch! It was the most delicious idea I had heard in the thirteen years since I had been discovered by Bruno Walter. I let out the cackle of glee which was to become my witch's trademark. That phone call changed the direction of my career.

Before I played that madcap witch's role, hardly anyone but my family and a few friends like Mario suspected I had a zany bone in my body. Early in my career, when I was thrown so young into a world still peopled by the great old men of music, I thought I had to be serious and majestic, even off stage. Reviewers perennially described me as "noble," and fans addressed me gravely as Madame. I was totally typecast – the lady-like square *Lieder* singer. In fact, when the Canadian music world heard I was to play the witch, Hermann Geiger-Torel, who ran the opera school, made no secret of telling people that he thought it was a terrible mistake. "She's no comedian!" he said. Little did that world know about my outrageous, raunchy side. But ever since that role, they've realized that it's my serious air which is the put-on part; the other part which lets it all hang out is the real me.

As soon as the *Hansel and Gretel* rehearsals began, I knew that this was the role I had been waiting for. Even the costume seemed inspired. Suzanne Mess designed a black waistcoat over a garish orange flowered skirt, which I wore under a wig of wild carrot curls that built into a phallic knob at the top of my head and fitted under my giant black pointed hat. It made me a dotty witch, not a sinister spooky one. The make-up took at least an hour to apply: it added warts to all my fingers and chin and a bizarre star on one cheek. Later when children would besiege me on the street after having seen the show, a lot of them would ask how long it took for me to put on my big false nose. Imagine trying to tell them that the nose in question was my own. My plastic surgeon, who had already taken his first of two passes at remodelling it by then, wouldn't have been pleased. But I think they were under the impression that I was wearing a false nose because I acted as if I had one. When I was preparing the role, I remembered reading something Spencer Tracy had said: that if you play a part as though you have a big nose, you don't need the make-up.

The costume, and Norman Campbell's brilliant coaxing as director, unleashed a craziness in me that I had never let out in all my years on the concert stage. I was having such fun clowning on the set that one day when Norman called a break, as I was walking past one of the cameras on my way to lunch, I leaned into the lens as a joke and stuck out my tongue. Suddenly we heard Norman's voice over the sound system from the control room: "Wonderful! Keep it in." On camera, with my face distorted by the closeup, my tongue looked like an enormous wicked snake and Norman spliced the shot into a scene where I stalked Hansel and Gretel through the forest.

Norman was a stickler for realism. For the final scene where Hansel and Gretel throw me into the oven, Murray Laufer had built an enormous bakelite contraption inside the witch's amazing mock-gingerbread house. It had an iron door with bricks underneath and a grate for an open fire. In rehearsal, I walked through the scene during which I was to sing "Tender Morsels," ending with Hansel and Gretel pushing me into the oven. Then Norman called for a take and I saw a stagehand light a real fire in the grate underneath. Norman said they wanted to shoot the flames, but that I was perfectly safe; besides, I'd only be inside a minute. Well, Hansel and Gretel pushed me through the oven door, which already was a tight fit, and slammed it shut. I crouched inside, doubled over, waiting for them to finish their duet exulting that the witch was dead. But the wait seemed an eternity. It must have lasted four minutes. I began to perspire, getting hotter and hotter inside that little bakelite cell. My carrot wig started to ooze streams of sweat and my make-up dissolved in rivulets. The heat became horrendous and I could only praise Suzanne Mess for designing a layered costume which kept me from burning off my backside. This was a sauna gone berserk. Finally, I heard Norman yell, "Cut!" and, believe me, if that take hadn't been good, they would have had to wait a day before shooting another. The witch had melted away. When a stagehand pulled open the oven door at last, I stuck my head out and cracked, "Toast, anyone?"

We didn't shoot the scenes in sequence and finally one morning Norman turned to me. "Well, Maureen, you fly today," he said. He led me into an enormous studio all painted a brilliant Wedgwood blue – floors, ceilings, everything, even the motorcycle which was parked in the centre of it. "What's that for?" I asked. "You're going to ride it," he said. Now, I had never been on a motorcycle in my life. But not only was I supposed to drive this Wedgwood-blue contraption around the studio in circles, I couldn't sit on the seat like some normal Hell's Angel. I was instructed to lie along it, as if I were leaning on my broom. Norman explained the technique of chroma-key to me: using certain cameras, he could shoot an image so that everything around it which was this particular colour of blue wouldn't be picked up by the lens. Then he could superimpose the image of me on whatever backdrop he liked – in this case, onto a broom swooping out a window and flying through the sky. It was magic time.

I climbed on my motorcycle and aimed the handlebars to follow the guideline they had drawn on the floor. Then, madly trying to steer in circles, I started to cackle. It sounds easy, but a singer can't just cackle like a normal witch or she would be hoarse instantly. I had to save my voice for the rest of the opera, which had some very difficult music. The only way for me to do it was as a vocal exercise, running up and down the scale. The script called for me to shriek in maniacal laughter for a full three minutes, but believe me, some of the screams on that soundtrack were for real. As the motorcycle picked up speed, I was petrified and half-dizzy, sure I was going to break my neck any minute. It was absolute insanity.

What a hit that show was! For years after, children would run up to me wherever I was singing in Canada, begging me to fly for them. I think the notion must have gone to my head. Later, whenever I was asked to repeat *Hansel and Gretel* on stage, I only agreed if I could take to the air. After all, I felt I had a reputation to keep up. When I performed it in Calgary, the theatre contracted the Boston Flying Company, which had helped stage *Peter Pan* in New York, to get me off the ground. But flying a sylph like Peter Pan is one thing and flying me is another. For days as we rehearsed, I kept asking the stage manager when the equipment I was to fly on would arrive and he kept assuring me that the only problem was a hold-up in Customs. The day of the performance, it was finally released. It took hours to install in the theatre. The opera was to open at 8:30 p.m., and at 5 p.m. the Boston Flying Company was giving me my first lesson in aerodynamics.

There was an enormous track running across the girders above the stage with wires criss-crossing back and forth, pulled with ropes by men below who essentially steered me. I was hooked onto the track through a wire from a metal plate embedded in a sort of corset that I wore under my costume. It had straps over the shoulders and under the legs, almost like a parachute truss, but of course it was so bulky that my costume wouldn't fit. We had to cut it open and re-attach it with fabric tape. And this with only hours to go until curtain time.

When it came time for the performance, the choreography called for me to walk out to the middle of the stage for my witch's dance, brandishing my broom, then to finish with a deep-knee bend which was a signal to the stage-hands to pull the ropes. Up I sailed fifty feet into the wings. All I could see was scenery – wires, ropes, a jungle of killer obstacles. Again, my cackling and shrieks came without the slightest prompting. I hurtled through the air at what felt like 100 miles an hour, sure I was about to decapitate myself. I would zoom toward one wall, catch myself with my feet, then push off at breakneck speed for the other side. When it came time to descend, the stage-hands caught me as I winged down, unhooked me, and I strode out on stage with my broomstick to break into a one-minute high B. It was always the best note I sang in the opera because in it you could hear all my relief at landing safely. The ovation afterward explained why I loved to do that part.

During the last performance in Calgary, I was making my first two aerial passes across the stage when I realized that I couldn't turn around to fly back again. I glanced down at the stagehands and they were all standing below with their hands covering their mouths in a look that signalled catastrophe. Suddenly, I started losing altitude fast, dropping like a rock. Two of the most strapping stagehands ran over and broke my fall. It turned out the wire had broken off the track. The audience couldn't see any of it and I managed to limp back on stage and make my high B, but everybody was absolutely shaken. Later, people kept coming up to me saying what a miracle it was that I hadn't been injured. "But don't worry, Maureen," the company manager said, "we took out a $1-million insurance policy on you." I just laughed, but I thought to myself: Honey, it wouldn't take long to go through a million dollars if I were a paraplegic. After that, I was pretty fussy about how anybody was going to fly me.

When I performed *Hansel and Gretel* again in San Diego, the opera company put an old one-time carney man in charge of my flight. He had once worked with trapeze artists, but I warned him that I was no trapeze queen. Before we started rehearsals, I went to the chief stagehand and slipped him a few hundred dollars. "Go and have yourselves a party on me," I said. "You're going to need all the strength you can get. I'm no lightweight." Those men had never known a gesture like that in their lives. They went out and bought pizzas and beer, brought it back and initiated me into the company of honorary stagehands. I've always appreciated the people who work in the theatre behind the scenes – the dressers and the hair stylists and the make-up and costume artists. If they don't like you, they can ruin your performance. I've seen tenors who were nasty to a costume-maker find suddenly at dress rehearsal that their neck piece has been made just a little too tight. Some performers forget that it takes more than what the audience sees on stage to create a work of art.

I feel I'm too old for the witch's role now and I've

finally put that part to bed. But it was my liberation. Suddenly people began looking at me in a different light and offering me comic and dramatic parts. That opera opened everybody's eyes to the fact that I could act and now I have a new lease on life as a character actress. Character parts were such a release for me. It's odd because in everyday life I'm very placid; I hate to create a fuss. But clearly I must have a melodramatic side to me that was just crying to be let out.

After *Hansel and Gretel*, meaty parts started to roll in. The next year I sang the role of the goddess Fricka in a Canadian Opera Company production of *Die Walküre*. The part was small, but again it allowed me to indulge in histrionics of a kind I had never had a chance to unleash before: a torrent of bitchiness. I hadn't been a screamer in my marriage, but when I strode on stage for Fricka's big second-act monologue, I let it rip, giving my stage husband Wotan hell for twenty minutes. No wonder some critics accused me of stealing the show. I would walk out of that theatre at night feeling absolutely refreshed!

Soon after, the Montreal Opera offered me the role of flibbertigibbet Mistress Quickly in *Falstaff* – a part that was a real vocal challenge, and comic, but in a classical sense. Then Brian Macdonald talked me into playing the outrageous wicked step-mother Madame de la Haltière in Massenet's version of the Cinderella story, *Cendrillon*, which we did first at the National Arts Centre in Ottawa before taking it to Washington, Paris, San Francisco and New York. The opera hadn't been staged in over a century so it caused a stir, especially in France, Massenet's home, and Frederica Von Stade, who played our Cinderella in the original production, had helped fan an interest in it by recording a part of it earlier.

Brian Macdonald is an inspired director and, as we rehearsed, he would see possibilities and work them into a scene. That production was organized slapstick. My costume was hysterical – an enormous balloon of red and purple which made me look like the Michelin tire man.

Halfway through rehearsal, Brian decided that it ought to descend from the ceiling. After the ugly stepsisters and I did our little dance in our pantaloons, suddenly, in keeping with the tempo, my dress came down out of the sky and dropped over my head. I unhooked it, so that I didn't get dragged up into the flies again, and we were off to the ball – all without missing a beat. At every performance, that scene stopped the show.

Cendrillon also changed people's idea of me. At the Paris production, who should appear backstage but my one-time British manager John Coast. "Maureen," he said incredulously, "I had no idea you could be funny!" I could see that he regretted having dropped me.

But the role which I found the most exciting to play was the one I ought to have held out to do as my debut at the Met: Klytaemnestra in Strauss's *Elektra*, which I sang for the Canadian Opera Company in 1983. To prepare for it, I did what I should have done earlier when I first ventured so disastrously into opera: I studied the part with a coach. In opera you're booked up sometimes four seasons in advance and so, a year before I was to sing the part, when I was in San Francisco performing in *Cendrillon* with time on my hands during the day, I found a coach named Philip Eisenberg, who had been a prompter both at the Met and with the San Francisco Opera Company. I could learn the notes of an opera by myself at the piano, but what he taught me was how to master the role on stage.

He had worked with *Elektra* many times and he would warn me to watch for a certain note and not to sing it softly because the orchestra always played very heavily at that point. He alerted me to the fact that at another point, when the stage directions called for me to run up a flight of stairs, I wouldn't be able to see the conductor at the moment and would be in danger of missing my cue. I learned to turn around at the top of the staircase and catch the conductor's beat. A singer has no way of knowing tricks like that from the music itself, and an audience doesn't realize what a difference tiny practical details such as those can make in a performance. An opera coach doesn't teach you how to sing; he warns you about the pitfalls of the music.

But some things you have to learn on your own. When I made my entrance in the dress rehearsal as part of Klytaemnestra's gala procession, I suddenly noticed with horror that I had no voice. Only minutes earlier, I hadn't been hoarse at all. Then I realized the cause: the boys who played my lackeys had walked onto the darkened stage and lit their torches, which had been soaked in coal oil. Breathing in that sudden ignition of oil smoke had wiped out my vocal cords. For the performance, I had to learn to stand at the top of a staircase in the dark and, as that scene opened, take a swig of water from a hidden glass, holding the water in my mouth as if I were about to gargle, so those deadly fumes filtered through my nostrils. In operas I've done since, I've also had to learn that when I'm being thrown across a stage, as I was in *La Gioconda*, I have to be careful not to gasp in any dust or I end up barely able to croak. But who ever thinks of telling a young singer to keep her mouth closed?

Klytaemnestra was also one of the most emotionally taxing roles I've ever sung. Playing a demented old woman with syphilis, covered in jewels to hide her festering sores, I had the most rivetting line: "I feel like an old piece of cloth eaten by moths." The part was twenty-five minutes of straight theatrics. In her final scene, she is ranting to her daughter and slowly sinking into madness until she sails off stage, where the audience can hear her dying with a final frenzied shriek in the wings. The reviewers noted that my off-stage scream was blood-curdling, but in fact it wasn't mine at all. Lotfi Mansouri wouldn't let me do it because screaming is very dangerous for the vocal cords. Instead, he hired a stage actress just to unleash that one final shriek.

The most vocally wearing part I've ever sung was the role of Madame Flora in Gian Carlo Menotti's one-act opera *The Medium*. I first did it at the Stratford Festival's

Third Stage in 1974, and, after it was such a hit, we brought it to Toronto's MacMillan Theatre for twelve performances. Madame Flora is a seedy old medium who has spent her life bilking people out of money with her séances, but who begins to disintegrate when she sees evidence that the spirit world she has been faking all these years might just be asserting its existence. Preparing for the role, I thought about the kind of faded old woman who had that sort of marginal existence and it came to me that she would have been the type with varicose veins and swollen ankles. I've always prided myself on my trim legs and skinny ankles, so I pondered how to fatten them up. I found a pair of my son Daniel's ski socks, cut off the toes and put them on under baggy lisle stockings with elastic around the knee. I wore an old sack of a housedress with my hair dishevelled and hanging in wisps, and later, when I looked at the pictures of myself in that part, it frightened me to see echoes of my mother in her later years.

In *The Medium*, I had to do a lot of shrieking and at times I felt I was just shredding my vocal cords. I loved the richness of that part, but it's the only role I have ever sung which left me both emotionally and vocally exhausted.

That production caused a small sensation and my American manager Harold Shaw wanted to bring it to New York. Harold had produced the original staging of *The Medium* there starring Marie Powers, for whom Menotti wrote it, but apparently the part began to get to her. She became so involved in it that she installed a *prie-dieu* in her dressing room and after a while she used to arrive early at the theatre and roller-skate up and down the sidewalk in front. She became a little strange. It was that kind of role. *The Medium* had something spooky about it which even demanded that it be played in a certain kind of setting. Despite his efforts, Harold never succeeded in finding a theatre for it in New York. He was offered the Rebecca Harkness stage at Lincoln Center, but you couldn't have played that opera in a glittering modern complex which was the hottest new piece of architecture in the city. It called for a setting which was creaking and atmospheric, where the audience could believe there were cobwebs and decrepitude in the air and that, at any moment, a clammy hand might appear at your throat.

After my role in *The Medium*, Brian Macdonald started to offer me other character roles which tapped my outrageous side. One was Bloody Mary in an Edmonton production of *South Pacific*. For it, he choreographed a hilarious number in which I jitterbugged with a chorus of sailors, wearing a mumu in bare feet, with a cigar dangling from my mouth. Then Sam Gesser booked me for a cross-country tour playing the lead in the musical *Mame*, which I felt was a part tailor-made for me. But the producer who was putting up the money failed to raise enough and cancelled out at the last minute. It was a disaster for me, since I had blocked out four months on my schedule to do it, but I hadn't signed a contract with him yet to protect myself. Filling up four months with last-minute engagements isn't easy and it taught me never to take a producer seriously before I have a contract in my hand.

In 1984, Brian talked me into spending the whole summer in Stratford playing the campy Queen of the Fairies in *Iolanthe*, my very first encounter with Gilbert and Sullivan. It was another case of taking wing. My character was a cross between Queen Victoria and Hermione Gingold with a magic wand. The costume had yards of tulle worked to look like fish scales, with a pair of wings tacked on the back. Underneath, I wore high-heeled Victorian boots, hand-made by a Stratford *bottier*, which were painted day-glo aquamarine. Brian knows I love to dance so he choreographed me a crazy little number with the fairies. But dancing in high heels, wings and all those yards of tulle, with a wand in my hand, was no mean feat.

I'm a self-taught dancer; when a choreographer shows me the steps, I usually pick them up right away. But of course, without lessons, nobody had ever told me that a dancer never makes a turn without pointing her foot in that direction first. I left my foot pointing straight ahead as I whirled around in rehearsal one day and I heard a crack. The small fine bone behind my knee had snapped out of place and lodged under my kneecap. It was the kind of pain you could feel in the pit of your stomach. Thank heavens it healed quickly.

That ought to have taught me a lesson. But I never know when to leave well enough alone. As we were rehearsing the exit that Eric Donkin and I were to make, sitting on rope swings at the end of the first act, I thought it looked a little boring. We devised a single-foot stirrup on my swing like the ones found on water skis. Right in the middle of the fairies' dance, I swooped across the top of the proscenium standing on my trapeze, one foot sailing out behind me in an arabesque, singing "Tra-la!" The audience went mad.

My friends were all startled that I was arabesquing about at my age, but, oddly enough, it was a much more innocuous scene that almost killed me. In the second act, Brian called for a sort of Victorian wagon to enter as a wacky symbol of the British empire. There was a platform on the back where I sat in a helmet and breastplate, holding a spear, looking like Britannia gone wrong. Douglas Chamberlain was driving the wagon, and a boy was pushing from the back as it circled the stage to exit by a backdrop of the Houses of Parliament and a wooden fence. But it was very difficult to manoeuvre, almost like a go-cart, and at one performance we missed the exit and smashed right into the fence. I flew off head-first into the wings. I landed with my feet in the air – Britannia with her skirt over her head. We were all in absolute stitches and I almost couldn't get my breath to go on to sing my big aria, "O Foolish Fay," which we had rewritten as a satirical ode to CBC newscaster Knowlton Nash. Afterward, people in the audience kept coming up wanting to know how I managed that trick every night and Brian joked that we ought to keep it in. It was a miracle I didn't break my neck, but I ended up with only a bruise the size of a fifty-cent piece on one shoulder.

I would love eventually to do a Broadway show such as *Gypsy* or *Sweeney Todd*. In fact, the Houston Opera Company once expressed interest in my playing Angela Lansbury's role in *Sweeney Todd*, but a combination of circumstances and my perfectionism made me miss out on that. Hal Prince, the director of the Broadway production, had insisted that I audition for him first in New York, singing "The Best Pies in London" from the show. I had asked his management to send me the music because I hate learning any song from a record. But the score didn't arrive in time and I couldn't find it anywhere, so when I flew to New York to audition for Prince at the theatre where *Evita* was then playing, I sang instead a medley of other pop songs, so he would know I wasn't just a concert singer. He was very impressed with my voice but I realized in retrospect that I had made a mistake. I ought to have risked sounding unprepared and learned the song from the record, no matter how imperfectly, because without it, Hal Prince just saw me as another pleasant middle-aged woman in a suede suit who sang pop songs, not as the mad pie-maker in *Sweeney Todd*. Losing that part was another of the rare disappointments in my career.

The only role of pure acting that I've done was a cameo appearance in a CBC-TV series called *The Great Detective*. I played a daft homicide suspect who was in the choir of a church where people were constantly being found hanged in the belfry, but even that part had singing in it of a sort. My character couldn't carry a tune at all and the script called for me to saw my way through a lullaby so disastrously off-key that the detective, played by Douglas Campbell, practically bolted from the room. The part was terribly difficult to do, but not because of the acting. Some people don't understand how hard it is for a person with perfect pitch to sing out of tune.

When I decide the time has come to retire from my singing career, I hope to carry on as an actress. Until then, I'm revelling in the character roles which keep coming my way. Last season, thanks to the Canadian Opera Com-

pany, within the space of three months I had three parts
which couldn't have been more different: the Mother Su-
perior under her wimple in *Dialogues of the Carmelites*,
the decadent Queen Herodias in *Salomé* and the dreaded
spinster Katisha in *The Mikado*, where everyone in the
cast sported dainty little Japanese socks, but I somehow
got saddled with dancing in three-inch wooden platform
clogs. I felt as if I were teetering on scaffolding. In that
COC production of *Salomé*, my Herodias was a little more
circumspect than it had been in an Edmonton staging of
the opera a few years earlier. Irving Guttman, the director
there, had the inspiration of casting the University of Edmonton football team as the soldiers and spear-carriers
who attack Salomé at the end. At the first rehearsals, we
would see these enormous brawny specimens standing
around, clearly disdainful of anything so sissified as opera, wondering what they were doing in it at all. By the
end, they were getting into their parts with such gusto that
I worried they might accidentally murder the poor singer
who played Salomé. As my slaves, I had two beautiful
young men with oiled bodies and, to keep me occupied
during scenes when I didn't have much to do, Irving had
worked out a bit of business where I ran my hands up and
down their torsos as any decadent queen might do. But
one of those poor young men was so mortified that, to
illustrate Herodias's decadence, we finally had to resort to
peeling grapes instead.

I often wonder if Mario Bernardi knew when he cast me
as the witch in *Hansel and Gretel* that he had unleashed a
monster: the ham in me. Now I have almost more of a
reputation as a crazy dame likely to pull any stunt on
stage than I do as a dignified concert singer. These days,
people expect me to be a bit of a character. That development is no surprise to my friends and family who for years
have never known what to expect from me. To them, I've
always been a creature of intuition, acting on impulse.

In Washington once, some friends who had come to
hear me sing at the Kennedy Center joked that I ought to

turn up for their church choir the next weekend. They were speechless when I took them up on the offer. That Sunday at the end of my solo, Handel's "Praise Be to Thee," the Secretary of the Navy, who was reading the lesson, turned to the minister and remarked, "Rather nice voice," and afterward several pillars of the church told me how lovely it was to have a breath of fresh air in the choir. I had made my friends promise not to reveal my identity and for me, to relive my old anonymous choir days like that was such a lark.

One night in New York I had gone to a midnight concert to hear my friend Bobby White sing and afterward, at about 2:30 in the morning, a group of us were on the way to a party at his brother's apartment on the Upper West Side. They were locking the car, and I had started to saunter up the street alone when suddenly, out of nowhere, two enormous black boys came hurtling by, chasing this skinny Puerto Rican kid. When they caught up to him, they began pummelling his brains out. The mother's instinct in me surged to the fore and I didn't even stop to reflect. I walked straight over to them and pulled those two hulks off their victim. "Pick on somebody your own size," I said. They must have been shocked because they took off like a shot. When I picked the boy up off the sidewalk, he was absolutely stoned – non compos mentis. He could have done with a doctor, but in two seconds he was gone too. My friends, who had witnessed the event, plastering themselves against a wall terrified, were aghast. "Are you insane?" they said. "Well, I think that if more people intervened when they saw an injustice like that, there'd be a lot less crime," I explained. "Yes," said Bobby White, "and a lot less singers!"

That same instinct to rush in where angels fear to tread landed me in a fight with ACTRA, the Alliance of Canadian Cinema, Television and Radio Artists. I was taping a CBC variety special called *Goldrush Follies* when suddenly a union official walked onto the sound stage and announced, "We're closing down the set. We have an unacceptable alien here." The CBC had hired a Gay Nineties singer named Joan Morris from New York, and the union had refused her a work permit on the grounds that she was taking a job from a Canadian. But the CBC had gone ahead and right there, in the middle of the taping, ACTRA pulled a hundred singers and dancers out of the production. Harry Secombe, the British music hall star, Doug Henning, the magician, and I refused to budge. My blood had begun to boil when I heard that phrase "unacceptable alien." To me, there is no such thing, above all in art.

The union decided to make an example out of me and called me before its disciplinary committee. Hundreds of members turned out for that meeting, which was just like a courtroom trial, with the press in rapt attendance. There were hours of speeches denouncing me, and among my most ardent opponents was Pierre Berton. I hadn't hired a lawyer because I had decided I was perfectly capable of defending myself. When my turn came, I took the microphone and pointed out that this wasn't a question of some jack-of-all-trades artist being hired; the person at issue was a ragtime specialist who had spent years cultivating her expertise. Here she was, a foreigner invited to perform in Canada, and she had found herself treated like some interloper off the street. Art should know no borders, I told them, and as much of a patriot as I am, I warned that such a narrow-minded suspicion of foreigners could only hurt our country.

"I'm a Mahler specialist," I said. "I perform in Vienna, Mahler's city, all the time and I've never once heard the Viennese raise their voices in protest that a Canadian is singing the work of one of their composers and putting them out of a job." The attitudes I heard at that meeting had made me furious and I added that, in my opinion, the trouble with the union was that there weren't enough international artists on its board; the only people who had the time to serve were those who weren't all that successful. Well, you should have heard the cheers, which only riled my ACTRA inquisitors further. In punishment, they slapped their heaviest fine in history, $850, on me and Doug Henning, and suspended me from appearing on television in Canada for a year. In fact, neither measure hurt me since ninety per cent of my income came from appearances abroad. But I appealed, and they eventually lifted the suspension, leaving me with a $500 fine for speaking out against the union. After that incident, what I had said obviously stayed in a lot of artists' minds. When it came time for the next election for Actors' Equity, the performers' union, some members put my name forward as a candidate for the governing council, without telling me, and I won. I had absolutely no free time to sit on their board, but I accepted and served a three-year term because I felt it was important to show that I was in no way anti-union. Since then, Equity has made me a life member.

My family has become used to the fact that I operate on whim. I never agonize over a decision. When we moved back to Toronto from Philadelphia because we had decided the children ought to know their own country while they were still teenagers – and because we thought the quality of Canadian public education was better – I had a terrible time finding a house to rent. Nothing was large enough for a two-career couple with five children, a live-in nanny and a housekeeper. We were a family that had become accustomed to a lot of space. Finally, the agent mentioned a thirty-room house for rent on Rosedale Road. It had been built by a Scottish railroad baron in 1928 and was so enormous that it had been vacant for ages. "It's a real white elephant," the agent warned me. Of course, I took one look at it and fell in love. "Quick," I told her, "I want to sign the lease right away. My husband is away at a conducting seminar in Mexico and I know when he sees it, he'll say that I'm mad." Sure enough, the instant Eugene laid eyes on it, he said, "What! Are you out of your mind?"

But we all came to adore that house. A reporter once described it as "runaway baronial" and it could have accommodated a large embassy. The dining room and music room were both panelled in mahogany and every room boasted a fireplace, even the entrance hall. There were six bedrooms on the top floor alone and butlers' pantries and backstairs popping up all over the place. The upstairs hall was so big that I used to wake everybody up in the morning and conduct family yoga classes in it. But the most incredible part of all was the rent: only $800 a month. Of course, it cost me a fortune to heat, but I still regret not buying that house.

Since then, I've lived in half a dozen other homes and, as my family knows, I can move at the drop of a hat. Last year I changed houses in the week between the opening of *The Mikado* and the rehearsals for *Salomé*. I had barely moved into my new abode when I decided to throw a cast party.

The children are constantly braced for me to do the unexpected. But six years ago at the party I threw for Susie's sixteenth birthday, I surpassed even their expectations. I had told them I would be away for a few days beforehand. Then I checked into the hospital and had a face-lift. I was prompted to do it, not because I was trying to stave off the tell-tale traces of old age, but because I didn't like the jowly look I saw on myself when I appeared on TV. A lot of my work involves television, especially as I'm moving into acting, and I considered it an investment in my career. The problem is that when you first emerge from the hospital after a face-lift, your face is black and blue and your eyes are swollen. you look as if you've been in a terrible accident. I put on dark glasses and came home and called in a caterer to arrange Susie's Sweet Sixteen party the next day in the reception room of the apartment building where I was then living. When the other children and Eugene saw me, they were aghast. "Why didn't you tell us?" they asked. "Because," I said, "you would have tried to stop me." Of course I'll never know what Susie's friends thought of this weird battered woman in dark glasses who was their hostess.

My children now are used to some of the more outlandish roles I've taken on, although I think they worry sometimes when I do something too much out of character that I might fall flat on my face. It was early on, when I started to accept more opera and acting roles, which often meant spending weeks at a time in a distant city rehearsing, that Eugene began to be wary of the new direction my career was taking. Over the years, we had been used to talking to each other on the phone every day, but when you're rehearsing an opera from morning till night, you often can't find a phone free at a break, and then when you do, you never have the right change. Also, the cast usually goes out to eat together later. Sometimes by the time I got back to the hotel at night, I would just collapse and accidentally fall asleep before I'd had time to call him. He began to get very nervous that I would become more and more involved in the opera and theatre world and not want to be a wife and mother anymore. For the first time, I realized that Eugene was jealous. "I'm afraid that opera is going to take you away from me," he said one night. I looked at him as if he were out of his mind. "Don't be ridiculous," I said.

TWENTY-SEVEN

Learning the Blues

IN 1974, WITH my Met debut looming in only a few months, I had decided that it was time for me to lose some weight. "Statuesque" is the word newspapers had always used to describe me, and I had made up my mind early in my career that if I was born big, I might as well flaunt it. As I told myself: If you're going to be big, be magnificent. For my performances, I had special gowns designed by José Varona, which were literally built to give me a presence. There would be chiffon or velvet flowing on the outside, but underneath there was a flexible skin with a zipper which would support me like a suit of armour while I was singing. Those costumes were works of art and they cost almost as much.

Singers tend to look on their weight differently than most women do. I regard mine as a cushion for the life I lead. I catch fewer colds when I'm carrying an extra ten pounds, but those ten pounds are also a cushion for the voice. When you're a bit heavier, there's a velour and sumptuousness to your sound that very few slim singers possess. If you're too thin, the voice gets reedy. That's why I really believe a singer needs to weigh more than the average person, although some opera stars obviously overdo it and are so heavy that they're endangering their health. Often it's a fine line to maintain and life on the road doesn't make it any easier. Most of us end up on eternal diets. When I was performing *Cendrillon* in San

Francisco, my friend Marilyn Horne was also there doing Rossini's *La Cenerentola*, the Italian Cinderella story, and one day I discovered that she kept herself on the straight and narrow by taping a photograph of a well-padded diva to her mirror labelled with a warning: "Monster Fat."

I seem to lose weight as easily as I put it on and, as friends point out, I'm always in the middle of losing twenty-five pounds – and always the same twenty-five pounds. But in 1974, with the promise of a new direction in my career as a result of my appearance with the Met, I decided to take drastic measures. I had hormone shots, and, in combination with following a very stringent diet, I lost fifty pounds. If I do say so myself, I looked fabulous. The transformation was so dramatic that people didn't recognize me and of course none of my clothes would fit. I had to go out and buy a whole new wardrobe. But the change was psychological too. I felt like a new woman.

I had decided that for my Met debut I was also going to rent a furnished apartment in New York so I wouldn't have to endure months in yet another impersonal hotel room. I had signed a lease for a flat, sight unseen, and one day early in the year, when I had a moment between engagements, I hopped on a plane in Toronto to fly down and look it over. I had booked an early-morning flight and I was sitting in the first-class section waiting for the plane to take off, when I noticed that the attendants seemed to be stalling before they closed the doors. Finally, the reason became clear: a businessman came rushing down the aisle and fell into the seat beside me. He was tall and distinguished looking with waves of silver hair, and he was absolutely out of breath. "Well, that was a close call," I teased him. "I'll bet you overslept."

"You better believe it," he shook his head. Then he did a double take. "Aren't you Maureen Forrester?"

We laughed and chatted all the way to New York. Before I knew it, we had landed at LaGuardia and he was insisting on dropping me off at the new apartment, which I had told him about. When I got out of his taxi on

Amsterdam Avenue near Lincoln Center, he promised to call me for lunch some day. I just smiled. A few hours after I had started to set up housekeeping in the flat, the phone rang. Even before I picked it up, I knew who it would be. "I'm worried about your cough," he said. "I just went out and bought you a heating pad."

I had been coughing on the plane, just as I always cough everywhere. I seem to have had non-stop bronchitis since childhood, but it doesn't have any effect whatsoever on my singing. Still, in all those years, I had never had a heating pad offered to me in what was obviously a come-on. Finally, he said, "Look, I'm lying. It's just an excuse to see you again. Will you have dinner with me?"

"Well, I knew you weren't all that worried about my cough," I laughed, "but I found your concern rather charming."

I felt vaguely guilty as I accepted his invitation, but I agreed to meet him for drinks and dinner in a well-known watering hole. After all, it was only a question of an evening. We laughed from the moment we sat down and it turned into one of the most madcap nights of my life. He swore he had a particular restaurant and jazz joint named Pete's in mind to take me to, but the cab driver had never heard of it and we cruised around Manhattan for hours searching for this place, in stitches the whole time. Finally we ended up eating paella and sipping champagne in a late-night Spanish dive with flamenco guitarists serenading us. At some point during that crazy dinner, it dawned on me that this was mad love at first sight and that it was mutual.

That realization, and what followed, was marvellous, but it also threw me into terrible anguish. Suddenly, I felt like a teenager once more, happier than I had been in a long, long time, but I couldn't escape the awful reality that we were both married. I felt sick about betraying Eugene. At first I tried to dismiss this as a mid-life fling which I would get over, but when he followed me to Boston the next day, then later, when we had both returned to Toronto, I saw that it was more than that. Over the next months, he would fly to see me wherever I was performing and if he couldn't make it, extravagant bouquets would show up in his stead in my hotel or dressing room. It was the first time in my life I had been on the receiving end of such expansive romantic gestures. A part of me was euphoric, but another part was in turmoil. I'm hopeless at deception and I knew I couldn't go on living a lie.

I finally told Eugene the truth and said I wanted a separation. He was devastated. He begged me not to move out and at one point, he even proposed that we carry on separate lives but continue to live together for the sake of the family. But I couldn't bear that kind of double life. Ever since my childhood, on stage and off I've wanted to bring happiness to people, and it was torture for me to see what I was doing to the man I had loved for so many years. I couldn't have stood to witness that pain daily so I persisted in my plans to find myself another house.

The children were stunned when they found out. For as long as they could remember, Eugene and I had constantly been holding hands and cuddling. Only a few years before, when we were still living in Philadelphia, Paula had walked into the house one day after a visit to a friend's home and announced, "You know, Mom, we're the happiest family I know." Everybody was under the same impression. Even I had thought we were happy – until I met someone else.

But of course, even armchair psychologists will acknowledge that meeting a man on a plane one day doesn't break up a marriage of fifteen years. In retrospect, I realize that there had been a breach growing between Eugene and me for quite some time. Certainly, it didn't help that I was always on the road. Eugene was forced into the role of "liberated man," left at home with the children week in and out and saddled with the domestic responsibilities. He had cooks and nannies and housekeepers to make the task easier, but he had no wife for companionship in the evening. His life was often lonely when he wasn't playing or teaching. My life was lonely too, a succession of airports and hotel rooms in strange cities. But to Eugene I'm sure it looked as if I was leading a thoroughly glamorous existence.

Often I would take a twelve-hour red-eye flight back to Toronto between engagements just so that I could spend a Saturday with him and the children, no matter how much I needed a rest. The instant I walked in the door, wanting to sink into a chair and catch up on the children's news, he would pour out the latest problems of the household to be solved – the tales of dishwashers to be fixed and bills overdue. It was up to me to handle every crisis. At times when I was travelling, I thought I couldn't bear the burden of making all the decisions. I would sit in my room and weep, feeling frustrated at being so far away, but wanting someone to share the burden, fifty-fifty. Yet because I can't bear to make a scene, I never told Eugene about that; I just went ahead and solved the problems. But there were times I dreaded coming home to the next crisis.

It must have been demoralizing for Eugene too that, just as his career had lost momentum, mine had become more and more successful. His early fears were coming true: the naïve young singer he had met in an Ottawa gym had outstripped the suave, worldly conductor. The pupil was outgrowing the teacher. At home too, as the children became teenagers, they had grown more and more independent, rebelling as all teenagers do. And of course, they rebelled against their father, the parent who was there all the time.

For a few years before our break-up, every meal in our house had become a hollering match. I, who grew up with a horror of scenes, found myself in a family of screamers. Someone was constantly erupting and stalking off from the table. Doors slammed, windows were broken; I'm sure that at times our neighbours thought people were being murdered inside our house. I would often have to leave the table because the arguments would tie my stomach in knots. But sometimes even I found myself drawn into the drama. Occasionally, in an effort to stop the screaming, I would seize a stack of dishes from the buffet, lift them over my head and let them crash to the floor, then stride out of the room. I lost a lot of crockery in those years and the children christened me The Iron Hand. Such scenes were not unusual in boisterous families but they took a terrible toll on me. I couldn't bear Eugene and the children screaming at each other and, if the end of our marriage came as a shock to us all, perhaps the least shocked was myself. I realized later that over the five years before our break-up, not all my acting had been confined to the stage.

Within a few weeks of telling Eugene about my affair, I decided I should be the one to move out. I felt it would be best to leave the children with their father because I spend so much of my time on tour. Irene Bird found me a nice apartment, and within a week the children appeared at my door announcing that they were there to stay. Suddenly I found myself with four teenagers living in a two-bedroom apartment. For the children, it was a difficult time. One day I found an old snapshot of Eugene and me in Susie's room on which she had written, "Mom and Dad before they broke up." Moments like that were absolutely agonizing. The guilt I felt was tremendous. I would get up every morning, look in the mirror and think: How could I have made them suffer like that?

Not long after we separated, I made my Met debut and Eugene, as an unwavering supporter of my career, insisted on coming to New York for it. I let him stay in my studio apartment there and, during a CBC radio interview with us both, he kept saying that it was the greatest day of his life to see me at last at the Met. But in private we were still spouting recriminations. I spent most of those hours before my performance in tears, which may be another reason why my debut wasn't a great success.

During the break-up, to my distress, my emotions intruded on a performance. Soon after I had told Eugene I was leaving him, I had to sing Mahler's *Third Symphony* in Montreal. As I sat on stage, listening to that incredible music, some of it so turbulent, I saw my whole life with Eugene passing before my eyes as if it were a film: the hopeful courtship, the lonely years in Berlin and London with Paula and then all the wonderful rich time as a family, climaxing in this heartache. As if I were hearing them for the first time, I felt the weight of the words the chorus was intoning: "O man, beware. What speaks the midnight hour? Deep, deep is pain and misery." I almost couldn't fight back the tears to sing and I realized that, once again, Mahler had read my heart.

My romance with the gentleman who had boarded the plane to New York that fateful day continued to bloom. In retrospect, it's astonishing that someone like myself, whom my children consider such a prude, could have carried on with a married man. But because I was so conscious of the unhappiness I was causing my own family, I didn't want to bring grief to anybody else's. At the same time if we were going to continue seeing each other, I knew I couldn't bear playing back-street woman, either. I was not the type to sneak about and hide. We began to go out to restaurants openly together and I introduced him to the children and my friends. Often Eugene would drop by when he was at my house and we would all sit there having drinks together, terribly awkwardly, but that was a little too open for my taste.

Aside from those moments, we had a wild romantic time. He was the type who would fly to Aspen to be with me for three hours. Once he joined me in Switzerland for two days and from there we caught a train to Paris. We almost missed it and we had to tear down the track, clutching the champagne we had bought for the trip. We spent the whole ride in stitches. I had never known a man like that, who had a sense of humour as outrageous as mine, yet treated me like a queen. I felt reborn. In a series of publicity pictures which were taken of me at the time, I looked absolutely radiant. Four years later, the same photographer shot me again and you would never know it was the same person. Sadness was etched in those portraits.

I ought to have seen the end of our relationship coming. My children all did. They had never liked or trusted my friend and from the start they had warned me that nothing good would come out of the romance. "If a man doesn't make a move to leave his wife after a year," Paula warned me, almost as if she were the parent, "he's never going to do it. He's taking you for a ride and we're afraid you're the one who is going to end up hurt." But I was stubbornly in love again. "Don't worry, dear," I would brush her concerns away. "It will work itself out. I'll handle this in my own way."

But gradually, signs appeared that even I couldn't ignore. He had offered to invest some money for me, which he promptly lost. Often I would drive him to the airport and, if he were in a hurry and leaving for the States, I would say, "Here's some American money. It will save you the time of changing yours at the airport." I never saw any of it again. In fact, it turned out that even though he was successful, he was having problems in his business. Slowly I realized that, because I was famous, he thought I was rich. Little did he know that, although the press reported I made $250,000 a year, I never had any of it left at the end. I'm a disaster with money.

One day in the fourth year of our relationship, I was in Ottawa singing in *La Fille du Régiment* at the National Arts Centre when I got a letter from him. In it, he said that his wife had fallen ill and he felt he owed it to her to spend more time at home. He suggested that we cool it for a while. There was something about that letter which didn't ring true to me, and when I told a friend about it, she was just as sceptical. She phoned me back later with news which was worse than I had feared: he had abruptly left his wife in the most heartless way and moved in with another woman. I was shattered.

I flew back to Toronto immediately and phoned him. I

said I had received his letter and asked if we could meet for coffee in a small, out-of-the-way restaurant. I made my voice cheery and casual. When I sat down at the table with him a few hours later, I found myself in one of the most difficult parts I've ever played. "How's your wife feeling?" I began. He blanched, and the truth began to ooze out. In the end, I just sat silent for a while. Then I said, "I have only one question to ask you. Does this new woman have money, by any chance?" He went scarlet and with that look, he told me all I needed to know. He asked if we couldn't still be friends. "No," I said. "I see now that you've lied to me from the beginning and for a person like myself, that's worse than death. I can't forgive deception. You're not worth my time of day. You've not only lost a lover, you've lost one of your best friends." I sailed out of that coffee shop with my head high and then I got in my car and sobbed.

I drove back home and for the next three days, I lay on a chaise in my garden and wept. The children were beside themselves. They had never seen me like that before. They didn't know what was wrong and they knew better than to ask me. I found out later they thought that a doctor had just told me I had an incurable illness. But for me, the bitter pill was the sense of humiliation and betrayal I felt. All my life I had trusted my instincts and it seemed an excruciating irony that I had been taken in by a man who turned out to be a slick charmer and a liar. It was terrible to think I had risked so much for him; I had broken up a marriage with a man who truly loved me. Eugene is such a good and scrupulously honest man and I had nearly destroyed him for such a deceitful character. I felt like a bloody fool.

Never in my life had I let my emotions show as I did in those three days, but at the end of them, I picked myself up and began to piece together my life again. "Look at it this way," Paula counselled me with her usual wisdom, "he made you laugh for three years."

Eugene, I know, was hoping we would get back together again after the affair broke up, but for me it was too late. We're still the closest friends, we spend all our family celebrations together, and I will always adore him. But for me, when a great love affair is over, it's over. That chapter is closed. Ever since I was a child, almost since the days of my disappointment with a girlfriend like Ruthie Maclean, I've been able to cut painful situations out of my life. I wish sometimes I weren't that way; it's a very sad thing not to be able to reach out again. But as Eugene points out, just as I'm always cleaning out closets, I'm an emotional cleaner of closets too. For me, yesterday is too late.

Sometimes now the children say that I need a new man in my life, but after such a betrayal, something went out of me. I can't imagine trusting anyone the same way again. I've become very wary and I'd rather spend time with my children, grandchildren and friends. Besides, I'm a lousy catch because I'm never around. When I look back on it, I realize that really all my life, despite my gregariousness, I've been a loner.

After that heartbreak, as always, music came to my rescue. I threw myself into my work. But gradually, I sensed that what I needed was a new challenge. I had taken on any number of zany character roles and people knew I might try anything. But one day out of the blue, Gino Empry, the publicist who books the Imperial Room at Toronto's Royal York Hotel, phoned me in Ottawa with what I thought was the most outlandish suggestion yet: he asked me to put together a nightclub act for their supper club. "Don't be ridiculous," I said, "you'd go broke." But Gino persuaded me that he was serious and later I called him back. I agreed to do it only if he booked me into the deadest two weeks of the season, so that the Imperial Room wouldn't lose money on me.

In my leisure time, I would far rather relax to the voice of Sarah Vaughan or Nancy Wilson than listen to the reigning diva of the day. And around the house, I love to sing low-down dirty blues. But in my professional life, what a change of pace. The evening before I was to open, I was booked to sing with the Orford Quartet, and the day after closing the twelve-night run, I was scheduled to fly to San Francisco to do Monteverdi's opera *The Coronation of Poppea*, with Tatiana Troyanos. I had only a few weeks to prepare the show, but once I started sifting through 200 pop songs to pick out a varied line-up of tunes which meant something to me, I was in absolute heaven. Here I was, after all these years, living out my band singer's fantasy from Danceland.

When I sing pop music around the house or in the car, I don't sound at all like I do when I sing classical music. In *Lieder*, you're lifting the voice over the orchestra and out into a vast concert hall. Pop music is inward and intimate, you're not using any muscle when you do it, so even though the Imperial Room only holds 350 people a sitting, I needed a mike. A *Lieder* program usually has at least two dozen songs, but for a nightclub act I needed only twelve. Listening to a Barbra Streisand album while I was preparing, I realized what made the record so rich was that every number had a different signature, so I commissioned arrangements from a dozen people. The only trouble was that, with so little preparation time, most of them arrived the night before I was to open. I'm a quick study, but that was a little too quick even for me.

The opening night audience was not your usual Imperial Room crowd. It included Lotfi Mansouri of the Canadian Opera Company, Walter Homburger of the Toronto Symphony, Pierre Berton, and my concert fans from New York and Washington. I only had time for one rehearsal with Howard Cable's house orchestra, but I wasn't nervous, although I'll admit it was the only occasion in my life when I'd ever had to worry about people breaking a musical spell by dropping their steak-knives. As Gino predicted, I had a wonderful time and the only thing that drove me crazy was the cigarette smoke.

I came out singing Jerome Kern's "Why Was I Born?" and continued on through Cole Porter's send-up, "I Like Pretty Things" to Neil Diamond's "You Don't Send Me Flowers Anymore." I always love the chance to talk to an audience about what I'm going to sing next, getting people into the mood, but you can tire your voice speaking during a classical concert. Doing pop music, I could indulge my penchant for the impromptu between numbers. Every night, I would introduce one of Eubie Blake's songs by telling the audience that when Eubie wrote it in 1930, the year I was born, little did he know that he was writing what would turn out to be a perfect theme song for me. Then I would break into my version of "A Great Big Baby":

> I've got lips and I've got arms
> I've got hips and lots of charms
> Come on somebody, step up, I dare ya
> Don't let my weight scare ya
> Cause I'm a great big baby
> Looking for a man to love!

Every time I sang it, the audience would howl and smack the tables. Nobody could believe that Maureen Forrester would sing a raunchy song like that.

The reviewers went wild. "Hey! The New Kid's Got It," said Wilder Penfield in the *Toronto Sun*, and the *Toronto Star* announced, "Diva Delivers Pop with a Dose of Laughter to Cure Anybody's Ills." For the next eleven days, I did two shows a night and almost every evening I would arrive at the Royal York to find letters waiting for me from women who had seen the performance. One wrote that she had cried all the way home in the car to Mississauga because I had made her think of so many moments in her marriage. In fact, I wasn't surprised by responses like that. I may have been using a different voice with less vibrato than when I do *Lieder*, but the emotions I called on were the same.

On one of those evenings, I walked out on stage, looked over the sea of tables and who should I see in the front row, sitting there as bold as brass? My former lover with his new ladyfriend. I couldn't get over the nerve. Even more infuriating, he had the cheek to hum along as I sang. All through the show, I never looked at him once. I wouldn't allow him that satisfaction. But that night there was a special note of poignancy to a number I had chosen from Jerry Herman's *Dear World*. "He stood and looked at me/ And I was beautiful . . . ," it began, with only a simple string accompaniment. And, as it built to a full orchestra, a few people in the audience might have noticed that I had trouble with my mascara at the end: "And then he walked away/ And took my smile with him."

TWENTY-EIGHT

Madame Chairman

NOT LONG after I had moved to my most recent address in Toronto, I woke up one morning to the sound of the garbage truck outside and realized that I had forgotten to put the trash out the night before. I threw on my clothes and was racing down the street after the sanitation workers with a green plastic bag in my hand. "Will you take this?" I panted. "Sure will, honey," the driver said. "But only if you'll sing me a song. I love your voice!" That's what I like about living in Canada. I might have had a grander career somewhere else, but there wouldn't have been the same sense of being a part of the fabric of the land. Canada has been good to me and I believe that artists who've become known here should put back into the country as much as they've taken out.

I have no patience with people who made it here and then promptly moved somewhere else to avoid paying their taxes. As a member of the board for the Order of Canada, I think twice about voting a medal to someone who doesn't pay his taxes here. I wear my own Order of Canada medal at every opportunity I get. Prince Charles admired it in the receiving line at the opening of Expo 86, where I sang Berlioz's *La Spectre de la Rose* as part of the festival kick-off. *"That,"* I told him, "is my pride and joy." Some people might have thought my response was just so much public relations but, in fact, one of the highlights of my life was finding myself the first artist to be named a

Companion of the Order in 1967, the year it was created. Among others awarded the same rank then were names which had been god-like to me as a young girl growing up on rue Fabre: former Prime Minister Louis St. Laurent; the neurosurgeon Wilder Penfield; the mayor of Montreal, Jean Drapeau; and Madame Vanier, the governor general's wife. To be included in that list of people who had contributed so much to this country was a thrill which will never wear off.

In return, I've never been bashful about trumpeting the country's virtues. Wherever I've travelled, I've made a point of singing the works of Canadian composers. Bailey Bird, my friend Irene's husband, a music publisher, encouraged many of the country's composers to write for me, and as a result I've had some stunning pieces to show off our talent. One of the first and still one of the most spectacular was Harry Somers's *Five Songs for Dark Voice* which he wrote for me to sing at the Stratford Festival in 1957, the year of my debut with Bruno Walter. People love the haunting mood of those songs, but they don't always understand the words, which are based on a short bitter poem by Michael Framm, written when he had been going through a very difficult time. Since then, almost every year someone has composed a work for me, from Harry Freedman and Oskar Morawetz to Robert Fleming, who wrote *The Confession Stone*. A few years ago, Murray Schafer composed a marvellous piece for me to sing with the National Arts Centre orchestra. It was based on the diaries of Clara Schumann during her marriage to the composer, especially at the end of his life when he was going mad, constantly hearing an A in his head, the note on which an orchestra bases its pitch. The work was called *Adieu, Robert Schumann* and after we performed it, Vincent Warren, a wonderful dancer, who was then with Les Grands Ballets Canadiens, came backstage. We both agreed it was so visual that it ought to be danced and, as a result of that conversation, Brian Macdonald choreographed a ballet version which has been a huge success every time we've done it. Murray also wrote a beautiful piece based on poems from *Thousand and One Nights* called *The Garden of the Heart*. I fell in love with it instantly but after reading the poetry later, I said to him, "I'm not a twenty-year-old girl, I'm a woman in my fifties. Can we add something to make it sound more reflective in a way – as if someone is looking back on this wonderful love story?" And so, Murray went back to *Thousand and One Nights* and found a fragment which I sing using a Middle Eastern technique involving the tongue and the back of the nose to create the sound of a babbling brook. "When you return to the Garden of the Heart," it goes, "take my body and lay it in a shallow grave and I will return as the dancing water."

If I'm teaching a master class, I always bring a sheaf of Canadian composers' music along. And if I'm singing at a music teachers' convention, I leave a list at the back of the room of the Canadian works I sing so people can request copies of the sheet music. I always sell at least fifty copies a session. Once a publisher phoned me. "Well, I can tell you've just been in Australia, Maureen," he said. "I've had hundreds of requests for Harry Somers's work from there!" I feel it's the duty of performers to showcase the compositions of their country. Musicians are the voices for their nation's composers. If we don't perform the pieces, how can we expect others to? To me that's fundamental to the notion of offering your country return service.

Still, one morning in December 1983, I had my belief in that notion soundly tested. Francis Fox, who was then Trudeau's Secretary of State, telephoned and asked me to become the new chairman of the Canada Council. I was flabbergasted.

"Oh, my God," I said. "Do you realize I sing 120 concerts a year? How much time does this job involve?"

"Only three or four days every three months to chair the quarterly board meetings," he told me. "Maybe twelve days a year at the most."

I've been kidding Fox ever since that he lied. I always seem to be in Ottawa or giving a speech somewhere. And all this for a voluntary position which pays an honorarium of only $325 a working day and travel expenses. What's more, almost from the moment I was appointed, there has been one crisis after another in the arts. I've been happy to do battle for the artists of the country, but I have to admit that I would have thought twice about saying yes if I had known my term would be non-stop red alert. What a job for a person who hates confrontation!

During that initial phone call, I had asked Fox to give me a few days to think over his proposition. In return, he asked me to keep it confidential. I understood his reasons since I knew I probably wasn't the first person to be offered the job, and if I didn't accept, whoever did wouldn't be thrilled to hear that I'd already turned it down. Fox had phoned the week before Christmas and in our household, where we celebrate everything, Jewish, Christian or pagan, things were absolute chaos. It wasn't exactly an atmosphere conducive to making a calm decision which would alter the next five years of my life. Irene Bird, the only person I confided in, told me I would be mad to take on another commitment. She pointed out how I was already constantly bemoaning the fact that I never had any time to myself. I knew she was right, but I phoned Fox back within a day and a half and accepted the offer anyway.

Of all the things I was constantly being asked to do, this post was something I really believed in. The chairman of the Canada Council is above all a spokesperson for the artists of this country. It was a way of putting my own voice to another use. Besides, I felt that I owed it to Canada. After all the opportunities and honours I've received, this was the least I could do.

I realized that if I refused, I would seem rather smug — essentially saying: Well, I've made it, the rest of you can fend for yourselves. At a time when the arts were under economic siege, I was one of the few people in a strong position to do the job. When I went to argue for money for artists, no politician could dismiss it as the whining of a ne'er-do-well or the sour grapes of someone who thought the government owed me a living. Ironically, I had made it without any help from the Canada Council at all. That put me in an even stronger position to make the organization's case.

I knew that for every Maureen Forrester, there were hundreds of talented young people across the country who had never had the luck I did to meet the Gilles Lefebvres and the Bruno Walters. Without a financial cushion during the crucial make-or-break-it years, many of them could easily have lost faith in themselves or been forced to give up their dreams to go into another line of work. I may not have had the Canada Council to help me, but I'd had J. W. McConnell, and I felt somehow that J. W. would be pleased to see that I was carrying on the torch, helping young artists just starting out.

My only personal experience with the Council had been when its Touring Office asked me to do regional tours through the small towns of Saskatchewan in April 1976, and six years later in Ontario. I really believed in their efforts to bring music to all the corners of the country which couldn't afford the block-buster fees of established artists. The first trip provided some of the best fun I'd had in years. Jean Latrémouille, the Touring Office manager, came along as a chauffeur and "roadie" and, during the long hours of driving across the Prairies, I would sit up front in the car with him and hold bubblegum-blowing contests. John Newmark, who rode in the back of the car, was absolutely appalled at us.

Wherever I had travelled in the world over the years, people in the arts wanted to know about the Canada Council. It was envied all over the globe. Even the Americans have no system like it which provides the financial foundation for the major arts groups of the country, free from any political pressure, and also gives grants to individual artists whose projects are judged by a committee of their peers. When I sang in Washington, senators would express interest in creating something like it there; some have even put forward a bill to create a copy of the Council's Art Bank, the first of its kind in the world, which buys Canadian artists' work under a jury system and, from that enormous warehouse, rents it out to public non-profit institutions to display – in the process, paying for itself. Here, starting out twenty-seven years ago with only the $100 million in death duties from the estates of two Canadian tycoons, Sir James Dunn and Izaak Walton Killam, the Council grew into something which has been a shining example to the rest of the world, but which I often felt Canadians didn't appreciate. I wanted to do my part in making sure that changed. Little did I know how right the newspapers were when they announced my appointment a few days later, predicting that it would be the most difficult role of my life.

Mavor Moore, the writer and director from whom I was inheriting the chairman's job, had told me it was a post which I could make as much or as little of as I liked. Mavor had been very outspoken, an articulate and intellectual advocate for the arts. But he pointed out that many of the Council's chairmen over the past quarter-century had kept very low profiles. I was under no illusions that the government had asked me to take on the post thinking I was some great intellectual. Clearly what they had wanted in choosing me was a high-profile artist with credibility – a kind of roving ambassadress of the arts. But I decided that I was not going to be just a title on a letterhead or a brochure. I would be a very active, visible chairman. If I was going to be an ambassadress, I was determined to be front and centre beating the drum for the Council.

A month after the government announced my appointment, as soon as I had a break in my concert schedule, I flew to Ottawa to meet the Council's director, Tim Porteous, who had run its day-to-day affairs since 1973, and his deputy, my old friend Gilles Lefebvre. They explained to me the Council's workings – how the staff prepares the grant applications and policy decisions for the twenty-one-member board to approve at its quarterly meetings. Then I told them my plan of attack: whenever I was singing somewhere in Canada, I would arrange to arrive a day early and don my chairman's hat, throwing a reception for the region's artistic community. I wanted to meet the artists of the country and hear what their problems were.

The Council started to organize the receptions right away. To save on expenses, we usually tried to hold them in an art gallery or a theatre lobby. For a year, from coast to coast, I met thousands of artists and listened to their gripes. From Charlottetown to Victoria, they flocked to those receptions as if they'd been starved for such an outlet for years. But finally after one in Vancouver, I decided that my scheme called for some revisions. The lobby of the East End Cultural Centre, which is home to some of the city's most exciting avant-garde art and theatre, was jammed with artists; they were hanging from the rafters. The cigarette smoke was so thick you almost needed a gas mask and the decibel level rose so high that I was shrieking through every conversation. The next day, when I sang the Brahms *Alto Rhapsody* with the Vancouver Symphony, I barely had any voice left. That's when I decided that I would talk to the country's artists the day *after* I did a concert.

In that first meeting with Tim and Gilles, I had been completely frank with them about my lack of knowledge of the Council's complex operations. "I'm going to need your help," I told them. "I promise to work hard but I'm counting on you to guide me through this job." Still, I had been a board member for the National Arts Centre for six years and also for Roy Thomson Hall; I couldn't imagine it would prove all that difficult to become a chairman. What an innocent I was. I had been in office barely two months when the first crisis hit the fan.

One morning when I was on tour, Tim phoned to warn me that I would have to come to the arts community's defence in a battle with the government over the taxation of artists. The issue had erupted into a furore three months before I was appointed when Toni Onley, the Vancouver artist, became incensed after a Revenue Canada auditor told him that he would be taxed on his unsold serigraphs, as if they were a factory's stock-piled inventory. Toni had promptly called a press conference on October 13, 1983, and threatened to burn all his brilliant prints on Wreck Beach in protest. Francis Fox had to dispatch a telegram from Ottawa begging him not to do it.

The government set up a standing sub-committee on communications and culture to look into the question of taxation of artists, who just don't fit into those neat slots Revenue Canada devises for ordinary citizens. The problem wasn't just Toni's; some of those measures were murdering other artists and performers, who found that suddenly they couldn't deduct travelling expenses or other costs basic to their survival. Even before I became chairman, the Council had asked to present a brief on the subject. Tim informed me that we finally had a date with the sub-committee on March 8. I've performed dozens of times on Parliament Hill – I even braved pneumonia to sing out Centennial Year at midnight on January 31, 1967, in twenty-below temperatures – but this was one part that I hadn't bargained on. Taxation isn't exactly my specialty. I'm my accountant's recurring nightmare.

I blocked out time between engagements to fly to Ottawa, and Tim, who is a lawyer as well as a gifted playwright and satirist, put together an excellent brief for me to read to the sub-committee in French and English. The council had also published a booklet of its recommendations for changes in the tax act, which we presented. I have to admit it was the only occasion in my entire career when I've had a case of stage fright. It's an awesome responsibility to speak for all the country's artists. When the MPs started to question me, I didn't feel embarrassed if I had to refer a technical question to Tim or a tax advisor we brought along, especially since I had been in office only a matter of weeks. But I had no trouble answering when one antagonistic member kept trying to be cute. It was clear he was out to knock the whole idea of the Council itself. "If my girlfriend writes a Harlequin novel, can she get a Canada Council grant?" he asked provocatively. "If your girlfriend writes a Harlequin novel," I said, "she won't need one." The whole committee room broke into laughter and it rather took the wind out of his sails.

In the end, after going to bat on that issue, the Council won a partial victory. Two weeks after our testimony, the minister of Revenue Canada announced an immediate change in the regulations which would allow artists to deduct their travel expenses. Then, three months later, he made other concessions, all of which helped to defuse the crisis, but they still didn't get at the fundamental changes in the tax act which we wanted – or at Toni's problem. In fact, it wasn't until two years later, in the spring of 1986, that the government finally decided artists could deduct the cost of their unsold canvases.

I was just recovering from round one when round two began. Barely a month later, I was again on tour when Tim phoned one morning to read me a story from the *Globe and Mail*, as he often did when I was on the road, so the press couldn't catch me by surprise. This article mentioned that the government was planning to include the Canada Council, the CBC, the National Arts Centre and several other cultural Crown corporations in a financial reorganization bill called C-24, which would have made them more "accountable" to the government. That word "accountable" was the red flag. Under the Canada Council Act, we're answerable to Parliament in an overall sense, and the Auditor General examines our books each year, but the one fundamental, sacred principle is that the government can't tell the Council how to spend its money. That notion of keeping the politicians at arm's length from the grant decisions means we can't be subjected to political pressures in distributing funds to the arts across the country.

"This is serious," Tim said. "We're going to have to fight them on this." In the next weeks, the furore, fed by the other arts organizations involved, exploded from coast to coast. The artistic community was in a state of outrage. Wherever I went – giving speeches or concerts – journalists would corner me, and I made no bones about my feelings on the subject. There was absolutely no reason for the government to take more control of our affairs. Our books were totally open to public scrutiny. "The government just wants to give out the money personally to make itself look good," I said.

The first board meeting since my appointment was scheduled for that same month. The meetings are two- or three-day affairs which start at 9 a.m. and are supposed to finish at 5 p.m., but never do. They often stretch stormily into the evenings, and even if they don't, we have receptions and working dinners. The board can't possibly review every grant application, but there are so many particularly troublesome policy and grant decisions to discuss that the Council staff prepares briefing books for myself and the twenty other board appointees who fly in from the provinces they represent. Some of those books contain as many as 500 pages. I do not exaggerate when I say we often sit down to stacks of documents which are nearly a foot high.

That first meeting was in the old Canada Council headquarters on Albert Street, before our recent move to save on rent. The board members took their seats at a horseshoe-shaped table facing the one at the front where I was to sit with Tim and Gilles and some of the Council's senior staff. The rest of the staff crowded into chairs along the walls of the room to keep an eye on their departments' projects like wary shepherds, ready to intervene to explain a point or argue a policy. There was standing room only. I assumed it was always that packed, but I discovered later that everyone had shown up to see this curiosity – the new high-profile chairman. Of course, with the arm's-length debate raging at full tilt then, this show had all the more riding on it. It was quite an agenda for my debut as a public official.

The board members are all successful citizens in their own right and each represents a region. Many of them have very strong views. Everybody thinks his own pet provincial company or art form ought to get more money. It's no easy task wielding the gavel and trying to lead them toward a consensus which will keep everybody happy. But after you've played Carnegie Hall and La Scala, a board-room of twenty-one independent spirits isn't quite so daunting. One thing we had no trouble agreeing on at that meeting was our opposition to Bill C-24. At the end, we issued a press release saying we "objected strenuously" to this effort to sabotage our autonomy and warned that it would lead to "unacceptable political pressure." That was putting it mildly.

But when the statement hit the papers, Trudeau's government didn't find such criticism mild at all. The reaction from on high was at first startled, then irate. It seemed that the powers in Ottawa weren't used to their agencies wagging an angry finger in public at the hand that feeds them. The word came down from the deputy minister to Tim that we had better cool it, which made him furious.

In fact, the whole problem of keeping the government at arm's length from the Council had begun even earlier. On February 14, 1984, Francis Fox had announced a little Valentine's gift to us: an additional $3 million. The understanding had apparently been that the money would go toward the country's Big Twelve – the major orchestra, theatre and ballet companies which were then under terrible financial pressure in an era of belt-tightening. All over the country, museums were being forced to close for as much as half a year and theatre companies had to cut back on their schedules. Reportedly, a letter came from the minister's office suggesting that this was how the $3 million ought to be distributed. I was singing in Europe at the time, so I never saw a directive to that effect and the Council publicly denied receiving one. Tim was adamant that we couldn't set a precedent by accepting a stipulation from the government on how we ought to distribute our funds. Instead of dividing the $3 million among the Big Twelve, he spread it evenly across all the Council's divisions and even created a new non-fiction program, an idea which had been on the back burner for years. I went along with Tim's defiance of the government's wishes at the time, but now that I have more experience, I think he was wrong to choose such a confrontational way of asserting the Council's independence. Fox's office – like the Big Twelve – was furious. That's when the government decided it wanted more control over the Council.

I flew up to Ottawa in June to present our brief protesting Bill C-24 to the Standing Committee on Miscellaneous Estimates. To bolster our case, the entire board in office at the time had joined me and, as I introduced them, the members stood one by one in the West Block committee room: William Kilbourn, Nicholas Goldschmidt and Celia Franca, to name only a few. There they were, all these heavyweights in the arts, Liberal appointees facing off against a Liberal government policy. It was quite an impressive show of strength. I pointed out that I was there not only as the Council chairman, but as an artist "on behalf of thousands and thousands of Canadian artists who are unanimously opposed to the Council's inclusion in the bill."

Again, Tim had prepared a strong brief for me to read. But I had a point of my own to make as an illustration of just how important the principle of arm's length was, even outside Canada. I told the committee how in 1982, when Lorin Maazel had been named director of the Vienna State Opera – the first American ever to hold the post – he was in the middle of planning his first season when an Austrian government bureaucrat intervened, objecting to this work or that singer. Lorin was so outraged he wasn't being allowed artistic freedom that he gave up the job, one of the most prestigious in the world. He said that he simply couldn't have that kind of political interference where every minister was adding his two bits about a Strauss piece or promoting his favourite soprano. That's what happens when you get government meddling in the arts, I told the committee. Everybody would be trying to get his friend a job. Why not leave the arts to be run by the experts – the arts community itself?

The debate before the committee got quite stormy, and near the end of it, as much as I hate a fight, I let some of my anger show. "If we've run the Council well for twenty-seven years, why did the government suddenly feel they had to take it over?" I demanded. "I wonder if they've thought about the cost of taking more direct control." It was a very successful presentation. But unwittingly, I had earlier fired a shot into the battle which may have played a role in the final outcome.

The Sunday morning before we presented our brief, I had had a meeting with Herb Gray, then the Treasury Board president, who was sponsoring the bill. He had asked for a get-together to resolve the impasse before we saw the committee, but both our weekends had been fully booked. I was scheduled for a dress rehearsal of *Iolanthe* in Stratford on the Saturday night, then I was to receive an honorary degree at the University of Ottawa on Sunday. "Well, I'm an early riser," I told him. "What about a 7:30 breakfast?" He gulped, but he turned up with two aides to meet Tim Porteous and me in a Four Seasons hotel suite. Essentially, Herb laid out the government's determination to press ahead with the bill. This new financial arrangement was how things were going to be and we would just have to accept that fact. Then without premeditation, I said, almost to myself, "Well, I feel so passionately about this I guess I'll just have to resign. The artists of this country will expect me to." I wasn't looking at Herb, but Tim said later that he went pale.

Some people credit that impromptu line with having reversed the course of the debate. I don't flatter myself at being able to make such a difference, but it turned out that, unbeknownst to me at the time, Pauline McGibbon, the former Ontario lieutenant-governor who was then chairman of the Arts Centre board, had threatened the same thing in a private letter to Trudeau. I'm no politician; I wouldn't try to get my way by laying my job on the line. I just knew that I couldn't hold up my head before the artists of the country if I accepted such an attack on the Council's independence. It would have been a betrayal of the trust they had put in me. Herb Gray obviously saw the damage to the government if two feisty, high-profile Canadian women quit in protest. And he knew I wouldn't be the type to exit quietly.

Within two weeks after we had presented our brief, the government backed down. Herb Gray announced that a sentence had been inserted in Bill C-24, exempting four organizations from its provisions: the National Arts Centre, the CBC, Telefilm Canada and the Canada Council. We congratulated ourselves on winning that battle and saving the Council – until a new government came to power the following September, and we had to start fighting the question all over again.

In a lot of people's minds, I was perceived as a political appointee – a Trudeau supporter who often sang at his official receptions and galas. It's true that I count Pierre as a friend, but some of those same people forget that all the disputes in the first months of my chairmanship were waged against his regime. When he announced his retirement that spring, his supporters asked me to sing "O Canada" at his final farewell, the night before the leadership convention opened to elect his successor, John Turner. That evening was a lovely, emotional swan song and, after the party, a small nostalgic group of Pierre's friends, including Paul and Jackie Desmarais and me, gathered back at 24 Sussex Drive. As we were leaving, Pierre came over to say goodnight.

"Maureen, you're doing a super job at the Council," he said. "Except for all these little altercations about arm's length."

"Listen, Pierre," I said, "you appointed me because you

knew I was a strong woman and I would defend the arts. You wouldn't want it any other way."

He just smiled. "*Touché*," he said and kissed me goodnight.

When Brian Mulroney became Prime Minister, there were some who suggested that I would be replaced as chairman of the Council, but they were clearly uninformed about the terms of my job. The chairman's appointment is for five years, regardless of the vicissitudes of politics. Besides, I wasn't chosen for the post because of my political opinions, but because I was an internationally known artist. The only time I've ever taken a political stand was when I was on the Arts Centre board during the campaign which ended with Joe Clark's brief term as Prime Minister. A reporter asked me what I thought of him and I said that frankly, as an artist, I couldn't vote for a man whom I had never seen in an art gallery or at any arts benefit. Right after the election, Joe came to the National Arts Centre where we were rehearsing an opera and he asked to meet me. Of course, I told him that I was delighted to see him there and hoped that he'd come back often.

I've known Brian Mulroney since long before he became Prime Minister. I'll never forget the night nearly ten years ago, after a benefit I had done in Montreal with Harry Belafonte, Nana Mouskouri, Pete Seeger and others, when I found myself at a reception with him in Senator Leo Kolber's home. I was standing in a group just at the moment Brian told Jeanne Sauvé, who was then a Cabinet minister, that he had decided to run for the Conservative party leadership. She advised him not to do it and warned that he would lose his shirt. I was totally naïve politically then, but it's a recollection which casts an interesting light on subsequent events. Later, at that same party, Brian and I ended up leading a sing-song of Irish ballads and old favourites. It's not everyone who can claim to have sung with the Prime Minister, standing on a coffee table in stocking feet.

Soon after the Conservatives came to power, we held our December 1984 board meeting, where feelings were running high, to say the least. In Michael Wilson's first budget a month earlier, the new government had cut the Council back by $3.5 million. Considering inflation, a $3.5-million loss was equivalent to $5 million. At the same time, the government had increased the budget of Marcel Masse's Department of Communications, which began making direct grants to arts organizations such as the National Ballet and the Montreal Museum of Fine Arts. The Conservatives had also begun their political appointments to the board, some of whom had no background in the arts whatsoever and who appeared to arrive determined to attack the Council.

In fact, between filling vacancies and replacing members whose terms were up, there have been fifteen new appointments in the two years since the election, which has meant some very turbulent board meetings. One new appointee in particular questioned every single expenditure, as if the Council staff consisted of bad children, trying to put something over on the country. Those cross-examinations wasted hours at a time when we had vital business to discuss. The atmosphere was tense and the Council staff's morale had plunged to rock-bottom as we emerged from that meeting to announce the death of important programs and services: our toll-free line for artists' inquiries, our short-film showcase, a program to train orchestra managers and our fund-raising and subscription department which was needed more than ever to help arts institutions pursue their own financing. The staff felt that our operations had been cut to the very bone, and to the arts community outside, it looked as if the government was out to destroy the Canada Council.

In fact, one rumour which was becoming more and more widespread was that some of those in power were out to destroy Tim Porteous. Tim had been known as a close friend of Trudeau's, had worked in the Prime Minister's Office, and was reported to be on the new government's hit list. The gossip persisted all through the winter and spring of 1985, poisoning the Council. Decisions weren't being made because everyone, Tim included, was waiting for the axe to fall. At the end of June, I couldn't stand the atmosphere of paranoia enveloping the Council any longer. I requested a meeting with Masse.

I had met him briefly before he had become Minister of Communications, and we have mutual friends in Quebec, but my first encounters with him in office hadn't been highly successful. Once, I had cancelled an obligation in order to fly to Ottawa to see him only to find that he didn't seem to have read the Council's briefing paper on the subject. At another meeting, one of his aides was constantly whispering in his ear. I finally told him that, besides being bad manners, behaviour like that created a terrible conspiratorial climate. Masse also set the terms of our relationship by always speaking, as well as conducting all his correspondence, in French; I'm always pleased to do business again in French, but he seemed to like to use three-dollar words that I didn't know.

Masse's ministry office was around the corner from the Council building then, but I met him in his huge Cabinet office in the West Block, which is sumptuously furnished with a magnificent view over the river. The meeting was in-camera, but there was nothing secret about my mission. I wanted to put an end to the rumour and gossip. I couldn't bear to see Tim being left like that with a sword hanging over his head, the victim of rumour and innuendo. It wasn't gentlemanly. But worse, it was paralyzing the Council's day-to-day operations. I wanted Masse to act quickly and cleanly and, one way or another, put Tim out of his misery. The present situation, I told him, was destructive to the Council and could ultimately backfire on the government.

Masse didn't tell me what he was going to do, but he hinted that he and the Prime Minister thought that people who stayed in one job too long became a little stale. I got the very clear feeling that they were getting ready to appoint a new director, one more agreeable to the Conservatives, but Massé promised me that whatever action was taken, he would tell Tim first, then me, before he told the press. I said that was all I could ask. I went straight back to the Council offices and, although I couldn't relate to Tim exactly what was said, I let him know the prospects didn't look good for him. But I told him about Massé's assurances that he would be the first to know if and when he was replaced.

I promptly got on a plane and flew back to Toronto for the July 1 long weekend. When I walked in the door, the phone was ringing. Tim was on the line. "So much for your bloody minister and his promises," he said. He had just received a call from Massé's deputy, De Montigny Marchand, who had offered him the job of vice-consul in Los Angeles. It was a terrible insult for a man of Tim's experience and background to be offered such a lowly job. He was livid, and said that De Montigny had told him he was being fired and that they hoped to make the announcement by the end of the next week. Tim told me he wasn't going to go quietly; he planned to call a press conference right after the holiday weekend. I said that I wouldn't stand in his way, but that I couldn't be part of it. As chairman of the Council, I couldn't afford to alienate the government at a time like that and it's never been my style to air dirty linen in public.

In that July 2 press conference, Tim went out with his guns blazing. He announced that his appointment was being "terminated" and used the occasion to blast the government's arts policies, warning that they would bring about the destruction of the Canada Council. As he knew they would, his denunciations made front pages from coast to coast. I tried to stay out of the controversy and duck the press at my country house. My number there is supposed to be unlisted but the phone rang off the wall.

It soon became clear that Tim had jumped the gun: the

order-in-council ending his directorship hadn't even passed Cabinet at the time, so the government was on perfectly firm ground when it disclaimed any decision to fire him. De Montigny Marchand denied in writing that he had ever told Tim he was being ousted. It may well have been that he didn't spell it out in so many words, but I doubt that the gist of his call left much doubt. To those reporters who did track me down, I kept repeating the same thing: the minister had promised to tell me if Tim was being replaced and so far I had heard nothing. I said I had no reason to doubt his word.

The day after Tim's press conference, Brian Mulroney's office called me. The Prime Minister said he was devastated by the furore and was perplexed as to why Tim felt compelled to call a press conference. I pointed out that all the rumours had contributed to the stormy climate and recommended that the government ought to handle the whole question cleanly, like surgery. Surely, I said, for a man of Tim's calibre who had given twenty years of his life to the public service, they could come up with a job offer and a settlement which weren't an insult. But the Prime Minister emphasized that Tim had been a "Trudeau pal." I argued that in fact he had taken on the Trudeau government in public as vehemently as he had the Conservatives. Don't worry, the Prime Minister assured me; he wouldn't do anything to hurt Tim because Tim's father had once been a law partner of his in Montreal. He said he was even quite fond of him. Most important of all, he promised that he would call me before he took any action.

In fact, what the government did was to leave Tim hanging out on a limb for the entire summer. They did nothing, neither officially confirming nor denying that his appointment was up. It was a very clever tactic because it took the wind out of his charges, while at the same time leaving him impotent. He was a man who had signed his own death warrant. It was cruel to Tim, who had only two choices: to quit, undermining his own case, or to wait for the inevitable axe to fall. Meanwhile, the government could take its time in finding his successor. Those were crucial months when the Council staff was preparing for our fall board meeting. But at headquarters, decision-making ground to a halt. Work was absolutely paralyzed. Everything was on hold.

I can't say that the government's plans were actually spelled out to me, but the Prime Minister's wife was having a baby then and I'm sure he had other things on his mind. The Privy Council Office did consult with me on the names it was considering for the director's job. Over the weeks, as the calls came to my cottage, the requirements for the post shifted. Originally the government had wanted a francophone woman, and one Quebec journalist even announced in her column that she had been appointed. That cut short *her* candidacy. Then, as the summer wore on, protests over Conservative patronage in Quebec grew and the short list took on a different character. Gradually one name began to emerge more frequently: Peter Roberts, the retiring ambassador to Moscow.

Things ended tragically for Tim that fall. His appointment was terminated in a terse, three-line order-in-council the same day Peter was appointed. There were no tributes or thanks for his service and, at this writing, he still hasn't been offered a job.

I had met Peter only once when the board of the National Arts Centre was considering him as a candidate for director. When we did meet after he was appointed to the Council in October 1985, he teased me: "Aha, I see at last you've gotten around to me!" Peter has been an effective new director and, as a trained diplomat, he doesn't use Tim's confrontational approach with the government. He forged a good relationship with Masse and he has taken the Council firmly in hand. He's charming and he has a way of speaking in Ottawa's bureaucratic jargon. He can talk about the arts in economic terms – production and distribution and cost-effectiveness – the language governments like. Peter also lifted a big load from my shoulders in taking on more speaking engagements.

At last, as we prepared for our October 1985 meeting, the non-stop crisis at the Council seemed to be calming down. I began to breathe easier. But too soon. Suddenly, Masse resigned in a scandal about his election funds, and once more, without a minister, decisions were frozen. Ironically, when Masse first came to office, the country's artists had attacked him as the villain of the piece – a budget-cutter who seemed to want to bring the arts to heel behind the Conservative party and use patronage to fund the companies he personally liked, making his own star shine more brightly. But by the time of his resignation, the artistic community had come to see him as its only champion in Cabinet, one of the few voices defending cultural nationalism. For one thing, when budgets were cut, he had come up with other funding sources. He had found money for the Canadian Opera Company in the Employment and Immigration's allotment on the grounds that the opera was an employer. He had also insisted on drafting a book-publishing policy and he promised one on film to safeguard Canadian content in those industries.

At first, I had my differences with him too. I thought he behaved with a slightly Napoleonic air. He was cordial to me, but I always felt at the time that I was being talked at, not invited into a discussion. I got the impression he was impatient with much of the culture outside Quebec. But after his terrible personal ordeal, when he was sworn back into office in December 1985, exonerated, I noticed a tremendous change in him. To me, he looked like a man who had been betrayed. He had a wounded look in his eyes. After that, with the arts community rallying around him, our relationship with him was excellent. I was very impressed with his efforts for culture in this country.

Masse had warned us early on that there wasn't much he could do for us in the government's spring 1986 budget, which was looming as a draconian measure. But a few weeks before it was brought down in February, rumours emerged which were later confirmed: Massé had found us an extra $10 million. Some critics point out that the Conservatives were just trying to mollify the artistic community before announcing approval of the sale of the publishers Prentice-Hall Canada to the American conglomerate Gulf and Western. I don't even question the motives. All I have to say is that they gave us more money when the arts in this country badly needed it.

But the story doesn't quite have its happy ending yet. As I write this, there has been a major debate over how we are to disburse the $10 million. The government wants it to go to the major arts organizations and companies – again. But the Council can't accept earmarked funds. A solution hasn't yet been worked out and in the interim, we've had to remain with our budget frozen, which essentially means functioning at cutback levels.

We now have a new minister, Flora MacDonald, who I'm looking forward to working with. We'd been running into each other at airports and government receptions for years before our formal meeting her first week in office. She's a fighter and she was one of the people in Cabinet who went to bat for the CBC when the government was slashing its budget.

But ironically in all this chaos, the government's qualms about the Council seem to have diminished. Soon after the election, one of Massé's closest friends, Jacques Lefebvre, was appointed as deputy chairman. The new board members who were Conservative appointees at first seemed almost suspicious of how the Council handled its affairs. They looked at some of the items as an accountant would, questioning why a company would get a grant when it was in the red for the third year in a row. But gradually, they've begun to see that the Council's mission is larger than economics. The reason we need a Canada Council is that there are economically disadvantaged regions which wouldn't ever be exposed to culture if everything were looked at on a pure profit basis. Now they realize that every part of Canada should enjoy the arts, not just the big rich cities which can pay for them. I think some of the confirmed sceptics on the board have even begun to believe that the Council is a well-run organization.

I still receive a lot of mail from people complaining that they've been turned down for grants. I try to point out that, just before my appointment as chairman, even I was rejected for a grant I was trying to get for a Canadian composer. You're judged by a committee of your peers and it's a democracy; not everybody can win with our limited funds. But at the Council, decisions are made fairly.

Still, sometimes I think this job calls for more of a politician than I am. I'm not the type to jockey for influence or say the diplomatic thing. I'm more comfortable expressing my own opinions, not those of twenty board members. I tend to call things as I see them.

I've also begun to wonder whether the chairman's term ought to be only three years. I don't know yet if I'll be able to fulfil my five-year mandate. I try to combine a lot of my official appearances with concert bookings and I'm reluctant to claim expenses or my per diem honorarium very often. I'm not being a martyr, believe me. It's all a part of my notion of return service. But all the time I've spent on the Council has cost me a $100,000 drop in income, which is no joke when, as an artist, I'm my own old-age pension plan.

Pondering a shorter term doesn't mean I'm any less committed to the Council. On the contrary. I think when the former government originally appointed me chairman, they thought they were getting a nice, cheerful motherly type who would neither excite nor disturb. But as they found out, they made a mistake. I believe strongly in the Canada Council and I think now that the country's artists know I'll put myself on the line for them. What I lack in bureaucratic skills, I've tried to make up for in public relations panache. I hope that Canadians have a better appreciation now of just what a gift they have in the Council. Recently a journalist asked me what I thought Americans were better at than Canadians. I didn't even need to think twice before answering: "Blowing their own horns." I often think Canadians don't have confidence in the resources and talent they possess. When you've had an international career such as mine, you see that when this country produces excellence as it has in a Margaret Atwood, a Jean-Paul Riopelle or a Glenn Gould, its artists don't have to take a back seat to anybody. We have to start believing in ourselves.

I'd also like to see more young people getting involved in the arts. As I told a recent graduating class, rising unemployment and shorter work weeks mean they're going to have more spare time on their hands; learning about the arts is a way of putting their leisure to use so they can enjoy more interesting lives. With my own family, I've got a personal arts-promotion program. I run them a cultural line of credit. Because they're all young or just starting families, without much extra money to blow on luxuries, I buy them subscriptions to the opera or ballet and make a deal to reimburse them for any theatre or concert tickets they purchase. With all the cultural riches there are in this country, it's a tragedy for any young person to become a soap-opera addict.

That's why, as the Big Mama of the arts' megabucks, I'm constantly pushing for more money for individual artists' grants. I don't want talented young people to leave their fields because they can't make enough for a square meal. Some of the harshest critics of the arts don't understand that it takes more years of training to become a violinist than it does to become a brain surgeon. Whenever I'm asked to speak to a businessmen's group or a convention, I always put in a pitch to the wealthy ones to leave some money to the Canada Council. Instead of a silly plaque on a building which people will just walk by and ignore, I ask them why they don't put their names on a prize or scholarship. It will live on forever – and besides, it's tax deductible. I've piqued quite a bit of interest so far and now I'm waiting for the bequests to start rolling in. As I tell them, "You can't take it with you. Life is a terminal disease!"

TWENTY-NINE

Joy Deeper Still

FOR YEARS, I've had a recurring dream. In it, I'm figure-skating on a vast field of white and as I raise my leg to go into a spin, the other leg lifts off the ground and suddenly I'm floating above the landscape like a figure in a Chagall painting. Whatever obstacles are put in my way, I soar over them. I am light as air, free, nothing can stop me. I always feel wonderful when I awaken and, if dreams are an unconscious measure of one's life, that vision runs true to how I look back on mine. Whatever troubles and pain I've had, I've managed to surmount them. I've leaped over every obstacle to land on my feet, and everything has turned out better than I could have plotted it in my childhood fantasies. Not long ago the composer David Warrack summed it up in the line of a song he wrote for me: "As fairy tales go, I'll take mine."

Even the moments I had most feared have become a kind of benediction. As the children got older and joined me on engagements during their summer vacations, I had the bright idea that they would find it more enjoyable if they could work at the same time. In 1977, when the Santa Fe Opera offered me the role of Dame Quickly in *Falstaff*, I accepted on the condition that the management rent me a big house and find jobs for three of my teenagers. Susie was still too young to work, but Gina helped staff the box office, Linda was an usherette (who fainted the first night), and Daniel was an apprentice stagehand, working sixteen-hour days for a pittance. They got a kick out of their employment at first, but Santa Fe in the summer was so hot that every bone in your body felt bleached from that unrelenting sun. By the time Paula had finished the course she was taking that summer and flown down to join us, the rest of the children were all leaving for home by plane the next day. Paula agreed to stay on and help me drive the car back to Toronto.

It was one of the rare occasions when the two of us had time alone together. On the last day, as we were packing and loading boxes into the trunk of my car, I started to reminisce about her childhood. I don't know what brought those long-ago days back to my mind, but once I had begun talking, the words just tumbled out as if they had a will of their own. Paula had heard most of my anecdotes before, but there was one that she hadn't: how she had been born in a Berlin clinic two years before her father and I were married.

I had dreaded that moment for twenty-one years. I was rewriting her personal history, and with it, our whole family's. All their lives, the children had believed the fiction about Eugene's and my secret marriage in Europe, and I didn't know how Paula would react to finding out that it had been manufactured. She has always been a very honest girl.

She was stunned. For a minute, she was silent and her big blue eyes misted over. Then she walked across the kitchen and threw her arms around me. "Oh, Mom," she said. "It must have been so hard for you. What a lot you went through alone."

During the drive later across the desert and on through the United States, we talked out the revised version of her life again and again. She kept wanting to go over it, because it was so much for her to grasp at once. For years, she had asked why she was called Paula Forrester Kash when her brother and sisters all had ordinary middle names, but I had always passed the question off by pointing out that I had been called Maureen Kathleen Stewart

Forrester in a tribute to my grandmother's maiden name. She had accepted the explanation at the time, but now she understood the real reason. I had been afraid that the truth might create a rift between us, but in fact, it made us closer. Paula suddenly saw me as someone who was more than Supermom with an eternal smile on her face and a flashy international career. She realized how strong I had needed to be to survive those early years.

There had been no reason for choosing that moment for my confession, but I had always known that at a certain time in each of the children's lives when I judged they were old enough to handle it, I would tell them. I didn't want them to hear some version of the truth from gossip or a malicious stranger and somehow pick up the idea that Paula had been an unwanted child. But I also knew they had to be mature enough to understand what can happen between a man and woman. I didn't want them to blame their father for anything, especially at that time when Eugene and I had just separated.

With each of them, I let the right moment present itself. It was only a few years ago that I finally told Susie, the youngest. Because the children never could be sure which of them knew and which of them didn't, they didn't discuss it among themselves. For a while, that was the hardest part for Paula: she had no one in the family with whom she could share this revelation which had shaken her whole life. In fact, what she didn't realize then was that I had already told Gina. Maybe because Gina is more like me – less emotional, a logical thinker with a very practical attitude to life – I tried the announcement out on her for size first. I had invited her along on a tour I was doing of Poland in the hopes that it would disabuse her of some of her leftist political ideas at the time and on the airplane I had blurted the story out. Gina could see how nervous I was about telling it. "But Mom," she had said, "it doesn't change anything. You and Dad loved each other and got married anyway. It's no big deal."

Her reaction was both a relief and an irony. I realized

then that my children had grown up in a different era than I had and to them stories like mine were commonplace. A whole generation of women was now having children out of wedlock, often purposely, and social or professional ostracism was unimaginable. I saw that after all those years of guarding my terrible secret, my children didn't think of it as terrible at all.

One of the reasons I had judged that Paula was ready to hear about her origins then was that she had just turned twenty-one and was already embarking on a woman's life herself. In 1971, when we moved back to Toronto, at her insistence I left her to board in Philadelphia with a neighbour for her last year of high school. She was a brilliant student but only seventeen when she graduated and I thought she still wasn't grown up enough to go straight into university. I convinced her to enrol for a year in the Canadian Junior College in Lausanne so that she could get used to meeting new people. I packed her off with pep talks about birth control and expected her to have a whirlwind social life. Virtually the first day she landed in Switzerland, she fell in love with a fellow student there, Pierre Berton's son Peter.

They went out together all through university and lived together after that while Peter established himself as an architect. Pierre and Janet Berton accepted Paula into their family as if she were another member of that enormous extended brood and, although it didn't come as the slightest surprise, we were all thrilled when she and Peter decided to get married. We agreed to hold the wedding on the Bertons' huge Kleinburg spread north of Toronto and somehow, the intimate little family affair we started out planning ended up as a 200-guest extravaganza. Paula said it was her dream wedding, but, taking a leaf out of her mother's book, the bride almost missed the ceremony.

Paula and her three sisters had all dressed in my apartment at Toronto's Harbourfront over champagne before we hopped into the limousines that I had rented to take us to the wedding. Just as she was climbing into the car,

Paula decided she was so nervous she needed to run up-stairs for a drink, so I told the driver of the first car to start on up to Kleinburg. In the confusion, the second chauffeur followed him. When Paula came back down-stairs, she found an empty driveway. She asked the door-man where the limousines had disappeared. He told her they had gone to a wedding. "But they can't go without me," she wailed. "I'm the bride!"

We had flown in Rabbi Abraham Feinberg from his retirement in Reno, Nevada, since he was the only rabbi available who would marry an inter-faith couple. Even though the wedding wasn't in a synagogue, Paula had insisted on having a *huppah*, the Jewish bridal canopy, which touched Eugene enormously. When we finally got her to the Bertons, the guests were seated in waves across the lawn, with two huge catering tents fluttering in the background for the massive buffet I had ordered. It was a brilliant summer's day and one of the most moving pro-ductions I've ever helped choreograph. A confirmed senti-mentalist, Paula had insisted that both Eugene and I walk her down the aisle, one of us on each arm. As we ap-proached the *huppah*, a single Scottish piper strode into view over the crest of the hill behind the rabbi, playing Beethoven. It might not have been traditional for a Jewish wedding, but there wasn't a dry eye in the house. The next day the *Globe and Mail* ran a picture of Peter and Paula on the front page and behind them sat Pierre Berton, wiping a tear from his cheek.

The newspapers treated the wedding as a dynastic merger. But only a handful of people knew what a special day it was for me – the happy ending to a tale which had begun so long before on such an uncertain note. Now Paula and Peter have had their first baby, Laura Naomi.

Gina and her husband Paul already have two little boys and I've turned into an absolutely doting grandmother. From the day he was born, I've sung to Ryan, her eldest, who can remember a ditty after hearing it only once. There may just be another singer in the crowd.

Over the years, I had noticed in other families that after the children reached a certain age, they scarcely ever saw each other. My children adore each other's company, and they're very supportive of one another. They wouldn't think of missing Linda's or Daniel's opening night or one of our birthdays. I decided that the way to keep that sense of family intact was to buy a big country house where they could all bring their husbands, boyfriends and children. A few years ago, when I did a Canada Council concert tour of northern Ontario, I fell in love with Muskoka and a particular patch of land nestled among the pines on a cliff overlooking a placid bay. I call it my resort. The huge house rambles forever and can sleep an army, and there are guesthouses scattered over the property. The crafts which I collect on my travels cram the pine shelves and we've run out of corners for the cushion covers I needle-point on my endless plane trips while I'm memorizing concert programs.

To the motorboat enthusiasts who roar by the dock, the flag which flutters over the water might look like any other Canadian Maple Leaf. But it arrived one day in the mail wrapped in brown paper from the Prime Minister's Office in Ottawa. It was the flag flown on Parliament Hill on December 6, 1981, the day the Constitution was sent to Britain for patriation after a ceremony at which I had sung the national anthem in alternating lines, English and French. "I thought you'd want to have this," Pierre Trudeau had written.

In summer, wildflowers bloom where Gina planted them on the front lawn, and a phoebe tirelessly tends her nest in the eavestrough over the door. My own brood arrives in assorted bunches, with friends and offspring in tow. Sometimes I drive up just for the day to find a moment of peace between engagements and obligations. I sit and watch the deer and hummingbirds feed. If I have music to learn, I perch at the baroque Heintzman baby grand in the living room and, looking out over the woods as I sing, I sometimes think of Mahler writing of the forces of untamed nature. The notes sail out over the bay and come back to me across the water. It's no accident that this corner of the bay is named Echo Rock.

The loveliest moments are at Thanksgiving when Eugene and all the children and grandchildren gather. Across the lake, the maples are scarlet among the birches and the long refectory table groans with gastronomic bounty; everybody contributes his or her special dish. And as I sit at that table, I can't help but count my blessings for the family that I always dreamed of being part of when I was growing up on rue Fabre. Seeing my children and grandchildren there, I'm convinced that I've led an enchanted life. There has been a lot of loneliness and sometimes I've needed a good stiff upper lip, but I don't have a single regret or any apologies to make.

I've known it all – a husband, children and a career which has surpassed my most extravagant ambitions. I couldn't advise a young singer to follow my example, because my route might not work for her, but I would tell her that if she loves someone and wants to get married and have babies, she shouldn't put it off. The more successful an artist becomes, the less easy it is to make time for those changes in her life and then suddenly she can wake up one day and find that it's too late. I look at some singers who've lived only for their reviews and I think how tragic to have only crumbled bits of newspaper left at the end.

There's a line that I sing in Mahler's *Third* which says what I believe I've had: "*Lust tiefer noch als Herzeleid* – Joy deeper still than heart's pain."

When I was young, I used to tell interviewers that I would retire by the age of forty. But forty arrived quite some years ago, and I'm still going strong, already booked up until 1990. I keep warning people that we ought to put a clause in my contracts these days which adds, "If she can still cut it." Every year recently I've promised myself that I'm going to start reducing my engagements, but then managers phone with a last-minute booking here or a benefit they think I might want to do there, and I'm back up to 120 concerts. At the same time, I have no illusions: I know that my voice doesn't have the lushness that it had ten years ago, and there are pieces I've put to bed now which just don't suit me anymore. But I can still sing because of the technique Bernard Diamant taught me. These are the years when my career is winding down, but they are rich in their own way. I hope that I won't have to wait for reviewers to start insinuating that it's time I left the concert stage. In fact I believe I'll have the sense to realize when it's time to exit gracefully. Still, just because I stop concertizing doesn't mean that I'll stop singing. I'll still be humming away to myself as I do now, in the street and in the bathtub. Singing is as much a part of my life as breathing. I joke that I'll probably be vocalizing on the way to my own funeral.

But I have a suspicion that the fates still have a lot of plans for me. On a brilliantly sunny Sunday in Waterloo, Ontario, last May, I slipped a fuchsia robe over my shoulders and donned a matching gold-braided cap to become the chancellor of Sir Wilfrid Laurier University. It seemed nothing short of miraculous that a high school drop-out like myself would end up with seventeen honorary degrees and students kneeling before me as Madame Chancellor. In my speech, I warned the graduates that they were living in a changing world and that the ceremony marked only the beginning of their course. Many of them might not be able to put their degrees to use directly to find a job and would have to consider a change in career plans. I urged them not to be too proud to start out with a humble post. "Life is like a bank account," I said. "You don't get anything out unless you put something in." That's the advice I've always given my voice pupils. There are so many young people who are talented, ambitious and good-looking, but the few who succeed are always the ones who pour their hearts and souls into the music.

If there has been any secret to my life, it is that I've

loved every minute of my chosen career. I walk onto a stage and I know I'm going to have a good time, and the audience senses that joy. Singing has opened doors for me that otherwise were beyond the reach of my imagination, and even when the hurdles in my path daunted me, music lifted me above them and took me out of myself to another universe entirely. Now there are so many things still left to do and songs still waiting to be sung. I swear, I've barely taken wing.

Acknowledgments

Ghost-writing is necessarily a process that must take place in the wings, but that doesn't mean it's a solitary one. So many people have helped to make this book possible through the generosity of their time and spirit that it's impossible to thank each one. But among those to whom a special vote of gratitude goes are: Merle Shain for her hospitality and wise counsel; Frances McNeely for her dazzling speed at tape transcription and wittily informed comments; Roberta Grant for her swift and graciously proffered research; Veronica Sympson for cheerily ferreting out even the most arcane facts, including the urinary habits of the koala bear; Elwy Yost for mobilizing his TV Ontario archives; and Tania Kamal-eldin for activating her word processor and taking such a lively interest in the project. Helen Murphy helped shed invaluable illumination on the workings of the Canada Council, and John Newmark shed light on everything by entrusting me with his own meticulously ordered files and memories. Eugene Kash unearthed a treasure trove of scrapbooks and generously shared his memories and insights, and to all the other Kashes as well, I'm grateful for their recollections. Ellen Seligman patiently helped sift and prod the manuscript to a finished flow, offering shelter, sustenance and friendship beyond the call of duty. And Barbara Czarnecki brought a fine eye and deft touch to the final stages of the project.

I would also like to thank Kevin Doyle of *Maclean's*, who allowed me the time out between earthquakes and trips to the Bay of Pigs to meet this deadline, and my colleagues Glen Allen and Ian Austen, who generously helped me juggle my journalistic load. But perhaps the greatest gift in any process such as this is cheerleading, and for that my thanks go to friends who kept the faith on the long-distance lines, and to my parents, James and Sherry Young.

Marci McDonald
Washington, D.C.